BORN TO
SHOP
GREAT BRITAIN

The Ultimate Guide for
Travelers Who Love to Shop

4th Edition

MACMILLAN • USA

For Mike and Aaron and Judy
In memory of Camelot

MACMILLAN TRAVEL
A Simon & Schuster Macmillan Company
1633 Broadway
New York, NY 10019

ISBN   0-02-860700-7
ISSN   1071-9717

Editor: Erica Spaberg
Production Editor: Matt Hannafin
Design by George J. McKeon
Digital Cartography by John Decamillis and Ortelius Design

SPECIAL SALES
Bulk purchases (10+ copies) of Frommer's travel guides are
available to corporations at special discounts. The Special
Sales Department can produce custom editions to be used as
premiums and/or for sales promotion to suit individual needs.
Existing editions can be produced with custom cover imprints
such as corporate logos. For more information write to
Special Sales, Macmillan Publishing, 1633 Broadway, New
York, NY 10019.

Manufactured in the United States of America

CONTENTS

MAP LIST

WHAT THE SYMBOL MEANS

· ·

 Suzy's Favorites

Stores, restaurants, and accommodations you should not miss.

TO START WITH

This is a new edition of *Born to Shop Great Britain* and it is also the debut edition with Frommer's. This guide has many of the basics that made it useful in its other incarnations and some new useful additions as well. While I'm afraid I can't take you, or Arthur Frommer, shopping in Britain on £5 a day any longer, I do know plenty of great things to buy in England and Scotland and Wales that cost a fiver, or less.

One of the biggest improvements to the guide is the very timing of the publication itself. We now publish *Born to Shop London* and *Born to Shop Great Britain* in alternate years, so from now on, a completely up-to-date guide to the United Kingdom's varied shopping scenes will be available every year.

We've also created a new first chapter in all of the guides, sort of a flashdance of a read for those on a business trip or in an incredible hurry who don't have time to do anything more than go for the basics. You want the best cashmeres in all of the United Kingdom and don't want to sort through multiple listings? Step this way.

Hugs across the sea to those in the United Kingdom who worked on these pages, especially Ian Cook, a part of the team since the beginning. He shot the cover photo and works as British correspondent on all the guides. Thanks and kisses to Ruth Jacobs who did research on antiques and factory outlets, drove me all over southern England, and promises to take me to Lovejoy Country next time.

For help in northern England, I send thanks and hugs to Elizabeth Jeffreys and Marie Mohan in Manchester; Carolyn Blain in Ashton; Jane Randall and Julie Obada in Stoke-on-Trent; Olive Ayre in Edinburgh; and the incomparable Malcolm Hawksworth, who arranged the cover for all of us.

Isn't this just the most beautiful *Born to Shop* cover ever? In case you're wondering where I am, we shot it in the courtyard of the Gladstone Pottery Museum in Longton. The gorgeous English blue and white I'm surrounded by is Spode's Blue Italian pattern. Not seen in the shot is the horse that pulls the wagon (off for tea, I guess) or the muscles Ian got from rearranging the dishes over and over again for this all-day photo shoot. Thanks to one and all, including Josiah Wedgwood and all my friends at Spode who packed and unpacked the dishes.

Chapter One

· · · · · · · ·

THE BEST OF BRITAIN AT A GLANCE

BRITAIN IN A FLASH

· ·

Searching the stones for the secret of life? Merely tracing your rolling stones? While exploring the British countryside you're going to have plenty of opportunities to shop. But if you're in a hurry, or you are in the planning stages of your trip, this chapter is for you. So, directly from my Filofax to yours, here is everything that Alice told the Door Mouse when she was ten feet tall.

If you are just going to London, please gather no moss and take a look at *Born to Shop London* for more in-depth shopping tips. Few of the stores listed in this chapter are in London. However, many of the listings make the assumption that you are using London as your hub city. If this is not the case, you may need more specific travel information in order to use this chapter in conjunction with your itinerary.

All listings in this chapter appear elsewhere in the book.

THE BEST DAY TRIP

· ·

This is not easy, so I'm fudging it just a little bit by giving you two choices, one easy and one hard.

1

Greenwich

While Greenwich has some super museums, the only days to take a serious day trip to Greenwich are Saturday or Sunday, when the town is filled with flea markets and crafts fairs. I happen to like Sundays a little bit better than Saturdays, but if Saturday is all you've got, spend the early morning at Portobello Road in London, then hop on the train to Greenwich for the rest of the day.

Bath

Because the train ride is almost two hours long, a day trip to Bath requires an early start—if you want to get in a full day of shopping. Aim to arrive in Bath by 10am, if not earlier. You can eat breakfast in the train station or on board the train if you aren't a morning person.

I suggest this as a Wednesday day trip, when there are a few more flea markets that also open early (at 6:30am), even though Bath is super every day of the week, even Sunday. The markets are what make a trip to Bath special.

Please note that a train ticket to Bath is expensive, especially if you leave before 9:30am (a peak round-trip ticket costs approximately $50). If you plan to take other day trips from London by train, you may want to consider purchasing a train pass from BritRail. It can lower your transportation costs.

THE BEST ANTIQUE MARKETS WORTH TRAVELING TO (FROM LONDON)

Assuming that you are based in London, I have also broken this category into two choices—the first one easy, the second one more difficult.

Alexandra Palace Antique & Collectors Fair

This is located right outside London, and while it takes some purposeful planning to be in town for, getting here isn't any big deal. Alexandra Palace is not actually a palace but an exhibition hall. This event hosts between 750 and 1,000 dealers in antiques and collectibles and is held several times a year. Call 181/883-7061 for the dates, which are determined a year in advance.

Newark

This takes a little bit more doing, so I'm classifying this as the hard trip. It is out of town, but can easily be done as a day trip from London. Take the train to Newark Northgate then get the bus, which will deliver you right to the gates. More than 3,500 dealers show. Call 01636/702-326 for dates and information.

THE BEST FACTORY OUTLET MALL

. . . .

BICESTER VILLAGE
Bicester, Oxfordshire

The drive is neither scenic nor picturesque—it's straight highway all the way. The "village" is an American-style factory outlet mall built in partnership with an American team.

While it's important to know American prices (Ralph Lauren, Joan and David, and OshKosh B'Gosh are some examples of American names that are more expensive in Britain), there were still plenty of values on my last visit—enough to make my heart sing. I thought the Cerutti 1881 outlet alone was worth the drive.

Bicester is only a half-hour drive from Oxford, so you can finish up your day there if you're not too knackered (British slang for pooped).

THE BEST SOURCE FOR POSTCARDS

· ·

EDINBURGH, SCOTLAND

The best postcards in Britain are sold from virtually all tourist traps in Edinburgh and strike me as enormously funny. There's a series of them, all of which share a running theme. One of my favorites features a picture of the Pyramids in Egypt and says "Greetings from Scotland." Maybe you just have to see them to think they're funny, but I can't stop buying them. It's that droll British humor.

THE BEST NATIONAL LANDMARK
WITH A GIFT SHOP

· ·

STONEHENGE
Two miles west of Amesbury and about 9 miles north of Salisbury, at the junction of A303 and A344/A360

THE BEST CASTLE GIFT SHOP

· ·

WINDSOR CASTLE
Castle Hill, Windsor

THE BEST MUSEUM GIFT SHOP

· ·

VICTORIA & ALBERT MUSEUM
Cromwell Road, London, SW7

THE BEST SERIOUS SHOPPING

· ·

THE POTTERIES
Take the train to Stoke-on-Trent and explore Stoke plus five other Pottery towns for more than 30 different outlet shops.

THE BEST SOURCE FOR CASHMERE GOODS

. . . .

HAWICK, SCOTLAND

THE BEST STORE FOR WHISKY

. . . .

MILROY'S SOHO WINE MARKET
3 Greek Street, London, W1

THE BEST AIRPORT SHOPPING

. . . .

TERMINAL FOUR, LONDON HEATHROW (LHR)

THE BEST PLACE FOR ONE-STOP SHOPPING

. . . .

ANY BRANCH OF BOOTS THE CHEMIST
ANY BRANCH OF THE BODY SHOP

THE BEST GIFTS FOR KIDS

. . . .

- Corgi cars and trucks are beloved by little boys, as are Britains' soldiers. They're sold at **Hamley's** in London.
- The Body Shop has a wide selection of products suitable for young children on up through teens.
- Football and rugby team merchandise appeals to boys. You can find it at any souvenir stand.
- Dr. Martens makes all sorts of gift items. While distribution is best in London, their goods can be found all over Britain and are the rage of teens in America.

THE BEST GIFTS FOR LOVED ONES

. . . .

- Hermès ties. I know they're French, but the prices in Britain are excellent and the prices at U.K. duty-free shops seem to be among the best in the world.

- **Aromatherapy products.** They relieve stress, jetlag, or tiredness and show your loved ones just how much you care. **Aroma Therapeutics** offers a number of products (available at **Harrods** and all department stores), including a travel kit for £30 that is a fabulous gift. **Culpeper the Herbalist** (with a handful of shops around the U.K.) also offers a wide range of aromatherapy products that make great gifts, including their Aroma Fan.

Chapter Two

. . . .

BRITISH DETAILS

WELCOME TO GREAT BRITAIN

. . . .

Hail Britannia and welcome one and all to England and Scotland, a little bit of Wales, and a lot of what's inside my shopping bags. Three bags full, of course.

Welcome to a country that is made up of several different countries all unified into one and welcome most of all to a place that almost speaks the same language you do. I'm leaving Wales out of that sentence for now. Welcome, friends—airfares are low, car rates are lower, and there's no time like now.

For those of you who are confused by the differences among the terms United Kingdom, Great Britain, and England, here it is up front.

- The United Kingdom (U.K.) is composed of England, Scotland, Wales, and Northern Ireland, as well as all those little islands offshore where they make great sweaters.
- Great Britain is the single island that includes England, Scotland, and Wales.
- England is just one country in Great Britain, a mere chorus in the refrain that makes up the whole.

So welcome to more than England. Welcome to regions that are still unique; welcome to tradition

7

and country charm. Welcome to circles of stones and Stonehenge, to tapestry and knitting yarn and needlepoint kits; welcome to the place that brews a number of single-malt whiskies.

Welcome to rolling hills, hand-built stone walls, half-timbered buildings, guest houses with hand-stenciled walls, and big country breakfasts.

Sure, London is part of the whole and you're going to love it whether this is your first trip or your thousandth, but more importantly, this book is a warm welcome to those who are ready to take in more than the big city.

England, Scotland, and Wales wait for you with open arms. More and more international airports are opening up to make access to the countryside easier (Manchester! Birmingham! Glasgow!) and, yes, cheaper. There are pounds to be saved in them thar hills (and valleys); there are shoppers' tales to be handed down to your grandchildren.

STRAIGHT TALK

• •

London is a great place; it's been a great place for some 2,000 years now. But the cost of living there is high, and the cost of visiting there can be down-right frightening:

- A drop-dead fancy hotel room in London costs at least £200.
- A drop-dead fancy room in the Cotswolds costs less than £100.

The first time I booked a trip to Britain without planning a stopover in London, I was cursing myself all the way down the departure gate. "Ten days in England and not one of them in London, what's wrong with me?" I wailed.

Then I did my 10 fabulous days in Manchester and northern England and do you know what? I didn't miss London one bit. I made new friends. I bought more dishes. I shopped at Marks & Spencer outlet stores. I didn't need London one bit.

Frankly, dear friends, there's a lot worth seeing and doing (and buying) out there in the countryside. Great Britain has so much to offer beyond London that I feel compelled to point out just a few itsy-bitsy but nonetheless important facts:

- You never really know a country, or its people, until you've left the big-time, show-off cities and gotten close to the land.
- In Britain, everyone speaks the same language you do (more or less), so it's very easy to get out and have a fine country adventure.
- Life is less expensive outside of London. You will save 25% on the cost of your holiday if you never set foot in London.

THE LAY OF THE LAND

· ·

Some people do their touring of England from a base camp in London; others move in a circular pattern and do not backtrack. In order to decide how you want to see the U.K., keep the following points in mind.

- The Cotswolds, although not very far from London, require a car and at least a weekend, if not longer.
- Scotland, some five hours away on the fastest train, obviously isn't for day trippers.
- Some cities can be piggybacked with others if you have a car, but are impossible to do together if you must rely on trains—such as Salisbury and Winchester, two famous cathedral towns. Despite the fact that they aren't much more than 30 miles apart, there is no train service between them! Plan carefully in order to save time and money.

When you know what kind of shopping you are planning, sit down with a map and plan your route carefully, paying attention to your mode of transportation. If you plan to ship everything you buy, you don't need to worry. But if you just buy small items as you go, you may find yourself buying new luggage and paying for extra baggage when you return to the United States.

Investigate excess-baggage rules and prices on the airline you're flying home, so you'll know how much you can safely carry on and how much you can check for free as well as how much it will cost you to add on luggage. Baggage rules differ widely among carriers and between destinations. British Airways has different prices for coming and going.

THE LAY OF THE VILLAGE

Never step off the train or drive into a town thinking that you can find your way automatically to the charming parts, the high street, or the best shopping.

Villages that consist of one street are pretty easy to scout on your own, but many villages evolved over centuries, and have a city center but no one single street for the best stores. Avoid frustrating and time-consuming searches: stop at a tourist information center or come with map in hand.

I now own a book of maps, published by **Automobile Association (AA)**, called *Town Plans of Britain*. This book, which comes in a variety of sizes, depicts the downtown centers of Britain's major cities. Use the maps in this book to get oriented, then locate the address of a particular shop on the bigger map—this is especially helpful if you are driving.

Even if you are on foot, always have your first destination in mind. You can wander all day and miss what makes a place worth visiting in the first place. I know. I've done it!

KNOW BEFORE YOU GO

I've worked with a number of national tourist offices, therefore I think I can say with some authority that the **British Tourist Authority (BTA)** is one of the best tourism bureaus there is. They offer a plethora of free printed information—everything from maps to brochures on car rentals and farm stays to complete books filled with details and inner secrets. And when I say free, I mean free. These same materials are available in Britain, but if you try to pick them up there, you'll have to pay.

There are several BTA offices in the United States. I use the main office in New York. Write them, explain your needs and interests, and wait for your mail carrier to tell you about his hernia operation: British Tourist Authority, 551 Fifth Avenue, 7th floor, New York, NY 10176. Tel. 212/986-2266.

Be sure to stock up on a London underground map, a BritRail map, all **BritRail** travel information, an InterCity train schedule, guides to the cities you plan to visit, hotel booklets, rental car ads, and tour promotions. You may also write to BritRail USA for its schedules and informative brochures: BritRail, 1500 Broadway, New York, NY 10036. Tel. 212/382-3737.

If you want theater information, the BTA will not fax it to you, but they will mail it to you. There are also a number of online services that can provide theater ticket buying information, schedules, and multiple reviews. See "Electronically Yours," page 13.

BOOKS ON BRITAIN

The Good Food Guide, which can be bought in the U.S. or the U.K., is the best guide for choosing restaurants all around the country. I count on it when selecting a place to eat, especially in small cities where I don't know anyone.

If you are going to be living in Britain for some time, or you plan to drive around extensively, or you consider yourself a major bargain hunter, you might want to buy a copy of Noelle Walsh's annual reference guide called *The Good Deal Directory*. Walsh writes a shopping column for one of the British newspapers. The book is a compilation of her columns and more. It includes outlet stores and discounters galore.

If you're traveling by train, the ABC *Rail Guide* (which you can buy at any newsstand at any train station in Britain) will become precious reading to you. I tried using the train schedules in the free brochures provided by the BTA, and they proved to be inadequate or outdated. If you are doing a lot of travel and insist on careful planning, you'll definitely want the ABC guide, which is published on a monthly basis. It costs about £5.

If you care about antique fairs and junk sales, please turn to chapter 6 for my recommendations of useful books and other publications specifically devoted to antiques and collectibles.

Now then, I have saved the single most important book for last. The book I recommend most highly is called *Johansen's* and it is not easily available in bookstores in any country. It is published in conjunction with MasterCard.

Why is this book so wonderful? Let me tell you. I was once looking for the perfect country hotel in the perfect location from which to take wonderful day trips. I faxed Cliveden, only to discover that all 21 of their rooms were booked (it was June). I panicked. In the end, I chose a hotel almost blindly from a faxed brochure and was nervous right until we drove up to the door. As it happens, it was one of the most gorgeous hotels I have ever stayed in (Wych Hill House, Stow-on-the-Wold in the Cotswolds); I was incredibly lucky.

If I had had a copy of *Johansen's*, however, I would never have had the agony or the ecstasy. I would have known what I was doing.

Johansen's is a large format trade paperback filled with color pictures (up to four per listing) of country hotels—all of which are our kind of places. There are no Holiday Inns. Each hotel is described, but the pictures are what makes it all worthwhile. The listings are arranged alphabetically by region.

It costs about £20 in bookstores or you may order it by mail. If you want your copy sent to the United States via surface mail, add £3.50; if you want it sent airmail, add £14. Write: Johansens', Horsham, West Sussex, RH13 8ZA; or call 800/786-9556 in the U.S. If you have to leave a message, someone from their offices will call you back; don't panic if it takes several days.

If you buy no other guidebook to Britain, this is the single smartest thing you can buy.

ELECTRONICALLY YOURS

. . . .

I confess to being virtually a techno-peasant. I'm not surfing the Net—I'm trying not to drown. However, I know that a lot of you can do all sorts of online watersports. And the fact is that this is an useful way to obtain tourist information, to get specific travel questions answered, and more. A number of firms provide such information about London and the U.K.; a few of them are listed below.

PROVIDER	ADDRESS
Time Out	http://www.timeout.co.uk
Manchester	GMVCB@MCR1.poptel.org.uk
London Guide	http://www.cs.ucl.ac.uk/misc/uk/london.html
Knowhere Alternative Guide to UK	http://www.state.51.co/uk/state51/knowhere

GETTING THERE

. . . .

From the U.S.

Several airlines will allow you to travel from the United States to Britain and enter at one airport (such as Manchester, or even Dublin in Ireland) and depart from another, often without additional cost. This can be much easier, especially if you are driving or training about the countryside anyway.

In fact, you can avoid London airports entirely. I'm not saying don't visit London, but I am saying that you don't have to use Heathrow or Gatwick. When you plan how to get there, be flexible about airports and connections.

There's no question that the **British Airways** (BA) and **USAir** liaison makes for many a code share and many a new gateway city, giving more and more access to Britain, especially to those who live outside of Manhattan. I almost always fly BA, partly because I collect their miles, partly because I fly them just about everywhere (yes, even to Hong Kong) and partly because I've grown used to their planes, their schedules, and their cute pyjamas.

Virgin has begun a code share with **Delta** so that now you can fly from Heathrow to New York on Virgin but with a Delta ticket, therefore enabling you to collect Delta miles.

Continental is really making a move on British skies and has revved up its number of flights into Manchester. Indeed, the two key words in alternative airporting are Chicago and Manchester. The city of Manchester is now so hot (you can also get there via American Airlines and United) that they've stopped doing extra promotions to lure visitors. They don't want to ruin the charm.

Airline Toll-Free Phone Numbers

American Airlines	800/433-7300
British Airways	800/247-9297
Continental Airlines	800/231-0856
Delta Air Lines	800/241-4141
United Airlines	800/241-6522
Virgin Airlines	800/862-8261

MILEAGE & PROMOTIONAL WARS

• •

There's no question that the best time to travel is when tickets are cheap, which is during the off-season (Oct–Dec and Jan–Mar, generally speaking). There's also something to be said for frequent-flyer mileage wars, which seem to be fought rather regularly as new gates open or carriers make strides against their competitors. Every time an American carrier makes inroads onto British soil, I find that British Airways retaliates with a tantalizing offer. Sometimes it's double mileage, and sometimes mileage awards actually go on sale.

If you regularly fly BA (or even if you don't), it pays to call its toll-free number before booking your flight to see what promotions it is offering. Option 3 on its voice mail message gives you promotional information.

GETTING THERE WITH A BARGAIN

• •

Cheap airfare is probably why our forefathers fought the American Revolutionary War (they just didn't know it at the time). If you're looking to go some-where but aren't sure where, try connecting through London on BA or look into their **World Offers** program.

World Offers, a program that is only available in the U.S. and the U.K., features a continually chang-ing list of cities to which incredibly discounted British Airways airfares are available. The fares are discounted because travel on the affected routes is light at the time. World Offers discounts are an-nounced in newspapers and on BA's toll-free 800 number. You never know what's going to come up for grabs, but if you're willing, it's a fabulous way to get somewhere and save money at the same time. You do get a real live, confirmed ticket, but the ticket isn't available until the last minute. Check with your travel agent, British Airways, any British Airways Travel Shop in Britain; or call 01345/222-111 in the U.K.

GETTING AROUND THE U.K.
· ·

By Car

If you are brave enough to drive around the U.K., you'll probably get the best value with a fly-drive package bought through your airline or the travel agent who arranges both portions of your trip.

There are numerous independent rental agencies in London, most of which offer better rates than the big American companies. The British Tourist Authority (BTA) can provide you with brochures and you'll find plenty of advertisements for these companies in your airline in-flight magazine.

Hertz (tel. 800/654-3301 in the United States and Canada) has a contract with BritRail. This means that they maintain the car rental desks at BritRail train stations, making them the most convenient, if not the least expensive, choice for many travelers.

Ian and I have become keen on renting from **Kemwel** (tel. 800/678-0678), which you can arrange from the United States (even if you are British) with a fax voucher. Prices are incredibly low and agencies can also be in or near train stations, depending upon the country.

If you are driving, I suggest that you stop by one of the Automobile Association (AA) retail stores—there are scads of them everywhere. They sell a lot of guidebooks, including a marvelous small paperback called the *British Highway Code* (99p), which explains British driving rules.

By Train

The best way to get around Great Britain, especially if you are terrified to drive, is to take the train.

Since it broke up, BritRail now has many separate legs. Furthermore, tickets can cost more if you wait until you get to Britain to purchase them. You can obtain any number of BritRail passes from your travel agent or by contacting BritRail Travel International, 1500 Broadway, New York, NY 10036 (tel. 212/575-2667) directly. Please note that these deals are only available in the U.S. Tickets must be purchased prior to departure.

The BritRail passes now available include:

- BritRail Pass for 8, 15, or 22 days or one month for anywhere in Great Britain
- BritRail Flexipass
- BritRail plus Eurostar
- England/Wales Pass
- Freedom of Scotland Pass

Before you can use your pass, you must present it at a BritRail ticket window at any train station for validation first. You cannot hop on a train and think all is forgiven.

Perhaps the best thing about a BritRail Pass is that you don't have to think after you've bought it. The second best thing may be that you are entitled to massive (30% to 40%) discounts on Eurostar (Chunnel train) tickets. You can also buy a BritFrance railpass or any number of other combinations.

Please note that with the breakup of BritRail, the firm is only called BritRail in the United States. The various lines have different names in the United Kingdom, so that you can get even more confused. And various lines have differing promotions. Thus it is that Great Western offers Business First tickets and seating, complete with amenities that would make Richard Branson proud. Yes, for just £1 you can borrow a CD player and use their library of CDs. Choose a video for your private video screen for £2. Great Western also offers Leisure First, a half-fare, first-class ticket that is sold to those spending Saturday night on the road.

Families can save as well. On certain promotions, grown-ups save 20% and kids travel for £2. A Family Railcard can be issued to two adults and up to four children can be added on. However, a Family Railcard is good for standard seats only. There's also the Young Persons Railcard for those aged 16 to 25.

In fact, if you are traveling with children of any age, don't use your common sense or go by American age breaks: Ask! BritRail defines the word *child* rather creatively.

It is impossible to get the cheapest fare unless you have the patience of a saint and the time of an immortal. You can ask three different ticket agents at BritRail and get three different answers. Having said that, here are a few tips to keep in mind if saving is important to you:

• Try to get a ticket agent to explain the differences between saver seats, supersavers, and super-advance return fares. All offer different amounts of discount depending on the day and/or time you travel.

- If you are going to Scotland from London, regardless of when or how you travel, a BritRail pass bought in the United States is your best value.
- If you buy the BritRail pass in the United States, you will get excellent value only if you travel a lot. You will have smooth sailing all the way, and will never be wrong. This pass was made for the type of traveler who can't handle hassles or confusion. It may not be the least expensive way of getting around England, however.
- If you are making day trips from a base in London and are flexible, you may do better without the U.S.-bought BritRail pass. Plan to travel "off-peak, cheap-day return." You can only travel after 9:30am, but you'll save 50% or more on the cost of the ticket. Using cheap-day returns on short-haul trips may cost considerably less than an unlimited-mileage BritRail Pass if you are going to places like Brighton or Oxford.

  If you are going further—such as to Manchester or Stoke—you will probably do better with a pass. I once paid $122 for the one-day, peak fare to Stoke-on-Trent; a four-day BritRail pass bought in the United States would have cost $139 and I would have gotten three more days of travel.
- If you must travel during rush hour but are still going and coming on the same day, ask for a cheap-day return with peak outward bound. If you insist on the freedom to use rush-hour trains, you'll save money with the BritRail pass.
- If you are totally baffled and don't know what to do, go to a ticket machine that says "Quik Tix" and buy an adult cheap-day return. If you owe the conductor more, he'll tell you. Sometimes the lines for tickets are so long you can miss the train.
- If you are doing a lot of travel, and a lot of long-haul travel, the first-class ticket is worthwhile. On short hops (of less than two hours) you're wasting your money.
- If you aren't traveling on a BritRail pass, find out if there is a promotion being offered called

BritRail Train Timings

TO/FROM	LONDON STATION	TYPICAL TRAINS PER DAY	MILES	APPROXIMATE JOURNEY TIME
Aberdeen	King's Cross/Euston	10	524	5 hrs. 45 min.
Bath	Paddington	25	107	1 hr. 11 min.
Birmingham	Euston	35	113	1 hr. 37 min.
Brighton	Victoria	35	51	51 min.
Bristol	Paddington	46	119	1 hr. 26 min.
Cambridge	King's Cross	31	56	1 hr.
Cardiff	Paddington	21	145	1 hr. 47 min.
Chester	Euston	16	179	2 hrs. 36 min.
Edinburgh	King's Cross/Euston	17	400	4 hrs.
Glasgow	King's Cross/Euston	8	401	5 hrs. 5 min.

To/From	London Station	Typical Trains Per Day	Miles	Approximate Journey Time
Manchester	Euston	16	180	2 hrs. 27 min.
Manchester Airport	Euston	16	180	3 hrs.
Oxford	Paddington	35	64	53 min.
Salisbury	Waterloo	18	84	1 hr. 21 min.
Stoke-on-Trent	Euston	11	146	1 hr. 43 min.
Stratford*	Euston	4	121	2 hrs.
York	King's Cross	27	188	1 hr. 57 min.
Gatwick Airport (Express)	Victoria	56	27	30 min.

Weekend Upgrade; it allows you to upgrade a standard ticket to first class for all of £5.

- If you plan on sleeping on a train and you have a BritRail pass, you must pay an additional fee for a couchette. Know the difference between a couchette and a wagon-lit. They aren't the same thing.
- Should you decide to make reservations (usually not needed for first class but a must for second, especially on the big trips such as traveling to Scotland), please note that you pay a few pounds per reservation with a BritRail second-class pass; for a first-class pass, there is no charge. During the holidays, reservations are essential.
- Never forget that you a dumb American. The train personnel will be more than happy to help you. Play it for everything it's worth.
- Don't forget that BritRail publishes a U.S. edition of an annual brochure that outlines not only all of its services, passes, and prices but also provides point-to-point travel information with prices so you can calculate if a pass will be financially beneficial to you. You can get this guide through either the BTA or BritRail; it is free. In it you'll find information on ferries, trips around the U.K. and to Ireland, ferries to Europe, and other important facts. Essential reading. You can book the Chunnel train, Eurostar, through BritRail (tel. 800/677-8585) and Rail Europe (tel. 800/4-EURAIL) in the U.S.
- Note that certain trains from cities outside London have now been designated Eurostar Link trains and are routed through Waterloo in order to connect to the Eurostar. Always note station names carefully, as there is often more than one train station in a large British city.

By Bus

If you have a BritRail pass, then you don't even want to hear the word *bus*, since your train travel is already paid for. However, if you have a four-day BritRail flexipass, you may want to save it for long trips and expensive routes and fill in with additional cheap-day return fares or the bus.

The bus is usually slower than the train, but it is tremendously cheaper. Very often the bus goes right into the heart of town, whereas a train stops at a station on the edge of town.

By Plane

Do consider getting around the U.K. by plane—it's not as far-fetched as it sounds now that British Airways has introduced the Europe Air Pass. It can only be sold to a U.S. citizen in the United States who has bought a transatlantic ticket to Britain (although the ticket need not be on British Airways). With this pass you qualify for a variety of discounted airfares to fly throughout the U.K.

The pass works as follows: Domestic U.K. and other destinations (as far away as Moscow and Tel Aviv) are divided into zones. Each zone has two prices for the fare: one price if you fly out of Heathrow and one price if you fly from Gatwick, Birmingham, Manchester, or Glasgow. Heathrow is more expensive.

BOOKING HOTELS

Don't forget to check with your airline frequent-flyer affiliations to see what you can book at a discount or through redeeming a few miles. Forte has a plan whereby if you book your room 30 days in advance, you get 30% off the bill.

Hotel Chains

I list specific hotels in each city I cover in this guide, but there are a few hotel chains with international reservation services and frequent promotions that can make it very simple for you to reserve a hotel room in Britain, particularly if you plan to stay in the countryside and have no any idea where to stay.

LEADING HOTELS OF THE WORLD   This fine hotel association, which generally claims the best hotel in any given city as a member hotel, has only a handful of hotels in Britain, but they are truly among the finest and best-located properties you can book, especially in the countryside. The brochure has a picture of each property; famous names—aside from **The Dorchester** and **Claridges** in London—include **Cliveden**, outside London, not far from Heathrow; **The Lygon Arms** in Broadway in the Cotswolds (see page 197); and **The Caledonian** in Edinburgh (see page 296). In the U.S., call 800/223-6800 for reservations.

PRIDE OF BRITAIN   This is another one of those chains in which privately owned hotels have banded together to make it easier for you. The brochure looks like a magazine; it's filled with color pictures of their properties as well as a map of Great Britain that shows you exactly where they are, and all the information you need to plan your itinerary accordingly. They have hotels all over Britain, but have a particularly heavy presence in the south and in the Cotswolds. There are three properties in London.

I stayed at one affiliated hotel—**One Devonshire Gardens** in Glasgow—and was quite impressed. One of the most famous hotels in Britain, it is drop-dead gorgeous and not wildly expensive (£140 for a double room with two occupants, including continental breakfast). Other castle and country manor–style hotels in the Pride of Britain chain fall into the £100 to £130 for two price range (breakfast is always included).

Call 800/828-5572 from the United States for reservations. This is a toll-free call to the U.K., so be aware of the time difference when you call.

LYRIC HOTELS   Truly, this is one of my best finds (I owe it all to Carolyn) because this chain is not well known in the United States. Their hotels are located outside Manchester; in Llandudno, Wales;

in Telford, Shropshire (an excellent base from which to explore Wales or The Potteries); in Stow-on-the-Wold (my beloved **Wyck Hill House**); in Gloucester—another great Cotswolds location; and in Surrey (a property that's more of a coaching inn called **Georgina Hotel**).

Not only do I stake my reputation on these adorable hotels, but they have incredible promotions for weekend stays and more. One recent promotion offered a double room for two at a castle hotel called **Madeley Court** for £55/night, off-season; £60, in-season; two nights cost a little over £100 for two.

To contact Lyric, write Lyric Hotels, Old Rectory Hotel, Meadow Lane, Haughton Green, Denton, Manchester, England, M34 1GD. I find it easier to fax them at 161/406-8781.

HILTON Hilton may be synonymous in your mind with big, glitzy, American-style hotels. Think again. Yes, the Hilton Park Lane in London is big and glitzy. But you can also book **The Langham Hilton**—a grande dame hotel that has been modernized with every new convenience.

The Hilton Mews in London proves they can do small and charming; **The Langham** proves they can do historical renovation.

In addition, Hilton has many promotional weekend rates and prices-in-dollars deals. Charm doesn't often enter the picture, but that may not matter to you. Last time I looked, there was a special discount for those with Delta plane tickets and American Express cards. Seems that with this promotion, you could get a room **The Langham Hilton** for $179 per night—this is so inexpensive by London standards (even *world* standards) that you may giggle right into your coin purse. Call 800/HILTONS in the United States for reservations.

FORTE The best thing about Forte is the ease of one-stop reservations; they have at least one hotel in almost every city in England. You can trust any Forte Grand hotel; others may be dicey. Sometimes you can get prices frozen in U.S. dollars and, if you're lucky, find a promotional deal that may include a free rental car, free breakfast, or other such amenities. Their Forte 30 program means you get 30% off if you pay 30 days in advance. Call 800/ 223-5672 in the United States for reservations.

BEST WESTERN If an inn, castle, or hotel in Britain is not signed with Forte, there's a good chance it's signed with Best Western, which has a large number of locations throughout England and a fair number in Wales and Scotland. I very much liked the **Marlborough Arms** in Woodstock, the **Dean Court** in York, and the **Grapevine** in Stow. All have excellent in-town locations. Children up to age 16 stay free with their parents; full English breakfast is included. Call 800/528-1234 in the United States for reservations.

HOME STAYS

. . . .

If you want more hospitality or more space than a hotel can offer, perhaps you want to be a paying guest in someone's home, or take up residence in your own apartment or country home. You can rent by the week or month. The following organizations all allow you to book a home stay through them.

THE NATIONAL TRUST They don't tell you the details and there's no one around to show you how to use the washing machine; linens and electricity are billed separately. Still, it's the National Trust. Sublime cottages and castles galore—some at surprisingly inexpensive weekly and monthly rates. Call 0712/229-251 for a catalogue; they also have offices in Scotland; call 0312/265-922 to make arrangements to book a home stay in Scotland.

WOLSEY LODGES This is a great idea, but I hear through the grapevine that the properties vary tremendously and there are no set standards of quality. Maybe you'll get lucky. Wolsey is a network of private homes that take in boarders. There's a color brochure featuring a picture of each home and a short description. You book directly with your host; to get a copy of the brochure, write Wolsey Lodges, 17 Chapel Street, Bildeston, Suffolk IP7 7EP, England. The BTA sells the brochure for $2.

BULLDOG This is also a private club, but on a much smaller scale. I've written at great length about this service in London, which is very individual and personal, and I also suggest you look into it for country stays. Bulldog is an organization of women who rent out a portion of their own homes to guests. The rate in the country is £55 for a single and £75 for a double. You pay a fee to join Bulldog and then make reservations based on need and location. It's a truly charming way to visit a country. Call 905/737-2798 in Canada and the United States for more information.

BEST BUYS OF BRITAIN

· ·

If you've followed the economic situation in Britain over the last 10 years, you know things there have changed tremendously and that the country has been dramatically hit by the international recession but has begun to come back with optimism in the last few years. High streets are booming and prices on goods continue to be high, but that doesn't mean you can't still find a bargain.

In fact, it was the recession that taught the British that bargain wasn't a dirty word; that sales can be held more frequently than twice a year; that it's okay to ask for a discount or drive for an hour to find a better buy.

People don't make anywhere near the salaries Americans are accustomed to making; daily bread costs a lot more than what Americans are used to paying for it. As a result, you'll notice that almost everything in the United Kingdom costs more than in the United States, particularly with regard to moderately priced merchandise. Nothing is moderately priced in Britain.

Because of this lifestyle difference, there are certain areas where Americans with comfortable salaries can benefit:

Antiques

Since an article must be 100 years old to be officially considered an antique, what I really mean is used furniture and household items. Whether you are buying furniture, old linens and textiles, silver, or ceramics, you can count on a big selection and pretty good savings in Britain.

The savings can be greater now that the VAT laws have been revised and you are entitled to a refund on antiques you purchase. Note that your antiques will only be cheaper if they were acquired by the dealer recently and he or she had to pay tax. Bargin and fix a price before you ask for a tax refund.

Collectibles

Royal memorabilia continues to sell, with the hottest items being Edward VIII coronation souvenirs. Rumor has it that Chuck and Di items are not going to be valuable, but I am holding onto my Fergie spoon (in box, mint condition) nonetheless in the hope that it will be an exception.

Books

Books are expensive in the United Kingdom, but you must consider that, generally speaking, you will find a wider selection of titles than in the United States. Businesspeople, please note: Many English-language business titles are available in the U.K. that can't be found in the U.S., even books published by American publishers. Britain has a number of cities that are famous for their bookshops, such as Oxford and Hay-on-Wye.

China

Even if you factor in shipping costs, china will cost less if you buy it in Britain. If you go to the factory outlets and are willing to buy seconds (of course you are!) you can save 50% to 70% off London retail. You can buy complete dinner service (for eight) of a fancy pattern from a big-name British manufacturer and bring it home for about $500!

It's not that I'm too cheap to pay for shipping, I have done it. But I prefer to pack my own china in wadded-up newspapers, snuggled between my clothes (and all those sweaters) in my suitcase, and schlepp it right to the British Airways counter where the gate agent attaches a champagne glass baggage tag to my suitcase to tell the world it's fragile. I can happily report that I have experienced no breakage, ever.

Needlework

Britain is a big place for DIY (do-it-yourself): Almost everyone knits or does needlework (called "tapestry"). If you remember to ask for tapestry, you'll discover that needlepoint kits abound in the English countryside.

Elizabeth Bradley and Kaffe Fassett needlepoint kits cost less in Britain than in the United States.

Home Decorative Items

Whether you shop at Laura Ashley or at Marks & Spencer, you'll find prices on home decorative items so dramatically lower than in the United States that you will be ready to redecorate your whole home, and then some. Laura Ashley stores are much more complete in England and offer a very wide range of styles in the home furnishings area—and we're not just talking cute little flowers anymore. A basic double roll of Laura Ashley wallpaper costs £8 to £10 in Britain at full retail and $27 in the United States. If you buy from the sale bins, you'll pay £5 per double roll.

Status Stuff

I don't usually buy designer clothes with impressive labels, but on my last visit to the U.K., I did some comparison shopping on a few items, and found that while prices in the United States and England can run awfully close to identical, there is a possibility of savings on the value-added tax (VAT) versus sales tax front. Whereas a Burberry raincoat was only $53 less in London than in New York, I must note that no one was standing on the corner of Fifth Avenue and 54th Street handing out $50 bills last week; $50 saved is $50 saved.

In case you want to run your own comparisons, the regular retail price of a ladies' trench coat at Burberry's is £495; on sale, it is priced at £275. The full retail price of a men's trench coat is £515; on sale, it goes for £295.

The Ferragamo shoes that I live in—low heels with the tuxedo bow—cost $165 (plus tax) in New York. The same shoes cost £100 in England, but then I get the VAT refund so they cost a little less. I'll take it.

Don't expect big savings on designer items, but if you spend enough to qualify for a VAT refund, you may come out a small percentage point or two ahead.

Chapter Three

· · · · · · · · ·

MONEY MATTERS

BRITISH ECONOMICS 101

· ·

If you are considering a trip to Great Britain, begin watching the dollar/pound ratio and talk to your travel agent about what deals can be guaranteed in which currency and what will happen to your investment if the dollar gets stronger.

This is where I start screaming, because I go absolutely stark raving mad when it comes to converting U.S. traveler's checks into pounds sterling. If you are not careful, you will be charged a fee *and* a commission! As in $15 per $100! We all knew the idea of a unilateral currency was never going to fly in the European Union, but the day British prime minister John Major called the notion "Euro-Crap" was the day I realized we are all doomed to convert and convert and convert.

- The rate of exchange you get is never what is listed in the paper, so you can forget about the bank rate.
- Buy traveler's checks in the United States from a financial institution with many branches throughout England. If you have a Barclay's service card, you will not be charged a fee for changing money in England. I stick with American Express. There is an American Express office in the prime part of every tourist city in England and Scotland, so with

care and planning you should be okay. If you have AmEx checks, AmEx will not charge you to convert them.

- Weigh the rate of exchange against any check-cashing fee. For example, we are staying at Hotel X and two blocks away is Bank Z. At Hotel X the rate of exchange is £1 = $1.58. There is no fee to hotel guests for changing money. At Bank Z, the rate of exchange is $1.55, *but* we must pay £3 in order to change money.
- Consider buying traveler's checks in pounds sterling while you are still in the United States.
- Always calculate the price of your purchases at the rate for which you bought your money—if you are paying in cash. The bank rate may be $1.53, but if you are paying $1.55, then divide accordingly. I once bought several items for friends at home, paying $2 per pound for each item. By the time my friends reimbursed me, the dollar had gained; they wanted to pay the going bank rate of $1.78. That's not fair. If you agree to shop for someone, agree to the rate of exchange ahead of time. Also calculate the fee for changing money as part of your price for the pound, in order to really understand what you paid for your money. If you change a $100 traveler's check every other day during a 10-day stay, that's five times £3, or about $25 that's just lost into thin air.
- Bank machines (ATMs) are more and more popular in Europe and are as easy to use in England as they are in the United States. American Express has its own private system that you need to sign up for. MasterCard and Visa have thousands of machines that allow you to withdraw cash in local currency. There is, as always, a small charge for each transaction, but this is possibly the single best way to change money these days. A bank machine is often called a "cashpoint."

VALUE-ADDED TAX

· ·

Value-added tax (VAT) is the equivalent of our sales tax. It differs from U.S. tax in that it is higher (17.5%) and is automatically added to the price of goods (not services, unless specified in the small print).

U.S. visitors may get a VAT refund from stores that participate in refund programs by meeting a minimum required expenditure. Stores may regulate that minimum—the fancier the store, the higher the minimum. Many stores say it is not worth doing the paperwork for less than £50, but a number of designer shops require you to spend £75 or £100. Harrods now asks for a £100 minimum.

There are three different companies now organized to do the paperwork for stores, so don't be surprised if your VAT forms differ. They all require the same information about you and your arrival and departure from the U.K., as well as a brief description of the merchandise, a stamped imprint from the store, and a final okay from a U.S. Customs officer.

1. Whether you are considering one purchase or several, ask about the store's minimum requirement before you decide if you want to buy it or not.
2. Make sure you leave a store with the proper paperwork and an envelope with either a frank (indicating postage has been paid) or a stamp on it.
3. Do not pack your purchases with checked luggage, as you must show them to Customs upon departure, and the Customs office is deep in the bowels of the airport, way past the ticket and baggage counters and past Immigration. If your purchases are too cumbersome to carry on, bring them in a suitcase to the Customs agent (a porter

will help you, if need be) in the London airport, and then go back to the airline desk and check your luggage. Allow time for this. If you do not have your purchases with you, take them to a notary public once you are home (in the United States) and have the forms notarized. Add appropriate postage to your envelopes and mail. Your refund will be processed properly.

Note to those flying out of Manchester: In Manchester there's only one agent in a tiny office just to the right of Immigration. Allow extra time. I once had to wait 20 minutes for the agent to come back from her coffee break to get my forms processed; consequently, I barely made it to my plane in time.

4. Indicate on the forms that you wish to be refunded on your credit card; otherwise you will most likely get a check in pounds, not dollars, which you will have to pay a fee to cash. Watch your refund dwindle before your eyes! My bank in the U.S. once wanted $15 to process a £15 check.

5. Don't be shocked if you lose a percentage of the refund to the retailer. Most shops charge a fee for processing your refund. All of the department stores do this. It's usually £3 to £5.

TAX REFUNDS

If you have been to several different countries in the European Union or are going on to other EU countries after you leave Britain, you must play by the new rules in order to claim a VAT refund.

Outward-bound visitors place their claim with EU Customs agents at their final point of departure from the EU. For example, even if you bought everything in Britain but are departing from Paris, you must file for a VAT refund in Paris, not London.

If you are leaving London but going on to Mombasa, you must file for a refund in London because Kenya is not a member of the EU.

THE VARIABLE AIRPORT REFUND

Because Heathrow is such a zoo, especially in the summer season, you must allot enough time to stand in line to show your goods in order to have your refund processed. One-half hour is the minimum amount of time you should expect to stand in line. It could be longer.

Of course, to beat all of the problems associated with congestion at Heathrow, you can use one of the alternative British airports—particularly Birmingham or Manchester. The lines here are a fraction of what they are at Heathrow.

On the other hand, please remember that I've had to physically go looking for the Customs officer in the Manchester airport because there is only one and the VAT refund system was rather new to her. This can happen, but Manchester is sprucing up its act, and you probably won't have any trouble.

Small airports are simply smaller and they have smaller problems. Enjoy them while the world expands.

BRINGING IT ALL BACK HOME

To make your reentry into the United States as smooth as possible, follow these tips:

- Know the rules and stick to them!
- Don't try to smuggle anything.
- Be polite and cooperative (up until the point when they ask you to strip, anyway).

Remember:

- You are currently allowed to bring in $400 worth of merchandise per person, duty-free. Before you leave the United States, verify this amount with one of the U.S. Customs offices. It may change. Each member of the family is entitled to the deduction, including infants. You may pool within a family.
- You pay a flat 10% duty on the next $1,000 worth of merchandise.
- Duties thereafter are based on the type of product. (Hefty levies on hand embroidery!)
- The head of the family can make a joint declaration for all family members. The "head of the family" need not be male, but whoever it is should take the responsibility for answering any questions the Customs officers may ask. Answer questions honestly, firmly, and politely. Have receipts ready, and make sure they match the information on the landing card. Don't be forced into a story that won't wash under questioning. If you tell a little lie, you'll be labeled as a fibber and they'll tear your luggage apart.
- You count into your $400 per person everything you obtain while abroad—this includes toothpaste (if you bring the unfinished tube back with you), items bought in duty-free shops, gifts for others, items other people asked you to bring home for them, and—get this—even alterations.
- Have the Customs registration slips for your personally owned goods in your wallet or easily available. If you wear a Cartier watch, be able to produce the registration slip. If you cannot prove that you took a foreign-made item out of the country with you, you may be forced to pay duty on it!
- The unsolicited gifts you mailed from abroad do not count in the $400-per-person rate. If the value of the gift is more than $50, you pay duty when the package enters the country. Remember, only one unsolicited gift per person per mailing.

- Do not attempt to bring in any illegal food items—
dairy products, meats, fruits, or vegetables (coffee is okay). Generally speaking, if it's alive, it's
verboten. Processed cheeses (hard cheeses) are
legal! Creamy cheese is illegal.
- We don't need to tell you it's tacky to bring in
drugs and narcotics.
- Dress for success. People who look like "hippies"
get stopped at Customs more than average folks.
Women who look like a million dollars, who are
dragging their fur coats, have first-class baggage
tags on their luggage, and carry Gucci handbags,
but declare they have bought nothing, are equally
suspicious.
- The amount of cigarettes and liquor you can bring
back duty-free is under government regulation.
Usually if you arrive by common carrier you may
bring in one liter of alcoholic beverages duty-free.
You may bring in an additional five liters on which
you must pay duty—at $10.50 per gallon for distilled spirits—so obviously you don't want to go
over your allowance unless you are carrying some
invaluable wine or champagne.

  You may also bring back 100 cigars and one
carton of cigarettes without import duty, but there
will be state and local taxes on the smokes. You
cannot trade your cigar/cigarette/liquor quota
against your $400 personal allowance. You must
be 21 or over to get the liquor allowance, but
you may be any age for the puffables. Thus an
infant's tobacco allowance is the same as an
adult's. Remember, no cigars from Cuba, please.

Some no-nos are governed on a statewide basis, so
check with Customs officials at your point of entry.
A few tips:

1. Elephant ivory is banned. Antiques made of ivory
must be accompanied by proper paperwork.
2. Tortoise shell is forbidden, no matter where it
comes from (unless, that is, it comes from a
plastic turtle!).

Chapter Four

· · · · · · · ·

SHOPPING STRATEGIES

THE MOSCOW RULE OF SHOPPING

· ·

The "Moscow Rule of Shopping" is one of my most simple and basic rules and pertains to all shoppers everywhere in the world, not just to those going to Russia, but to those going to Great Britain or any-place where many cities and towns will be visited. The rule is: *Buy it when you see it.*

It's that simple. Unless you are doing a huge day of comparison shopping and have nothing else to do with yourself but comparison shop and schlepp back to previous reference points, or you are pick-ing up an item of which there is unlimited stock in a million towns and valleys along your regular travel route, you should buy it when you see it, since you may never see it again.

Don't make yourself nuts during a day's outing or a week's holiday. Even if you are overpaying slightly or it inconveniences you to carry it all day, if you love it and have to have it, buy it when you see it.

The Moscow Rule of Shopping does break down when you are shopping for antiques or knickknacks, since condition and novelty are two factors that you cannot account for. To help you sort out your feel-ings, ask yourself these questions:

1. Is this a touristy type of item that I am bound to find all over town? If so, wait.
2. Is this an item I can't live without, even if I am overpaying? If so, buy it now.
3. Is this a reputable shop, and can I trust what they tell me about the availability of such items? Will they hold it for me? If the answer is yes, wait.
4. Is the quality of this particular example so spectacular that it cannot be matched anywhere else? Buy it now.

Regular retail prices on brand names in clothes and china are the same all over Britain. However, sale prices vary from store to store, and are notoriously lower outside of London.

COUNTRY HOUSE SALES

A newish concept that is taking Great Britain by storm is the country house sale. This is a fancy tag sale (read *yard sale*) held in a stately manor. If the owners can't handle the burden themselves, they turn it over to an auction house (usually Sotheby's, but Christie's also performs this service). Just to get into the houses is considered a dream come true for locals; tourists rarely even hear about such sales. There is a viewing before the sale, so if you don't trust yourself with your allowance, you may enjoy a nonsale day. Watch newspapers and local magazines for advertisements or ask your hotel's concierge.

ENGLAND BY MAIL

To really understand retail in Britain, you have to understand the mail-order business. To maximize your time and fun in Great Britain, you may find ordering goods by mail order an additional bonus.

Britain is a small country. Not only is it small, but it's got a fabulous postal service. There are two mail deliveries a day and first- and second-class mail. You can mail something today and it will be received in Scotland tomorrow. Honest.

Meanwhile, British retail is owned mostly by the multiples, all of which have catalogues. People who are too busy to get into stores use catalogues heavily. In fact, if you think catalogues are popular in the United States, there is double or triple the interest in Britain.

There are therefore two different branches of mail order at work in Britain: catalogues from the big multiples for people who are too busy to get to town and catalogues that offer unique goods that come from specialty sources that could not afford to open on every high street in the United Kingdom and stay in business. Some catalogue firms provide specialty items (clothes for petites, lingerie, etc.) and others offer a full retail line in an attempt to simulate the experience of shopping the store, floor by floor, as you flip the pages.

Some of the catalogues are such big business and are so elaborately produced that they are sold at newsagents along with regular magazines; this includes department store catalogues and major multiples such as Laura Ashley. In fact, one of the newest trends in publishing in Britain is the cross-over from catalogue to magazine; see page 42.

It's difficult for an American tourist who is only in town for three days to get into this, but if you are back and forth a lot, or have friends and/or family in Britain, or want to branch into things that no one at home has, you may want to get more interested in shopping by catalogue. You may have goods shipped to you in the United States (watch out for the duty!) or mailed to you at your hotel to be held for your arrival. *Note:* The Windsor catalogue is for Americans in America.

British Catalogues

BRORA If your trip to the United Kingdom does not bring you to Scotland, poor you. Make up for it by phoning 171/731-7672, which is the London phone number for an old Scottish mill that sells tweeds and shetlands and even cashmere and does a marvelous country look.

CULPEPER THE HERBALIST You can read my rave about Culpeper on page 69; this is a catalogue it actually makes sense to order from while in America because there really aren't any stores like this in the United States. They have a huge international mail business in place and things cost so little to begin with that the price of the item and the shipping together aren't unbearable, although there is an £18 minimum for international airmail. Surface mail to the United States has a £10 minimum.

HARRODS Catalogue sold at newsagents; there are small promotional catalogues that come in the mail to charge customers; there's a special January Sale Catalogue that's available to you in the United States so you can shop without flying over; and then there's the "big book," which is the magazine sold on newsstands.

HARVEY NICHOLS Catalogue sold at newsagents.

KINGSHILL The British designer's collection: designs by the likes of Caroline Charles, Paul Costelloe; bags, accessories, and even jewelry—also a new, lower priced catalogue called Diffusion. To order, call 1494/890-555 in Great Britain. There is also Kingshill Diffusion; same phone number. Overseas orders are no problem.

LAURA ASHLEY This catalogue is so big it looks like a magazine and is sold with other magazines at any newsagent's stand. Catalogues are intermingled with magazines, not placed in a separate department.

RACHEL GRIMMER Jumpers (that's sweaters, to you Yanks), similar to Bill Baber. For a copy, write c/o 21 Devonshire Place, Harrogate, HG1 4AA or call 1423/524-236. Catalogue costs £1.50.

REID & WATERERS   Simply great garden catalogue; any American who is into serious gardening
should be on the phone already—call 1815/723-225
for a copy.

WEALTH OF NATIONS   This is sort of a fancy
ethnic costume dress-up catalogue but the prices are
fair and the selection so wide you won't look like
you are wearing your last vacation. The number of
classical ethnic pieces is astonishing. Just about
everything costs under £50. Some of the clothes
are sold at Liberty of London. For a catalogue, call
171/371-5333.

THE WHITE COMPANY   Linen and white work,
some from the Orient, at seemingly fair prices. Also
wool blankets, Irish linen, and other bed and bath
needs. Call 171/385-7988 or fax 171/385-2685 for
a copy. Not to be confused with **The White Shirt
Collection**, which carries a nice line of women's
blouses. Call 171/833-3388 for their catalogue.

MAGAZINE OFFERS

. . . .

I am always shocked at the amount of private label
retail that is done on behalf of British publications.
One look at a British newsstand tells you that British publishing is alive and fabulous, but did you
realize that many women's magazines and home
and garden magazines have their own fulfillment
houses so that they can provide "special offers" on
merchandise?

    An example of this trend is a full-page advertise-
ment I just spotted in *Country Living* for the "Cardigan of the Year," a patterned blue knit sweater
priced at £33 (about $50). Most of the clothing items
sold through magazines are priced and styled rather
conservatively, partly because this is Britain and
partly because people don't like to make mistakes,
especially when ordering clothes through the mail.

MAGAZINE EVENTS

. . . .

One of the things that truly slays me is the intimate relationship various British magazines appear to have with their readers. I am constantly awed by the number of special offers and events planned by these magazines. Events often feature special sale events held once or twice a year or even mini-conventions and showcases. Weekends away, do-it-yourself classes, special trips, and opportunities to shop when stores are closed are also arranged. Some of these events are free, some require a ticket but are free, some have registration and require prepayment in full, and some are "buy a ticket at the gate" events.

Almost all of the home and garden magazines have these events; two of my faves are sponsored by *Country Living* and *Homes and Garden*. Who could resist an invitation to the "Summer Grand Sale" at Riply Castle in North Yorkshire? It's a crafts fair-cum-antique show with 80 dealers and costs £6.50 to attend. You clip the registration form from the pages of the magazine and mail it in. A variety of dates are available. Amazing.

ENGLAND AND THE SPREE

. . . .

It's very hard to plan a shopping trip to England when you know full well that, culturally speaking, the English only shop twice a year (during sale season). Furthermore, the dollar has been dancing a little bit lately and one is no longer sure what's cheap and what isn't. Therefore, a few modest rules:

- Nothing in London is cheap.
- Items sold in the countryside can be well priced, fairly priced, or even thoughtfully priced—some simply offer good value.

- Antiques and silly finds still make the best gifts, offer the best prices, and send you home with the kind of shopping stories you will live to tell until you are 90.

SOCIOLOGICAL REAL ESTATE

Once you get out of London, you'll find that most small English cities are organized in more or less the same manner. They all have a high street, which is the main road through town and the primary shopping street.

Bigger cities have a small network of streets for retail business; often part of town is devoted to antique shops. There is almost always a single building that is the antique center for that city—it may have anywhere from eight to 20 stalls. A few have more than that. The antique neighborhood is not usually in the main part of town; it may or may not be within walking distance of the high street. Antique dealers tend to gravitate to slightly lower-rent areas, as do up-and-coming shops. The bigger the city, the more chance there is for alternative retailing in out-of-the-way places.

The "Tourist Trap Rule of Shopping" insists that any city that boasts a famous landmark has not only a plethora of souvenir shops, but substantial retail business clustered either near the landmark or on the way to the landmark. Hence Laura Ashley is across the street from the Shakespeare Museum in Stratford-upon-Avon. There's a mile of solid shopping from Edinburgh Castle to Holyrood Palace.

FACTORY OUTLETS

There is a factory outlet business in Britain, just as in the United States, and it seems to be growing by leaps and bounds. In fact, the first outlet mall to open in Britain is in Hull (on the coast, 40 miles east of York). It's called **Hornsea Freeport** (after Freeport, Maine) but only has a dozen or so outlets including **Austin Reed, Laura Ashley, Aquascutum,** and **Knickerbox.** Just as many shops associate themselves with famous landmarks inside a town, these outlet stores seem to find a patch of real estate that is in the middle of nowhere but is within an hour of somewhere, so you can get to the outlets en route to a tourist destination. The outlet village in Bicester is a mere 15 miles from Oxford.

Any "factory outlet" located on a high street is not a real outlet. Real outlets should be in out-of-the-way locations (preferably in factories or in manufacturing towns), and should require a car to get to them. Any outlet conveniently placed for easy tourist access should smell fake. Even in Wales.

Note that what the British call a "mill shop" is more likely a free-standing outlet or a unit inside a real factory. Outlet malls, a newer phenomenon, have been mostly built in partnership with American outlet mall developers and resemble traditional U.S.-style outlet malls, only they have fewer tenants. In the United Kingdom, 60 outlets in a mall is considered a big mall. Some malls include: Bicester (say "Bista") Village, Bicester, Oxfordshire; Clarks Village, Street, Somerset; Cheshire Oaks, Ellesmere Port (between Manchester and Cheter), Cheshire; Hornsea Freeport, Hull, East Yorkshire; Jackson's Landing, Hartlepool (The Borders); K Village, Kendal (Lake District).

Mill shops and factory outlets have become such a hot new thing that manufacturers who used to keep their outlets a secret are now bragging about having such resources. At any Jaeger mill shop you can get a printed brochure with the addresses of all the Jaeger mill shops and outlet stores. Check the travel section of any bookstore in the United Kingdom for books about outlets. *The Good Deal Directory* by Noelle Walsh comes out once a year; Gillian Cuttress writes a series of regional guides to mill shops and outlets called *The Factory Shop Guide.*

SHOPPING TO SAVE

· ·

The more you shop and the more you mentally adjust to the cost of living, the more you will come to think in British prices. Believe it or not, you will come to think of the buying power of $1 as the same as that of £1. When someone says, "It's only 10 quid," you'll automatically translate that as "only 10 dollars." But 10 quid is anywhere from $15 to $20. Yet the buying power is on parity even when the actual sums are not, and you will be hard pressed to justify measure for measure if you keep translating costs from pounds to dollars and prices back home.

Under these conditions, shopping to save takes on a new challenge.

- If you are interested in British-quality big-name clothes or designer goods, check U.S. prices at regular retail and on sale before leaving home. Write them down, if need be. Also keep state taxes in mind. Your only savings in this category may be on the difference between U.S. sales tax and a value-added tax (VAT) refund (see page 33).
- Avoid American names in Britain even if they are on sale. I call this the "Coals to Newcastle Theory of Retailing." As it happens, sometimes American designers—less well known in Britain—get marked down to very low prices in big sweeping sales, and they bear consideration at times like these. But for the most part, The Gap is outrageously expensive everywhere in Britain (even on sale) and Ralph Lauren's goods cost the exact same amount they do in the United States.
- Know your collectibles market or your antique furniture prices and selection. Most people who buy large pieces in Britain do it for the choice, then the savings. Since it's unlikely you can take an armoire on the flight home as carry-on luggage, figure in the cost of shipping. Although this rule of thumb can break down under close

scrutiny, I find it useful to think of shipping costs
as being twice the price of the item I want to ship.

• If you are decorating, know your fabrics, your
wallpapers, your prices, and your measurements.
You can expect to find some unbelievable bargains
in Britain, so be ready to pounce. One roll of
British wallpaper is equal to almost two rolls
of American wallpaper. If you need help, go to a
local Laura Ashley and play dumb.

• If you are shopping to have fun and to send home
a few pieces and only possibly to save some money,
you will accomplish all these goals. If you are
seriously shopping for an entire house, know
your stuff or take an expert with you, or go on a
shopping tour with an expert. She may get a percentage of what you buy, but you will get the added
advantage of her expertise. Remember: An expert
who has a reputation to lose will never steer you
wrong.

ABOUT THAT DUTY-FREE SHOP

All of Heathrow has turned into a shopping mall.
It's almost as if providing departure gates for
inbound and outbound aircraft has become the
airport's second priority. As the years pass, the
various terminals seem to actually compete with each
other, not just for carriers but for branch stores.
Please note that the firm that was hired to set up
this mall-shopping concept has been hired by several American airports to redo American airports.
Pittsburgh is the U.S. showcase, but Indianapolis has
also signed up.

Meanwhile, back to Heathrow. Since I invariably
fly British Airways, I am most familiar with Terminal Four at Heathrow, so let's use it as an example
in discussing duty-free shops.

I once bought my friend Lilla a bottle of the
Lagerfeld fragrance Sun, Moon, Stars at the duty-
free shop in Terminal Four thinking this was a

Tie One On: The Hermès Tie Report

For the most part, an Hermès tie in the Bond Street Shop costs £62, but qualifies you for a VAT refund of 17.5%, which brings the cost of the tie to you down to £55. For you math phobics out there, this means that the tie costs about $88.

Unless there is some sort of wonderful promotion going on, such as the one described below, an Hermès tie at the Hermès counter in the Terminal Four duty-free shop costs £55—the same price.

An Hermès tie in Paris costs 550 F, which means (with an exchange rate at the time of writing of 5 F= $1) that the tie costs over $100. With a less favorable rate of exchange, the tie costs even more.

Last but not least, let's keep in mind the price of an Hermès tie in New York. It costs $135, plus N.Y. sales tax of over 8%.

Who said there aren't any bargains in Britain?

divine gift: it was new, probably not available in the United States, and tax-free. Boy, was I wrong! When I got back home and saw that Saks Fifth Avenue had Sun, Moon, Stars and was selling it for less than what I paid for it at Heathrow (which was the regular retail price, no less), I couldn't believe it. Not to mention the fact that the dollar was trading at $1.50 to £1 at the time.

This one experience pretty much burned me on the duty-free shops at Heathrow until the time I went back and discovered that Hermès ties were on sale at the Hermès counter for £50 each if you bought two (they are normally £55). Needless to say, I forgot my past experience and bought two ties.

ABOUT THE OTHER AIRPORT SHOPS

Talk about your captive audience! Anyone shopping at an airport doesn't have many bargain choices. Magazines cannot be marked up, so stock up, but souvenirs are very expensive (buying them at your hotel is cheaper).

Note that both the Manchester Airport and Heathrow have amazing shopping opportunities, but these shops are divided into two categories: those before you cross immigration and legally "leave" the country and those in the duty-free zone. Most of the good shops in Manchester are located in the airport itself, not the duty-free zone.

ONBOARD SHOPPING

For the most part, the duty-free shopping selection on airplanes is very small and will not satisfy a serious shopper. And yes, you have to declare whatever you buy and pay duty on it to Uncle Sam when you arrive home. I recommend taking the duty-free brochure off your airplane when you arrive in the United Kingdom so you can use it to help you run price comparisons in the duty-free shop at the airport before you leave the United Kingdom. If you find that you can do better shopping onboard your flight home, don't buy anything in the airport and wait for takeoff.

Chapter Five

. . . .

BRITISH DICTIONARY OF LIFE & STYLE

AN ALPHABETICAL GUIDE

. . . .

In this chapter, I've put together a small dictionary of the words, terms, and revelations that help me to survive on the road in Great Britain. As an American, I am constantly floored at how many language, lifestyle, and cultural differences there are between Britain and the United States. I also work more closely with local types in this book than in any of my others, partly because I can't drive in Britain. As elsewhere, I am dependent on the kindness of strangers to get around. My friends in the United Kingdom have been kinder still. They teach me new words daily.

Anyone who thinks Brits and Americans speak the same language is sadly mistaken. Ask questions about definitions that don't make sense to you.

A.F. Price tags marked with the initials "A.F." are almost always attached to ceramics. These initials mean the item is "at fault." It is therefore priced below market value because it is cracked or chipped. If you see no damage or signs of repair, ring the piece with your finger and judge by the sound you hear. If there's an interior weakness, you will hear it because the piece will ring with a flat, dull sound rather than a pure, high-pitched clink.

Andirons   Also known as firedogs, these are two metal stands inserted in fireplaces to hold firewood.

Aran   Islands off Ireland's western coast known for their fishing sweaters, which are made in different cabled patterns. Long ago, the patterns identified the village a fisherman was from, an aid should his body be recovered from the sea. Shoppers in all parts of the United Kingdom call these sweaters either Arans or fisherman sweaters.

Argyle   A dukedom, a castle, and a sweater—or a pair of socks! Argyle patterns are knitted with colored diamonds counted in, and can be rather intricate.

Aromatherapy   The practice of using natural plant and herb oils and extracts to heal and otherwise promote general physical well-being—an alternative form of treatment used for centuries that is now part of the New Age. Aromatherapy is especially big in Britain where several firms specialize in selling ready-made products created with the proper essential oils and extracts or the ingredients themselves so that you can mix your own. Oils and extracts are never to be taken internally but are ideal for mixing with an oil base to create massage oils, body lotions, and potpourri. See the box on page 52 for an alphabet of herbs and essences used in aromatherapy.

ASDA   A chain of grocery stores, most of which are modern and new.

Bangers and Mash   Sausage and mashed potatoes, my favorite thing to order at Langan's Brasserie.

Bank Holiday   On a bank holiday, the banks are closed but the stores are not. At least, the big stores in the big cities are open. In small cities, it can go either way. Bank holidays are established ahead of time and are somewhat related to the season (there's a Spring Bank Holiday, a Summer Bank Holiday, etc.). Like American holidays, many are rigged so that they fall on a Monday. When planning a trip,

Culpeper's Alphabet of Aromatherapy

As you've probably gathered, I'm wild about aromatherapy. Here's a handy primer to the essential plant and herb oils and essences found in these products, courtesy of Culpeper the Herbalist.

Aniseed Used as a room freshener to help nervous tension.

Basil Can be helpful in inducing sleep.

Bay Used in massage oils to relieve aches and pains.

Bergamont The ideal room freshener: citrusey, fresh, and uplifting.

Chamomile Used in massage oils to relieve aches and pains.

Caraway Used in the bath for its aromatic qualities.

Cinnamon A powerful antiseptic.

Citronella A wonderful insect repellant.

Clove Strongly antiseptic.

Cypress Used in the bath to relieve piles.

Dill Refreshing and calming; used in the bath.

Eucalyptus Massage into chest when diluted with massage oil, or put in bathwater.

Fennel Used in facial steams.

Ginger Can be added to massage oils for aches and pains.

Jasmine An antidepressant; used to relieve menstrual pain.

Juniper Excellent in massage oils for relieving rheumatic pain.

Lavender Can help to calm nervous headaches. Can be vaporized in room to induce sleep. Added to a bath, it relaxes and refreshes. Be careful when you inhale; extremely strong and able to burn skin. Should be diluted with massage oil or water.

Lime Very refreshing, used in the bath and to freshen rooms.

Mandarin A bath fragrance used to encourage sleep.

Myrrh Healing, anti-inflamatory, and antiseptic.

Neroli Used in the bath to provide calm.

Nutmeg   Stimulating. Has the reputation of being an aphrodisiac.

Orange   Thought to improve skin elasticity. Relaxing and sedative in the bath.

Peppermint   Powerful digestive and antiseptic.

Pine   Stimulating in the bath.

Rose   Excellent in cases of tension, worry, and sadness.

Rosemary   Good for headaches and depression.

Rosewood   Excellent bath and massage oil.

Sage   Warm, soothing bath ingredient, ideal for helping one to relax.

Sandalwood   A relaxing room freshener.

Spearmint   Used in footbaths and as a mouthwash.

Tea Tree   Used in a hot bath in case of flu.

Thyme   Added to rinse water, can help to fight dandruff.

Vetiver   Traditionally used to scent linen.

Ylang Ylang   Soothing emotionally.

---

especially to the countryside, check to see if any bank holidays coincide with your stay, as they can really affect your schedule and your shopping plans.

Barbour   The maker of weatherproof coats in certain specific styles that are de rigueur for English country life. Few other brands will do (maybe Burberry or Aquascutum), and no other brand is acceptable to Sloane Rangers. Their waterproof coats or jackets are called wax jackets (the wax makes them waterproof). Several other brands make wax jackets. This one is considered the best; they are also expanding the line into footwear, etc.

Battersea Boxes   Battersea is an up-and-coming London neighborhood; a Battersea box is a small enamel box that can be round, oval, or cylindrical and usually measures no larger than an inch or two across. They were originally made from 1750 to 1840; old ones are highly collectible, but reproductions are currently made.

Halcyon Days is the most famous maker of reproduction Battersea boxes, but there are two or three other companies that also make them. To be authentic, the box must be enameled; ceramic copies are available for much less money. In addition to boxes, there are also Battersea enamel wine labels, watch cases, and small gift items.

BHS   The initials and store logo for British Home Stores, a chain of department stores that cater to the middle class. Fancier than Kmart, but the quality of their goods is about the same.

Bilston Boxes   A style of Battersea box, made in the shape of an animal.

Blue and White   Those who collect blue and white transfer ware call it simply "blue and white," and the world knows. Those who collect Chinese export porcelain (see "Chinese Export Porcelain," below) also call it blue and white, and the world smiles. Both styles are high on everyone's rave list, but export is far more expensive.

British collectors are very serious about their blue and white and most of them collect British transfer wares, not export. Prices are high, and there is much talk about marks and some fair amount of quoting from *The Blue and White Dictionary*, which weighs a ton, costs a fortune, and is imperative if you are really a collector.

Transfer printing is thought to have been developed by Josiah Spode in the late 1700s, but it caught on so quickly that no one is certain who got there first. The technique is extremely difficult but can be oversimplified to be understood: The pattern (almost always a scenic, but sometimes a floral) is engraved on a copper plate; the finished engraving is rubbed down with cobalt paste; a softened (in soap or oil) piece of tissue paper is laid over the paste, removed, and then laid onto the china, thus imprinting the pattern and completing the transfer. Since anything can go wrong, there are frequently seconds.

Some people collect blue and white in all patterns; some collect a specific pattern; others collect from certain makers or periods. Age and condition affect value; a covered sugar bowl from 1790 (this is a real example), with a fault, sells for £199. See page 56 for information on Chinese export; see page 54 for information on famous blue and white patterns; see page 54 for more on transfer printing. See the Blue and White Room at the Spode factory in Stoke-on-Trent (page 282) if you really want to lose your mind.

Bone China   Pottery is made by firing clay; bone china is made of ground bonemeal (animal bones) and clay, which makes it lighter and stronger than pottery. Bone china is a type of porcelain made famous by English potters.

Brogues—Traditional English shoes with little holes tooled or punched into the leather in a pattern around the toe and front of the shoe. The fringed flap that is sometimes attached through the shoelaces is called a "ghillie." Oxford brogues are the dressy shoes some Americans now call oxfords.

Bucket Shop   This is what we in the United States call a consolidator, a discount travel agent that sells discounted airfares and packages. Most bucket shops focus on selling packages to the Continent to the local population. However, if you are considering a side trip from the United Kingdom—such as a visit to Paris—you might want to book your arrangements through one as well after you arrive. Bucket shops advertise in the back of *Time Out,* a weekly cultural magazine sold on newsstands, and operate mostly in London. Since unethical, fly-by-night bucket shops do exist, have your brain turned on when you deal with one and make sure you're satisfied with what you are being offered before you hand over money.

Burberrys   Thomas Burberry was a draper working from a little shop in Basingstoke (Surrey) in the mid-1800s when he realized there was no weather-proof apparel on the market. He developed the fabric gabardine, which King Edward VII called "Burberry." Burberry soon devised the raincoat, as well as other weatherproof gear for sportsmen, ex-plorers, and world conquerors. (Lord Kitchener went down in his Burberry.) The company expanded, obviously, and now produces ready-to-wear for men, women, and children, as well as "weatherproof apparel." The plaid lining in beige, cream, and red is the trademark of the company and has become a status symbol.

Busby   The big, fat, tall (and heavy) black fur hat that some of the guards wear on royal watch.

Car Boot Sale   The car's boot is the trunk. A car boot sale, literally translated, is one in which people sell things from the backs of their cars. It's actually a tag sale or garage sale or whatever you want to call it, very often in a large parking lot or an open field and people do set up tables next to their cars, so it's not like you have to rummage through some-one's car boot.

To attend, you sometimes have to pay an admis-sion charge of a few pounds (which goes to the charity if this is a charity event). The quality of the goods is the same as what you find in a typical American yard sale. The season is late spring, sum-mer, and early fall. For specific addresses and dates, buy a copy of *Antiques Fairs and Markets Diary* (see page 84) or ask your hotel concierge when you check in. Car boot sales are also advertised in local newspapers, but not the *Herald Tribune*.

Chinese Export Porcelain   Porcelain made in China for the European (and later, American) markets. It often copied popular European styles but not trans-fer styles. When the English still did not know how to make porcelain, export china came to England on ships, and was very costly and very chic. Royals and nobles collected it, and there was talk of people going bankrupt in the early 1700s from investing too heavily in blue and white. Porcelains are from the Yuan and Ming periods in China.

Chippendale Thomas Chippendale the Elder (1718–79) was a furniture designer who published his designs, making him widely known in his time and a legend in ours. His name denotes works created in the 1750s and 1760s in the rococo style, with two other influences, Chinese and Gothic. Most Chippendale-style furniture is made of mahogany, which is sometimes referred to as Jamaica wood.

Chipping An old-fashioned term for market. Cities with the word Chipping in their name (Chipping Camden) were once market towns, and are usually worth visiting today. I happen to think a market groupie should be called a chippie, but the English language disagrees with me.

Clarice Cliff An Art Deco artist and one of the most famous "Pottery Ladies," whose hand-painted work is signed and extremely hot in the current collector's market. One of her patterns is appropriately called Bizarreware—you will recognize it immediately because of its orange colors and bold, Deco-like exuberance. There is Clarice Cliff signed transfer ware, but it's not worth very much. There's also a big market in faux Clarice, which is signed and very difficult to spot. Beware of Bizarreware that's too cheap; make big-time purchases only through a reputable dealer. Every fall, Christie's South Kensington (see page 92) has an annual Clarice Cliff sale.

Clotted Cream More like whipped butter than anything else, clotted cream is a substance that has no direct equivalent in the United States. It's not butter and it's not whipped cream, or even sour cream. It's rich, it's gooey, it's best on toasted scones and under jam. It is illegal to bring clotted cream into the United States, because it is a dairy product.

Coalport Bone china factories established in the late 1700s and still in existence today. Famous for antique blue and white transfer patterns with high cobalt (deep blue) content.

Corn Exchange Many a small city or village has a local Corn Exchange, which is most often on the main square. It is usually the location of the local antique market.

Cream Tea Cream teas are advertised as such. This does not mean that you get cream with your tea or that the house tea is creamy. Rather, this is a set package that includes a pot of tea, scones (usually two), clotted cream, and jam for one price. The cream in the title refers to the clotted cream. You can order tea and scones à la carte—without the clotted cream and jam.

Crown Derby A China pattern. It was Crown Derby (say "Darby") in the beginning, back around 1750, but Queen Victoria changed it to Royal Crown Derby in 1890, when she went nuts for their bone china. Princess Anne registered for Royal Crown Derby when she was married.

Deerstalker A type of hat most associated with Sherlock Holmes. It has a small brim or peaked front, and earflaps that can be worn down in cold weather (or while hunting) and then tied up when not needed. Sold in many tourist shops, particularly in the Borders.

Earthenware Pottery fired at relatively low heat that requires glazing for use; the substance of most primitive and peasant pottery.

Fair Isle A specific style of knitting that originated in Scotland but is now famous throughout England, in which several colors of yarn are knit off bobbins to form intricate lines or patterns (often flowers) in various shades that are worked across the sweater (entire or the yoke portion) in stripes.

Kaffe Fassett His first name rhymes with "waif," so it's a one-syllable name, not two. This American designer is a living legend in Britain, where his knitting-and-needle designs have been displayed at the Victoria and Albert Museum. Buy kits at **Liberty** or Ehrman in London. If you thought Missoni was special, get a load of this guy's stuff.

Fete Yes, it is a party, but it's a shopping party. A fete is an open-air sale much like a church bazaar and almost always sponsored by a charity (or church). Unlike a jumble sale or a car boot sale, most of the merchandise at a fete is new and handmade (or homemade). Usually held in the summer or on bank holidays, these down-home events are a good opportunity to check out knitting bargains.

France Where the English go to buy wine, beer, and champagne. Also foodstuffs and fashion.

Glengarry No, this is not the name of the marching tune of Custer's Seventh Cavalry, but close. It is the name of a brimless hat created in Scotland and worn with the whole outfit; you'll know it by the ribbons down the back.

Gum Boots Wellies (short for "Wellingtons," high boots named for the duke of Wellington). You'll need 'em if you go hunting or fishing or tromping around in the mud; good for car boot sales the day after it rains.

Hallmark When you care enough to make the very best you put your signature or guarantee on your work. If you are a silversmith, that is your hallmark. English smiths have been using hallmarks since the 1700s; there are books and charts of the English hallmarks to help you place (and date) what you buy for proper valuation.

Hepplewhite A style of furniture named for George Hepplewhite, who may not have been the originator of the designs but was the publisher of a book of collected designs popular in the late 1700s. The term has come to stand for neoclassical lines.

Honey-pot City   The British refer to cities with natural tourist attractions and/or historical charm (read "cute") as honey-pot cities. All the retailers have to do is sit back and count the money that comes in from visitors (British and foreign) who naturally want to visit these destinations. Examples include Chester, York, and Stratford-upon-Avon. Because they have become such enormous tourist destinations, honey-pot cities may have a crass commercial edge or lack the authentic charm you seek. Non-honey-pot, no-name cities are the answer to your prayers.

Horse Brasses   Victorians decorated harnesses with brasses made in shapes or ovals with designs on them. They are now collected. There are said to be as many as 3,000 different designs. Collectors look for dated or commemorative brasses, patina, and smoothness from wear.

Jacobean   A popular furniture and architectural style in the 17th century: heavy oak furniture that is rich and ornate and copiously carved. Lines are straight and symmetrical. Supporters of the royal line through the Stuarts were known as Jacobites.

Jasperware   A matte-finished stoneware developed by Josiah Wedgwood that is overlaid with white figures in the traditional Grecian style. The finish is available in various colors, although blue is the most famous. Widely collected; still produced.

Jumble   Jumble is junk, and they sell it at jumble sales, which are pretty much like flea markets and can be wonderful (or awful if you are unlucky). They sell mostly used clothes, which are the rage in England these days.

Large Double   This is a size of sheet (or duvet cover) stocked by Laura Ashley. It will fit a queen-sized American bed, they say.

Charles Rennie Mackintosh   A Scottish design leader and spiritual head of the Glasgow School (known for Art Nouveau works), Mackintosh was an architect who also designed furniture and a tearoom or two. See it (The Willows) in Glasgow.

Minton Minton began in Stoke-on-Trent in the 1790s, producing first earthenware and then bone china. It's known for the quality of its figures and for gilding work (22 karats). Queen Victoria used Minton; various members of the royal family have followed suit. Now part of the Royal Doulton Group. (See page 280.)

Narrow Boat Painting At first you'll think it's tole, but this folk art painting style has rules as to the colors that can be used and the types of flowers that can be drawn—and how they must be drawn. Decorative tinware cannot be used for eating. Sold in the countryside at fairs and fetes, and at Liberty in the housewares department.

Old School Tie Public schools (which are the equivalent of private prep schools to an American) and colleges all have their own ties, which students and grads wear to show their colors to the world. This is taken very seriously by the British, and no one—absolutely no one—would wear a tie from an institution that he was not associated with. The very notion that Americans buy these ties as souvenirs or because they like the colors is galling to an Englishman. Also note that snobbish Brits need the ties to tell them who is good enough for them and who is not, as each school has a social status attached to it.

Oleograph No, this isn't a painting made with margarine. An oleograph is a reproduction of an oil painting—done either on board or on canvas—that from a small distance looks quite sensational, but when you get very close or use your eagle eye you can tell that it's a photographic process almost like a postcard. They're commonly sold in British flea markets and many frame shops, and are usually reproductions of Dutch masters. In a good frame, they can be fabulous.

Paisley Paisley is actually a city in Scotland (a suburb of Glasgow, to be exact) where shawls of the paisley pattern were once manufactured; hence the name. The pattern itself came from India and Kashmir, and became stylish in England and on the Continent. The shawls are highly collectible and are very expensive; expect to pay from $500 to $1,000 for one. Ralph Lauren has made them hot in America; look for the difference between a handmade shawl and one made on a jacquard loom. Also look for wool versus wool and/or silk. Although the shawl looks like it should be soft, the hand is usually quite stiff. Condition is a major factor in price and value. Paisleys from Kashmir, which exist in the marketplace, are very expensive—a good one is more than $1,000, and possibly more than $2,000.

Pewter An alloy of tin and copper, possibly with lead as well, it has been made since medieval times and serves as the poor man's silver. Church services and later table services have been created from pewter for centuries. British settlers brought pewter to the United States in 1635.

Pimm's Actually, it's Pimm's No. 1 Cup and it's gin. Sometimes people order it as a Pimm's Cup; most simply say "Pimm's." This is a summer drink, appropriate only in mild weather and somewhat associated with "The Season" (see page 63). It's served in a tall glass with ice and garnished with fruit and cucumber. To be made properly, the gin is mixed with sparkling lemonade, a product not available in the United States. Pimm's can be mixed with Sprite or 7Up but it tastes slightly different. Don't let that stop you.

Plaid To an American, a plaid is a pattern of squares of color. Actually, these patterns are more properly named tartans. A plaid is a piece of clothing: a large shawl in a tartan fabric, worn over one shoulder.

Queen Anne A style of 18th-century furnishings most often represented by walnut veneer, curved legs, and a simplicity of line with elegant style. The furniture was made in the early 1700s, not only during the reign of Queen Anne herself but also during the prior reign of William and Mary.

Regency A style of furniture of the 18th century and the beginning of the 19th century, very similar to French Empire. Rosewood is popular, as is inlay; designs are neoclassical. The late Georgian period is referred to as Regency, although the actual regency occurred in the years 1811 to 1820, when the prince of Wales (later George IV) was regent for his father, the infamous George III. The architecture of the period is more often called Georgian.

Royal Doulton Delicate but tough is how Doulton described his china, one of the many brands used by Her Majesty the Queen. The company was granted its royal warrant in 1901, adding "Royal" to the name. Famous for its Toby mugs and figurines. (See page 286.)

Royal Worcester The royal warrant goes back to the late 1700s. The firm makes bone china, figurines, and other collectibles.

Sainsburys One of the most popular chains of grocery stores in England, with new, modern markets.

Season, The Ah, to be in England in June when the weather has arrived and with it, the social season appropriately called The Season. Officially, there are certain events that are part of The Season (Grosvenor Antiques Fair, Royal Ascot, Wimbledon, etc.), but this is also the time that people get married and have parties, so it's really the season for being alive and for appreciating all that is British. Note that many of the events in The Season are sporting events (polo, tennis, rowing, horse racing) one attends to watch, not participate in. Social calendars to the official Season are printed annually; a free insert is usually available in *Harper & Queen* beginning with the March edition. Note that The Season brings with it very strict rules about dress for men and women. Proper head gear is essential.

Sheffield Plate   Sterling silver fused to a lesser metal base, creating a silver item known today as "plate"— not as valuable as sterling silver but is still highly collectible. Silver plated on copper began to become popular around 1750.

Sheraton   A furniture style of the 18th century based on works by the cabinetmaker Thomas Sheraton (but not created solely by him); neo-classical pieces in mahogany, satinwood, and painted furniture, often with inlay. The style was in vogue from 1790 to 1805.

Sixpence   Not minted since 1970, the sixpence is traditionally what the bride places in her shoe for good luck. You may buy sixpence from coin dealers or at antique fairs; Maggie Sheerin turned me on to Elizabethan (Elizabeth I) coins. I actually bought one for my son's bride; it'll come in handy in about 15 years. Prices range from $25 to $40. An excellent wedding or shower gift for the person who will appreciate what it is.

John Smedley   A knitting mill known for shirts made of the finest Sea Island cotton, which begin around $50 for a short-sleeved polo and escalate quickly. A very "in" brand, sold in men's shops around England; try S. Fisher in the Burlington Arcade in London. Factory shop in Yorkshire.

Spode   Josiah Spode (not to be confused with Josiah Wedgwood) began his china factory in Stoke-on-Trent in 1770. In 1833 the Copeland family bought in; Robert Copeland is still at the firm carrying on his family tradition. Today Spode is part of the Royal Worcester Group (see page 282). Spode is believed to be the father of transfer printing. The firm still produces several transfer patterns in blue and white (see "Blue and White," above), as well as in other colors; it also produces one of the most famous Christmas patterns in the world.

Sporran The leather (and/or fur) pouch worn in front of the kilt; hangs from a belt worn on the hips.

Staffordshire Technically, any pottery made in Staffordshire is indeed Staffordshire, an awfully broad definition since almost all the bone china factories are now in Staffordshire. Furthermore, the figurines are generally called Staffordshire by those in the trade, and the dishes are called by their own names or marks. There are several potteries that use the word Staffordshire in their names and marks, but stores that specialize in Staffordshire sell figurines.

Stoneware Clay firing at higher temperatures produces stoneware rather than earthenware. Mason, the pottery house known for its ironwares, developed a process that is protected by copyright and called Ironstone.

Tesco One of my favorite supermarket chains, with branches in suburban London—even downtown stores called Tesco Metro—and all over England.

Toby Mugs You actually know what a Toby mug is, you just might not know it by its proper name. Okay, let's visualize. Close your eyes and think of Winston Churchill, Henry VIII, Margaret Thatcher, or other famous faces in ceramic form. What should come to mind are the jugs or mugs that are three dimensional with the face forming the body of the mug and an accessory to the personality forming the handle. The mugs have been made for more than 100 years and are therefore dated according to runs. Some people's faces are made for decades; some go out of fashion. The test of value is related to age, condition, marks, and the actual finesse of the modeling—just how well sculpted is that face?

Tole Before pottery could be perfected to hold heat, tinwares were commonly used. A small percentage of that tinware was painted—most frequently with floral motifs—for decorative use. Although little survives from those early days, the practice of decorating tin (especially trays and small objects) remained popular in England and in the United States up until post–World War II years. Tole trays are considered highly collectible; value is based on age, condition, and ability of the artist. Signed work is slightly more valuable. Because paint chips easily from tin, it is difficult to find an old piece of tole in good condition.

Transfer Printing   Chinaware when decorated by hand was costly because of the talent and labor needed to paint patterns. The development of the transfer printing process made it possible for less skilled workers to produce patterned china at a faster rate, which brought down the price. Transfers were perfected over the years and became quite elaborate. Judge their value by intricacy of the pattern and placement of the transfer on the ceramic—the harder-to-reach places (inside the cup's rim or bottom or handle, for instance) make a piece more valuable. Transfer wares can be made in one color on white, or in many colors. (See "Blue and White," above.)

Valances   Don't skip over this one. A valance is not what you think—in Britain, anyway. It is a bedskirt; so there. You buy them in the sheet department of any department store or at M&S or Laura Ashley. A valance like one you hang with the curtains is called a "pelmet."

Waxed   A process whereby fabric or leather is treated with a waxed coating that makes it somewhat shiny and also water repellent—an important accomplishment in a country where it often rains. Most often found in "waxed jackets" (of which Barbour is the most popular brand) or "waxed leather" handbags.

Wedgwood   Josiah Wedgwood is one of the fathers of modern pottery. Check out their brand of tea—a great gift item.

Willow (Pattern)   The traditional blue willow pattern is an English design based on a Chinese design, and is reproduced on dishes made by many firms. Many people call all blue and white transfer patterns "Willow," which is technically incorrect but understood by buyers, collectors, and dealers. Transfers are sold through transfer banks, so several makers produce the exact same Willow pattern, but on wares of differing degrees of quality. Buyer beware. The actual Willow pattern has elements in it that tell the story of a maiden who lived in a fine house but who fell in love with a laborer; they ran away together (over a bridge) and lived in a little house across the water from the big house. Daddy was not happy and came after them, killing the husband. Their souls were reunited in the form of two lovebirds, which fly above.

Wine   London is considered the wine capital of the world; rumor has it that if you want to know anything about wine—especially good, cheap wine— you should ask an Englishman. The English are also widely varied in their knowledge—it's not just Spanish and French wines that they buy and drink. They know them all. Brazilian? You bet. The supermarkets are filled with good but well-priced private label brands. Newspapers and magazines are chockablock full of reviews and information. Auctions are widely attended and bought up. There are even wine stores and societies that deliver to your door; just phone or fax in your order. Sorry, no transatlantic deliveries.

AN ALPHABETICAL GUIDE TO INTERNATIONAL CHAINS & SHOPS

• •

Alexon   Say you're a British woman who is more drawn to European style than American style, who is actually more comfortable in a pair of jodhpurs, and who doesn't really even care about fashion at all, but if pushed will pick a soft flowered skirt, a blazer, and a knit blouse in the moderate-to-expensive price range. Where else to go but Alexon? It's a chain not unlike Rodier, but with a totally different concept of fashion. Perfect for Princess Anne. Because of this image (and higher prices to match), there is not an Alexon shop on every high street, but there are a number of them in Britain and all over the world. They even have branch stores in the United States.

Austin Reed   A chain of stores selling men's and women's traditional British clothing from the big makers—the place to shop where you can't go wrong if the Brit Look is your need. Branch stores tend to be in need of renovation. All the sturdy and steadfast British big names are sold through these stores and you can sometimes bump into something fashionable.

Bally   The venerable shoe company Bally of Switzerland has numerous other Bally divisions all over the world. Bally of Britain is a great place with great quality, featuring fashionable men's and women's shoes and handbags at moderate to high prices. Some of the shoes are made in Europe and imported to Britain; some are made in Britain—thus you'll find a range of prices. Expect to find several Bally shops in any given city; there's one on almost every high street.

The Body Shop   The Body Shop is a phenomenon: Inside is a world of environmentally responsible soaps, scents, and other beauty products. Prices in the United Kingdom are almost half the prices in the United States.

Boots   In the Queen's English, Boots is a chemist. To Americans, Boots is a drugstore. But what a drugstore: It carries just about everything. Some have take-out food departments, although I've never seen a full-fledged grocery store. The best thing about Boots is that it has a huge selection of health and beauty aids, usually at reasonable prices. There is always a pharmacy, sometimes an optical shop, and always a selection of small appliances such as hair dryers, should you discover that your American model will not work in England. (It won't—different plugs.)

There is a Boots in almost every city in England and Scotland, most often located on the high street. In London, there's a store in every major trading area. Some are bigger than others, but you'll rarely be disappointed with a Boots.

Cotswolds Woollens A small but growing group of sweater shops, Cotswolds Woollens is perhaps the most classy of all the sweater chains, and does not sell discounted merchandise or pretend factory leftovers. This is a first-rate fashion shop selling machine-made, traditional English patterned sweaters. You'll find both Fair Isle designs and pictorials. There's cotton and ramie in summer and wool in winter. Prices are fair—in the under $100 range for a cute sweater. This is the place for the sweaters with the rabbits, the ducks, or the kitten pattern knitted into the front.

Culpeper the Herbalist Despite the popularity of **The Body Shop** and **Crabtree and Evelyn** (which is actually an American firm that looks British), Culpeper the Herbalist has found its niche selling the same kinds of things in a different manner. Culpeper shops are not as elaborately decorated as the competition, and thus feel more low-key and down-home. They offer soaps, essences, and oils, as well as other beauty products. Among our favorite items are a variety of pillows filled with herbs to give you better sleep and sweet dreams. You can also buy fresh herbs in little pots in season.

Dash A chain of stores specializing in sweat-suit fashions in high-style looks and great colors at moderate prices; there's a branch store in almost every city. Part of the Woodhouse brand and therefore sold at Woodhouse outlet stores.

Droopy and Browns   This is where you shop if you are hobnobbing with Sloane Rangers. Droopy sells work clothes and dressy dresses for those who wear Benetton and pearls (together) on weekends. Prices are moderate (about $200 for a dressy dress), so you get a lot of value for your money. There aren't tons of these stores, but you should be able to find one in most major cities. For heaven's sake, don't think the word *Droopy* in the name of the store means they sell droopy clothes.

Edinburgh Woollen Mills   In this case, the name is better than the chain. Edinburgh Woollen Mills is one of those factory-direct sweater shops with bins and tables and racks and lots of mediocre merchandise that you are expected to believe is being sold at outlet prices. If the weather turns and you're chilly, there's nothing wrong with picking up a sweater here, but we doubt you'll find anything exciting. The shops in some cities border on tourist traps.

Habitat   A chain of home-furnishings stores originated by Sir Terence Conran and later sold. They sell the lean, spare, smart look Conran is famous for, at quite moderate prices. Many of the stores are in rehabbed spaces and are interesting architecturally. There should be one in every big town you visit. Sir Terence has moved on to open his own **Conran Shop** stores that sell more pricey merchandise and are even more stylish than the **Habitat** shops. Don't get them confused.

High and Mighty   A small chain offering men's fashions for large-sized men, with well-made and reasonably priced merchandise; a true find for the oversized gentleman. You'll also find stores back home in a few cities.

H&M Hennes   This is a Swedish department store chain that operates several specialty stores around Britain catering to teens and other young-at-hearts who crave hot fashion and the latest style at low prices. The clothes may not be made to last, and the

fabrics may not be the finest, but you can find all
the new looks at readily affordable prices. In London and most college towns. They plan to attack
France next. Watch out, world. Great good fun, even
for middle-aged ladies. H&M stands for Hennes and
Mauritz, but most signs in the U.K. say either H&M
or Hennes. Don't be confused, it's the same store.

Hobbs An excellent chain for well-made, sporty,
and dressy shoes at the top end of the moderate price
range, but not so over the top that you can't afford
them. They have clothes now, too.

Jaeger A classic British resource, sold in its own
shops and in many department stores. It has a way
with wools in particular, and strides the fine line
between boring English clothing and high fashion.
For quality you can always trust Jaeger. Wherever
you buy, the value is good. Clothing is automatically coordinated, saving the working woman lots
of time. Outlet shop in Yorkshire.

Janet Reger If you've ever wondered what the True
Brit woman wears under her rather safe and standard clothing, you might be shocked to discover how
frilly and fancy her underthings can be. Janet Reger
is the Victoria's Secret of the British underwear
crowd: more sophisticated than many (and more expensive), but not so pricey and fancy that it's totally
out of our range.

Jigsaw One of the best examples of what a British
multiple can (should) be, Jigsaw is a fashion chain
selling hip but wearable fashion for young women.
The line is such that a lot of merchandise is on the
cutting edge (which means good, frequent sales) and
much of it is for women under 40. Prices are moderate; the stores are always high-tech chic; and there's
always something to see and be impressed with—
even if you are just sizing up the hot looks. This
chain is just beginning to move into the international
market.

Jumpers   Shops selling mostly sweaters in the traditional English manner of either cables, ribs (solids), or simple florals. Prices aren't too high; there is some coordinated clothing.

Knickerbox   The Knickerbox business is one of the major success stories in recent retail history. The underwear buyers from Marks & Spencer—famous throughout the land—went out on their own and opened Knickerbox. Almost immediately, it became a gigantic multiple with shops in every mall, kiosks in every train station, and even high street stores in high-rent districts. The underwear (bras, panties, camisoles, etc.) comes in cotton and silken varieties and in jazzy and even risqué styles. Prices are about the same as those at Marks and Spencer: moderate, but not dirt cheap.

Laura Ashley   If you love this look get ready to spend! Savings in Great Britain can be huge. Hit a sale and go wild. Some of the stock you'll find is not sold in the United States. The line encompasses everything that has to do with the home as well as dresses, kids' wear, and sleepwear. Chintz fabrics cost less per meter. Each store has its own closeout policy. You may see baskets filled with discontinued wallpapers (in double rolls, for added bargains). We think this is one of the world's best deals.

Liberty   No trip to London is complete without a visit to Liberty of London. Liberty is a department store that rambles around a bit (it's in several buildings all clumped together) and is best represented by the part that is a whitewashed, half-timbered building of Elizabethan and Jacobean style. There is no store in the world that compares with this store (particularly the old part). Branches of Liberty are located in most cities. They tend to be half-timbered on the outside and adorable, and they sell the traditional Liberty prints and Liberty merchandise, but they lack the oomph of the main store. Because Liberty prints are so identifiable, they make good gifts; the store also has its own foodstuffs, like jams and mustards.

Marks & Spencer Sometimes called "Marks & Sparks" but more often simply called M&S in the local vernacular. A chain with stores everywhere, M&S is a department store with a private label (it offers its own label only, which is called **St. Michael**) selling everything from clothes to food to home furnishings. It is famous for its cotton underwear. The home furnishings departments are sometimes housed in separate stores.

Miss Selfridge There is a Miss Selfridge department in the main London Selfridges store, but you'll find free-standing stores all over. Its specialty is the young, kicky look at inexpensive prices—this is a find for teens or for those who want to dabble in a trendy look without spending too much money. Also makeup and accessories.

Monsoon A chain of low- to moderate-priced women's fashions made in India in current styles but of fabrics inspired by the mother country (India) and therefore gauzy, colorful, sometimes ethnic (but not always), and very distinctive. The look is very popular with the teens-through-20s set. They also own a group of accessories stores (**Accessorize**) as well as some evening dress-up shops (**Twilight**). Nice scent as well.

Mothercare A gigantic chain of stores selling maternity and brand-new baby needs as well as kids' clothes and things like strollers and plastic dishes. Well designed, good quality, moderate prices. There are some stores in the United States, but they pale compared to even a branch store in the United Kingdom.

National Trust Britain's National Trust preserves the great castles, manor houses, and historical landmark homes of the realm—and has a little business in gifts on the side. Most of the shops are identical;

all sell gift items, cards, games, jams, and things either inspired by designs in the great houses or in reproduction or souvenir form. Much fun for finding a typically British gift.

Next   Every city in Britain has a handful of Next shops—some sell women's clothes, some sell men's clothes, some sell home furnishings, some sell kids' clothes, some sell accessories to go with the above. Next sells a total lifestyle look that is modern, with a classic European edge as opposed to the Laura Ashley sweet-flowers routine. Don't miss their X stores for the teenage set; very avant-garde and hip, with wild architecture.

Oxfam   A chain of stores selling used clothing and imports from the Far East for charity.

Paperchase   The "in" place for paper goods. Paperchase offers a wide range of paper products—everything from greeting cards, stationery, Filofax pages, and party items to a variety of materials for the serious artist.

Past Times   Taking centuries of British heritage (from Druids and Romans to Victorian times) as their credo, this chain of shops sells gift items (all reproductions) that are the kinds of things you would find in a museum gift shop. There is truly something for everyone here; even the kids will like it. The shops aren't big on ambience, but the merchandise is well lit and easy to see. They also have a catalogue.

Penhaligon   Especially well known for its toilet water and soap that men adore, Penhaligon holds a royal warrant. Its products are produced according to the original formulas of William Penhaligon, who began his business as a barbershop in 1841. It's very Olde England in here, and we love to sniff around.

Pied à Terre   Despite this seemingly French name, this is one of the biggest names in English shoes.

Pied à Terre is a resource for high-fashion shoes at not too outrageous prices.

Pitlochry of Scotland Yawn. I think this "factory outlet" chain has the most boring traditional clothes in all of England. If you're into heathery wool skirts with a matching crewneck, or a cardigan sweater (worn with a plain white blouse, of course), this is your kind of place. Every now and then this store does turn out something I find interesting, but it can best be counted on for the staples of women's woolens.

Principles Hot, with-it fashions at low (for Britain) prices, with plenty of designer knockoffs and in-step accessories. From the outside, many of the stores look like Next. Don't be confused, because the looks inside are definitely different. Redefining itself under financial stress. Stay tuned.

Reject China Shop I must warn you: There may not be any bargains here, but it's still the best place to check first. The shops are usually packed with British and American patterns. They are used to tourists, and make shipping a breeze. Catalogue, telephone, and mail orders can be done with a credit card. Prices on some items can be 20% less than the usual retail prices; you can deal on big orders. Firsts are often priced the same as in nondiscount stores!

Richards Richards has patterned itself after the American chain of Ann Taylor but has lost its way. The Richards point of view is simple: clothes for the working woman, at prices she can afford. Certainly worth looking at, but don't expect too much and you won't be disappointed.

Sacha Sacha used to be a fabulous British shoe source for hot styles at less than Charles Jourdan prices. While this is still its function in the marketplace, the shops have gotten worn and overcrowded, and the merchandise gets cheaper each year. We don't think the stores have as much class as they used to. Still a good source for someone on a budget.

The Sock Shop   There is not a train station, an underground station, or a high street in the United Kingdom that does not have a branch of the Sock Shop. Despite the popularity of these stores (selling socks and panty hose and sometimes underwear and umbrellas), I remain baffled. Yes, the styles are incredibly cute, but there are no bargains.

Sue Ryder   Another charity shop, this one more like Goodwill. They sell used clothes and household items, and are most often found on the high street.

The Tie Rack   The Tie Rack is to necks what the Sock Shop is to feet.

Waterstone's   One of several popular bookshops, rather like B. Dalton in the United States, Waterstone's is a typical British mass merchant, with a wide selection of everything, including travel and Tintin books. Waterstone's now has a branch in Boston and is bringing British book retailing to the United States.

Chapter Six

· · · · · · ·

ANTIQUES & COLLECTIBLES

COLLECTOR'S HEAVEN

· ·

For such a small country, Britain has an amazing
number of antique shops, antique fairs, and car boot
sales. Sure, some of this stuff has been brought over
from foreign countries over a period of centuries,
and some of this stuff is fake or reproduction or
truly worthless—but the extent to which people in
the United Kingdom collect and sell what they find
amazes me. Furthermore, prices can be quite good.

I am not talking about the availability—
or prices—of museum-quality antiques. David
Mlinaric, the star interior designer who works with
Jacob Rothschild, has confided to me that it's really
hard to find museum-quality antiques these days.
He often shops in Paris or works with craftsmen to
reproduce the missing piece from a matched set. I
don't live in a place like Spencer House and, needless to say, Jacob Rothschild does not frequently
drop by my house for coffee. I'm talking about
articles that pass themselves off as antiques. Junk,
in other words.

I like junk. I like junk so much that I am willing
to plan my trips to the United Kingdom around finding it; I am willing to sit on a train for a few hours
to get to it; I tally the success of a trip based on how
the junk rated and how I was able to pack it up and

bring it home. I'm happiest when the junk is cheap and in disrepair and I have come up with a brilliant way to remake it or re-create it in another format. Junk gives me permission to be creative, to buy and play and fall in love again and again.

While London has more than any great city's share of antique shops, antique malls, flea markets, vetted events, and junk, it's only when you get outside of London that prices drop and your ability to haul home a real find increases.

So what are you waiting for?

If you learn nothing more from me and from this guide it should be that Manchester is the name of your new best friend. Manchester is the gateway to the best low-priced jumble in England. Manchester is the secret of dealers and the deal. But Manchester is not the only secret.

THE PROFILES OF BARGAINS

. . . .

I was in England with my girlfriend Pat recently and was planning to schlepp her along on a day trip to Bath. "Oh, I'm so glad we're going to Bath," said Pat. "That's where the American dealers get all their good stuff."

While Pat is partially right, this isn't the whole picture. Despite its countless (and sometimes supreme) flea markets, Bath is a tourist town. Even though it caters to antique dealers, it focuses on the high end of the trade. I like Bath just fine, but I think that real dealers go to much more out-of-the-way places and suffer far more for their art than one suffers on a day trip to Bath.

There's no question that if you are willing to prowl, your best bet is the Manchester Circle. I call it that because this term encompasses the destinations that ring Manchester from Chester to Liverpool.

I like Brighton. You will too if you are serious, know what you are doing, and don't mind a hard day's night. You will have to search in order to suitably work Brighton; nothing is what it seems there. I don't send mere day trippers to Brighton.

I like Warwick because it's easy.

I love the Cotswolds because they are perfect, visually, even if they're not the best place for finding a bargain.

I've never been to Suffolk and Lovejoy country, which my friend Ruth tells me is lined with warehouses filled with old furniture.

I do love Bath; I just don't think it's in the same category as the funky places with the funky finds.

DEFINING ANTIQUES

Just to keep us all straight on what we're talking about, there is an official definition of what an antique is and it comes directly from one of the world's leading authorities: Uncle Sam. The U.S. government defines an antique as an object that is 100 years old or older. Due to new EU regulations, you must pay duty on antiques.

Since much of what you can buy in a flea market is not 100 years old, it is defined as a collectible. My husband calls it junk, but that's another story altogether. As always, Uncle Sam wants you to pay duty on collectibles.

KNOWLEDGE IS POWER

Stories abound of smart shoppers who purchased A, B, or C in a flea market and then sold it at Sotheby's for hundreds of dollars or even hundreds of thousands of dollars.

My favorite story of this kind involves a woman who was interested in porcelain and spent most of her time in museums and libraries, studying pieces on display and reading books. When she spied a particular piece at a flea market, she knew that the match to it was in the collection of a Dutch museum.

The dealer had no idea of the true value of the piece but the shopper did. She later sold her piece at Sotheby's, making a great profit. A round of applause for the intrepid shopper, please.

The beauty of shopping antique markets, fairs, and shops is that there is a hierarchy to it all and that hierarchy is related to knowledge. If you are willing to do what I call "down and dirty" shopping, you have a great chance of finding a serious bargain. If you only like white-glove shopping, you will get the best possible antiques available in the world, but no bargains.

Here are few tips to get you started:

- Items sold at a car boot sale or yard sale are always the least expensive because the person selling the goods usually doesn't know what he or she has. This person is merely cleaning house or emptying the estate of a recently departed family member. Because of their ignorance, you have the greatest chance of a score.
- Flea markets are one level above a car boot sale because the stalls are paid for by people who know they can make a profit; they are usually professional dealers. The better the dealer, the more he knows about what he's selling and the more likely he is to fix a reasonable market price. Depending upon his need for immediate cash, he may be flexible on price.
- Shops are almost always owned by dealers, people who think they know what they are doing and think they know what they own and what it's worth. They have higher overhead than people who buy a stall at a weekend market and, therefore, higher prices. You are also paying for the fact that they have preselected their wares based on their expertise or at least their well-trained eyes.
- Vetted antique fairs and dealers with trade associations not only know what they are doing but are so enraptured with their areas of expertise that

Trick of the Trade

How can you be sure a dealer is reputable? The very best test you can give a shop is to ask the shopkeeper to explain a certain piece to you. If he or she gets wound up with energy, spews forth an encyclopedic paragraph or two, and seems willing to spend the day talking about the object and its type, you've found someone to trust.

they will happily give you an earful on the subject of whatever it is that you are considering buying. These people know their stuff, know the market, and have the highest prices but yet offer the best guarantees on what it is you are considering buying.

- Auction houses—especially the best ones—employ a staff of experts who spend their time studying the goods and the marketplace; they are paid to learn, and will often turn their knowledge over to you free of charge. The best collectors in the world have their own contacts at auction houses and are often tipped off as to what to buy when an auction approaches. Auction catalogues also provide a good education in price and availability. In fact, if you would like to learn about high-end goods, auction houses are an excellent place to start an education.

AMERICAN VERSUS BRITISH INTERESTS

The person who is going to get the best buys in Britain is the person who knows the most about what he or she is buying. It also helps to know the variations between American and British interests and prices. Since demand for the same objects is rarely parallel, certain objects can be more readily available and better priced in the United Kingdom or the United States.

To learn the differences in the marketplace, you're going to have to do a lot of shopping.

Life is tough.

BOOKS & MAGAZINES

. . . .

There are tons of books, magazines, and even self-published tomes that serve the local population. If you're the type who likes to spring for artsy hard-cover books replete with gorgeous color pictures, there are plenty of them in every British bookstore you walk into.

In addition to illustrated books, there are also price guides, annual yearbooks with names and addresses of shops that belong to various associations, and so on.

For many years I have bought a book called *The Antique Shops of Britain*, which is published annually.

While it doesn't list all the dealers in any given city and doesn't give anything resembling an overview of the British junk scene, it's a good jumping-off point for the uninitiated. Just don't think it's the only book you'll ever need to own.

British Antiques Fairs, by Peter and Jennifer Hornsby, is a guide to the 100 best antique fairs in Britain by a husband-and-wife team who have been exhibiting at fairs for more than 25 years. It is sold in British bookstores.

There are a variety of specialty publishers whose works are difficult (maybe impossible) to find in bookstores but who sell directly to the public through their ads in collector's magazines.

After you've finished at the bookstore, you may want to hit your favorite newsagent. The really good, big newsagents have the best stock of antique and collector's magazines. Frequently I can't get everything I'm looking for at one stand. Don't wait for the airport because many of the best antique magazines are not carried by airport newsagents.

The number of magazines with information on antiques is legion; they also come in a variety of styles geared to price points and interest. *Antique International* costs £4.25 (whoa!), is extremely slick, and only features the kind of dealers that terrify me. They do have excellent educational articles, however. My favorite magazine is *BBC's Homes & Antiques,* a monthly, which costs less than £2 and is filled with easy-to-read features and color pictures of collectibles and what they're worth. It's made for people who are out there "junking" for the fun of it.

One cannot underestimate the position the BBC has come to play in the antiques market in the United Kingdom—all due to the success of its television series *The Antiques Roadshow.* In this show, a small group of antique and collectibles experts visit various sites around the United Kingdom to look at real people's junk and tell them what its worth (much to the people's astonishment).

In addition to the magazine mentioned above, the BBC now publishes a series of pocket guides called *Antiques Roadshow Pocket Guides.* Each guide addresses a different kind of collectible (dolls, toys, and games; pottery and porcelain; clocks and watches, and so on) and is written by a different expert. You can buy the entire set at a slightly discounted price.

Aside from the specific glossy magazines geared toward collectors, there are magazines for people who are renovating homes (a big hobby in the United Kingdom) that are filled with tips and sources for buying antiques. Don't ask me why I recently clipped out the full-color article titled "How to Thatch a Roof." It came complete with a source guide for thatchers (Margaret not included) and I was enchanted.

Even the venerable *Country Life,* a weekly magazine that comes out on Thursdays, has information on antiques, auctions, and salvage.

There are two small-format publications—not often found at newsagents but usually sold at

antique events and fairs—that I find essential for
my kind of shopping because they are guides to the
actual events that are being held at specific times
and dates. *Car Boot Calendar*, a desktop-published
wonder that appears every other month and gives
a list of what's on and where, is one. Another is
Antiques Fairs and Markets Diary. Formerly a little
booklet, it has now gone upmarket with a color
cover and some color pictures inside. This guide,
which costs £1.50, lists flea markets and jumble sales
throughout Britain by region (London and southern England are considered one region). It is truly
the bible for someone who is seriously searching.
This item can be hard to find; I usually get mine
from a dealer's stall at either the Jubilee Market on
Mondays in Covent Garden (London) or the weekend fairs in Greenwich.

Finally, *The Sunday Times* lists area antique fairs
and events by the week.

SPECIALTY TOURS

If all this is beginning to sound like great good fun
but perhaps too much for you to cope with, you
may want to go on an organized tour led by an antique dealer so that you get a little expertise thrown
into the bargain. Such tours are extremely popular
among American tourists and originate in all parts
of the United States.

George Read gives workshops and seminars
around the United States that teach shoppers how
to get the best buys; he also leads specialty weeklong
tours to England. Call 803/853-8366 or write GE
Read Associates, 97 E. Bay Street, Charleston, SC
29401.

Hammersmith and Co. runs eight-day tours of
England and combination packages of both France
and England along with additional special events.
About half the people who go on these tours are
dealers, so you'll be surrounded by knowledgeable

folks, but you'll have to have quick hands. Write P.O. Box 694, Brockton, MA 02403 or call 508/586-0067 for details.

Bedford Hills Travel, 83 Adams Street, Bedford Hills, NY 10507 does its trips from a hub in Manchester, which is an indication they know what they are doing. Phone 914/666-6444.

EXCLUSIVE PROMOTIONAL EVENTS

In addition to private tours that leave from the United States and tours sponsored by British travel agencies, there are also exclusive antique and collectibles events. They are very often sponsored by magazines and include a day out at a fair or a lecture by a certain expert or two. Transportation may or may not be included. You must usually call or write ahead for a ticket as the number of seats can be limited, depending upon the event.

LOCAL TRADE ASSOCIATIONS

If you'd like to plan your own tour but could use some help determining which shops are worth visiting, you can write to assorted antique dealer associations to ask for a list of their members. Most associations have standards for membership, so that while you won't get a complete list of every shop in a given village or hillside, you will get a list of reliable dealers who have reputations to keep.

BADA (British Antiques Dealers Association). This is the grandmother of them all. It offers a free list of its members and advice on buying antiques. To contact them, write BADA, 20 Rutland Gate, London SW7 1BD or call 171/589-4128; fax 171/581-9083.

LAPADA (London and Provincial Antiques Dealers Association). Another biggie in terms of its reputation and that of its members—more than 700 top-notch dealers are listed with LAPADA. They also run their own shows and fairs. For information, write LAPADA, Suite 124, 535 King's Road, London SW10 0SZ or call 171/823-3511; fax 171/823-3522.

CADA (Cotswolds Antiques Dealers Association). Their informative booklet (often given away in Cotswolds antique shops) can be yours before you leave American shores if you write and ask for it to be sent to you. Contact CADA, Barcheston Manor, Shipston-on-Stour, Warwickshire, England.

FAIRS & EVENTS

Antique and collectibles events can be scheduled in any number of ways—some towns have a weekly antique market; in others, a local church or school sponsors an annual jumble sale whose proceeds go to a charity. Weekend car boot sales are also common.

Some antique fairs, especially the fancier ones in London, are social events to which tickets are hard to come by. Others are events, not particularly social but quite annual or biannual, that have their own group of regulars.

Certain fairs are held at a specific time of the year annually; some are held purposefully on British bank holidays, which do not appear on calendars printed in America. (A good reason to buy a British calendar while you're there.) The best way to find out when these fairs are held is to call the organizer directly. In many cases, the frequency of a fair is based entirely on the availability of the hall.

Dates to upcoming events are booked usually 16 to 18 months in advance, so you can plan an upcoming trip quite easily. Most of the better organizers also have a mailing list and will send you whatever materials they have as soon as they are available, even if you are a civilian.

CAR BOOT SALES

. . . .

Few actual antiques are sold at car boot sales. Much junk can be found; some sales have a section where new merchandise is sold—socks, hardware, bedding, and so on. I've bought everything from a Manchester United football team coffee mug with a chocolate Easter egg inside (£2) to a few odd dishes and pieces of glassware at car boot sales.

The British car boot sale is equivalent to the American yard sale. Instead of setting up at your home and praying for people to drive by, mere mortals take a space—often called a pitch because it's where one can pitch a tent—at an established field and bring their goods there. The price of the space is usually around £10, so you get both the mom-and-pop variety of seller as well as people who think they have a knack for this kind of thing and find that they can make a little extra cash on weekends.

Regular Car Boot Sales

Lewisham Centre Sales are held on Sundays in this covered multistory car park (how romantic). Because of its location, rain cannot close sales. Lewisham is not far from Greenwich; it's a suburb of London labeled SE13.

Trafford Park On Sundays, car boot sales are held in this venue, which is not too far from central Manchester, although public transportation to it is limited.

Norwich As at the above venues, Sunday is car boot sale day at Norfolk Showground. It's indoors.

Brighton Held in the train station parking lot. Couldn't be more convenient. Sundays only.

Peterborough This town is halfway between London and York and has several different car boot sales on Sundays in different venues.

Some people bring a table to set up their goods; some use blankets—others literally sell out of their car's trunk ("car boot" in Britspeak).

Car boot sales are usually regional; ask your hotel concierge if there's one nearby. Originally, I thought they were only held on weekends but Ian says there are plenty held during the week, especially in the summer. Car boot sales are advertised in local papers and are listed in *Car Boot Calendar*. If you travel to the United Kingdom frequently and wish to order your subscription, the U.S. rate is £16 (£8 per year in the United Kingdom). Single copies are not available from the main office. A few final tips: A car boot sale is sometimes called a "boot-fair" in Britspeak. Please remember that weather affects car boot sales more than any other type of antique fairs, since these are the most cheaply run and may be held in fields or in parking lots or airstrips. Fields get muddy—Wellies are preferable to Ferragamos. Covered venues are often advertised as such because it guarantees the shopper won't get rained out.

Many car boot sales are scheduled for bank holidays; there's usually one or two on Boxing Day—the day after Christmas—because that is a day on which there is no traditional retail.

JUMBLE SALES & FETES
. . . .

Jumble sales are events at which mostly used clothing is sold. They usually take place in a church or a public space with the proceeds benefiting a local organization. They are sometimes called fetes—as in the French word for party. Don't get too excited, but poke into one if you pass by.

FLEA MARKETS & STREET MARKETS
. . . .

Flea markets are established events at which dealers take stalls. A few of them are held on specific days and have become famous—Portobello Road in London is the best example, but I'm keen on Tommyfields outside of Manchester on Wednesdays and Greenwich on Saturdays and Sundays. Greenwich has several events in different venues; see pages 150–151 for details. For some reason, *flea market* is not a preferred term in Britain—*antiques fair* or *antiques market* are more popular terms.

MARKET DAYS
. . . .
Most small English towns still have traditional markets where food and durable goods can be bought from stalls at prices that are competitive with regular store prices or slightly less. Some cities have markets every day; some have markets only on certain days of the week. In most cases, one day of each week is devoted to selling articles of clothing and furniture rather than food and vegetables.

For a list of antique market days in the Manchester area, see pages 247–248.

Don't expect market day to be overwhelmingly glamorous, but it can afford you with a good buy.

BROCANTE
. . . .
Brocante (say "bro-cahnt") is the French word for the type of junk I like to buy. The word has begun to creep into the British vernacular to dress things up a little. Nonetheless, any event that features brocante has affordable goods for sale.

ANTIQUE FAIRS
. . . .
Organized antique fairs are presented on a regular basis by professional fair organizers and host dealers. These are folks who make their living working a circuit of what they consider the best fairs for their

wares. There's something almost medieval about this practice.

Fairs are ranked by the type of goods they sell. To differentiate among them, I always think of it this way—a "fair" sells junk and a "show" sells important goods. Some fairs are vetted, which means that a committee has met to pass muster on the goods presented to make sure they are in kind with other goods and are genuine. Many fairs are organized around a specific time period in history or a type of collectible. Admission may or may not be charged.

Some such fairs include: **Art Deco Fairs**, usually held around London in Kensington Town Hall, Greenwich, or Battersea; **Period Fashions and Vintage Clothing**, usually held in London; and **Antiquarian Books**, sold at regular antique markets as well as at specialty events for book buyers.

ANTIQUE SHOWS

An antique show is a serious event. Vetting is the norm. Admission is charged and vendors and patrons take it all very seriously. You dress to show your standing in the community of collectors, therefore there is no need to worry about wearing expensive clothes—they won't cause a dealer to raise prices on you.

ANTIQUE CENTERS

Since most shows and fairs are weekend or occasional events, many towns and villages have a local antique center where dealers can set up permanent stalls or showcases. Some of these centers have 10 to 20 dealers, while others may have 100 or more. I follow the same rule of thumb when shopping antique centers as I do when shopping fairs—bigger is worth my trouble, smaller is only interesting if I'm in the area anyway.

London has a large number of excellent antique centers; outside of London it gets more spotty—there are plenty of so-called centers, but you may be disappointed in them. A few of them use a system of glass showcases wherein the goods are locked up and a person "on duty" shows you the goods by unlocking the cases. I find this can put a crimp in my style, but it hasn't kept me away.

AUCTION HOUSES

The most famous auction houses in the world, Sotheby's and Christie's, are based in London but have small offices in various places in Europe and the United Kingdom (although a recent trend has been to close down small regional offices in both these places).

There's no question that the serious stuff is auctioned off in London at Sotheby's and Christie's, or at one of a handful of other auction houses with international reputations that are quite good (see box below). *Born to Shop London* has a complete list of London auction houses.

Auctions held outside London tend to be more casual events where perhaps less is known about the provenance of the goods and prices are therefore lower. I went to an auction outside Manchester that was more like a circus act. You can find these in New England as well, so it's not peculiar to Britain, but do understand that there are hoity-toity auctions and there are funky auctions. Funky is not found within London.

The auction season in London follows the international season of cultural and sporting events. All auctions have previews during which you can inspect the wares or lots to be sold. Some of the fancier auctions admit guests to preview or auction by catalogue only. Catalogues can be bought at the house, by subscription according to topic of interest, or at some newsagents in London.

London Lots

Most of the auction action in London and across the United Kingdom is through the two biggest houses in the world: Christie's and Sotheby's. Important auctions tend to be in London even if goods have to be sent there. Every now and then an auction is held in a manor house, but usually the London showrooms will do.

CHRISTIE'S
85 Old Brompton Road, SW7
(Tube: South Kensington)

SOTHEBY'S
34-35 New Bond Street, W1
(Tube: Bond Street)

There are two other houses in London that do not have the international reputations of the above two but are just as famous locally and throughout Europe:

BONHAMS
Montpellier Street, SW7 (Tube: Knightsbridge)

PHILIPS
101 New Bond Street/7 Blenheim Street, W1 (Tube: Bond Street)

Dealers who want to buy by the lot should check out a trade resource called **Lots Road Chelsea Auction Gallery** at 71 Lots Road, SW10 (Tube: Fulham Broadway). The average price of a lot is between £100 and £200. They sell antiques, junk, collectibles, and contemporary wares. Call 171/351-7771 for more details. They are only open for half a day on Saturdays, but are open all day Sunday.

Just as there are post office and police auctions in Manhattan and most big American cities, there are similar auctions in London. Contact Dowell Lloyd, 118 Putney Bridge Road, SW15 (Tube: Putney Bridge); local phone: 181/788-7777 for information.

If you've never been to an auction, catalogues can demystify the experience. In them, auction houses explain in simple terms how to buy at auction or by sealed bid.

Don't forget that after you've agreed on a purchase price, a buyer's premium is added (usually 15%), in addition to value-added tax (VAT).

OH, SAVE ME: ARCHITECTURAL SALVAGE

I get incredibly excited when I walk into a warehouse and see piles of radiator covers, miles of sinks and washbasins, a few claw-foot bathtubs, and about an inch of dust on everything.

Despite this, I have never renovated a house; in fact, I have never even bought architectural salvage. But I love to look at it. Because so many people in the United Kingdom live in old houses and like to keep them up-to-date within the style of the original decor, there is a large business in architectural salvage and reproduction housewares in Great Britain.

There are warehouses all over the United Kingdom (especially in Scotland) where you can buy a church steeple, wood siding, a floor, a barn, a cupola, or a bar. And much more. Needless to say, almost every shopper at a salvage yard needs to arrange for delivery or shipping—which most salvage warehouses arrange for you automatically. Sometimes it is even included in the price. Ask!

Remember that people in Britain think nothing of jumping in the car and driving an hour or two to another part of Britain to look for just the right part to complete their do-it-yourself project. Below is a listing of the most famous resources in the more commonly visited areas of the United Kingdom.

Please note that there are approximately 1,000 salvage dealers in the United Kingdom and Ireland; some of them specialize in certain types of merchandise, others take whatever comes their way. Price is

most often related to the condition of a object and
the relative scarcity of its material. Some of the best
deals can be found in alternatives to higher-priced
goods. For example, Cotswold slate tiles have
become outrageously expensive because they are in
high demand. In response, dealers are now selling
buff-colored concrete tiles that are 40 to 50 years
old. They look almost as charming, but at a fraction of the cost of slate.

Most salvage resources are open seven days a
week, with different hours on weekends. Call for
exact hours and directions. Many provide restoration services and shipping.

Architectural Salvage Store, Chorley Wood (30
minutes from London); local phone: 1923/
284-196.

Drummond's of Bramley, Guildford (30 minutes
from London); local phone: 1483/898-766;
fax 1483/894-393.

Edinburgh Architectural Salvage Yards,
Edinburgh and Glasgow; local phone: 141/
556-7772 (Glasgow); local phone: 131/554-7077
(Edinburgh).

London Architectural Salvage and Supply Co.,
London EC2; local phone: 171/739-0448.
Shares space with Westland and Co. (see below).

Solopark, Cambridge; local phone: 1223/
834-663.

Tunnel Avenue Antique Warehouse, Greenwich;
local phone: 181/305-2230.

Walcot Reclamation, Bath; local phone: 1225/
444-404.

Westland and Co., London EC2; local phone:
171/739-8094.

FAMOUS ANTIQUE TOWNS

I've had some very disappointing experiences in certain English towns and villages that are known for

their antique shops. For some reason, I've seen a negative correlation between "cute" and good shopping. Cities such as Chester have left me cold with their high prices and fancy shops, whereas unheard-of areas, such as Boughton, right outside of Chester and without any apparent charm, have warmed the cockles of my heart.

Please don't get me wrong: I'm not complaining about the city of Chester. It's a beautiful photo op. I'm just saying that after years of hearing how cute Chester is and how wonderful the antique shops in the heart of town are, when I finally got there, it didn't meet my expectations. There is a string of shops and they are very attractive, particularly the one that is built into the city wall. But I was done looking at the shops in five minutes. In fact, largely because of this experience, I'm thinking of developing the Cutie-Pie Theory of Retail: The cuter a place, the less good its bargains are.

I've checked out "The Lanes" of Brighton and "The Pantiles" of Tunbridge Wells and wasn't particularly impressed. And it wasn't even raining. I do cover antique shopping in Brighton, but I send you elsewhere; you won't even find Tunbridge Wells listed.

Conversely, I've been to cities that Londoners like to joke about, such as Manchester, and gone nuts for the true charm and serious finds there. Contrary to everything I've said thus far, I confess that I like Harrogate, one of those honey-pot antique cities that I ought to hate. Go figure. I've never been to Melford, which became famous through the British television series *Lovejoy*. Harrogate is Seriously Cute; Melford looks average from the pictures I have seen but is getting a big reputation among locals.

I also like The Cotswolds, which can be classified in the same category as Harrogate. I'm not adverse to Cute but I am sometimes confounded by it. So I guess the lesson is: Let the beholder of Cute beware.

WHERE THERE'S CUTE THERE'S FAKE

. . . .

I have this other rule that is just sort of a small rule with a warning attached. This is an international rule and the situation is actually not as bad in the United Kingdom as it is in many other parts of Europe.

Imagine that you live in an adorable city that receives a large number of tourists every year. You decide to open an antique shop and you do so-so, but you can't believe how stupid and uninformed most of your customers are—not to mention how price driven they are. Over a period of time, partly to stay alive and maybe to get rich, you begin to buy your "local antiques" in France, Spain, or the Far East. You buy anything you think might have the right "look" but a lower price tag, so you can move the merchandise. This is called capitalism.

While I understand this practice, I am offended by it. Be aware that it exists and you'll run a smaller chance of getting taken.

BIGGER IS BETTER

. . . .

The question I am invariably asked about particular flea markets, car boot sales, and antique fairs is, "Is it a good one?" Obviously, anyone's definition of good is going to vary depending on her budget and what she finds over a series of visits. I've come to base my professional answer not on how well I have fared but simply on how many dealers attend. The number of dealers at an event tells you a number of things beyond an actual head count.

High-end, extremely tony dealers do not go to large events, since they are by nature selective and only want to show with their own kind.

Junky dealers do not show at vetted fairs.

The more dealers, the less likely the event is to be vetted and the better your chances become of finding fun junk and good prices.

So let's talk numbers. A big show has at least 450 dealers; 700 dealers is a huge show; and 2,500 dealers is pretty much inconceivable (but incredibly fun). My personal rules of thumb:

- Don't go out of your way for a fair of 25 dealers or less.
- Consider attending a show with 100 dealers if your time isn't limited.
- Seriously consider making an effort to get to a show with 250 dealers, especially if it takes place on a day of the week when several different shows are in one town.
- A show with 500 to 600 dealers is considered in the trade to be an up-and-comer—worth attending and worth watching.
- Arrange your trip to London or Britain around a show with 750 dealers or more.

The largest show in Britain is held a few times a year in Newark; there are anywhere from 2,500 to 3,500 dealers at any given show. You do not need a show this big in order to have a good time, but if you are looking for the memory of a lifetime, book now. See page 103.

PRICES

. . . .

I always judge a vendor to be fair if he has prices marked on his goods—regardless of whether I am at a car boot sale or a London showroom. Items with price tags that are written in code make me especially angry because the code tells the dealer what he paid for an article as well as how long he's had it. He can glance at the code and know instantly how willing he is to part with the article and how flexible he can be on its price. Dealers who have no tags whatsoever make up prices on the spot based on how well dressed you are and even your accent.

It is rare that you are expected to pay the asking price, even on an object with a price tag. If you are a dealer, or even a dabbler with proper business cards and credentials, identify yourself as such when you first start talking about pricing. You can expect a 10% trade discount.

You must pay VAT on antiques.

BARGAINING

If you hate the very idea of bargaining, but you realize the price on the price tag can be negotiable, you can simply say something like, "Is that the best price?" or, "Can you do a little better on the price?" This is a nonthreatening attitude that may result in a small discount.

If you seriously know what you are doing and you know what the fair market price is, you can get more aggressive, particularly if you see a flaw in the goods. Simply quoting the market value for an item in the United States to a British dealer seldom has much power, however.

PREVIEW EVENTS

Just as the big shows have charity previews (air kissing is even practiced in Great Britain!), most other shows—especially the big, good junky ones— have previews for the trade. You can pay an early admission fee (higher than the regular admission) and get in a day early. Admission may be as high as £35 or as low as £10. (It's to separate the dealers from the tourists.)

Some previews are strictly trade only at which time you must present a business card with your cash.

Calendar of Major Fairs

The major antique fairs are held on an annual basis and are as regular as rain. They are rather upscale and therefore not an accurate reflection of the entire scene I've described thus far. They are a great starting point for exploring the antiques and collectibles market, however.

January

• **West London Antiques Fair**, London
• **LAPADA Fair**, Birmingham

February

• **Olympia Antiques Fair**, London
• **Chester Antiques Show**, Chester (one hour from Manchester)
• **Harrogate Antiques Show**, Harrogate (one hour from Manchester)

March

• **Chelsea Antiques Fair**, London
• **Manchester International Antiques and Collectors Fair**, G-Mex Centre
• **Shepton Mallet Spring Antique and Collectors Fair**, Shepton Mallet

April

• **International Antiques Fair**, Birmingham
• **Scottish Antiques Fair**, Edinburgh
• **Harrogate Spring Fair**, International Centre

May

• **Aberdeen Antiques Fair**, Scotland (one hour from Edinburgh)
• **BADA Fair**, London

June

- **Olympia Antiques Fair**, London
- **Grosvenor House Antiques Fair**, London
- **Sussex Country Fair**, Barkham Manor near Uckfield

July

- **Armoury House Fair**, London

August

- **West London Antiques Fair**, London
- **NEC August Fair**, Birmingham
- **Chiltern Antiques Fair**, Racecourse, Windsor
- **Melba Fairs Giant Fleamarket Racecourse**, Cheltenham
- **Chester Racecourse Antiques Fair**, Grandstand Pavilion

September

- **Kensington Brocante Fair**, London
- **Chelsea Antiques Fair**, London
- **Northern Antiques Fair**, Harrogate
- **Chiltern Antiques Fair**, Racecourse, Windsor
- **Melba Fairs Giant Fleamarket**, Racecourse, Cheltenham

October

- **LAPADA Show**, London
- **Chiltern Antiques Fair**, Racecourse, Windsor
- **Melba Fairs Giant Fleamarket**, Racecourse, Cheltenham
- **Anglican Arts and Antiques**, The Athenaeum, Bury St. Edmonds

- Yorkshire Tabletop and Furniture,
  Racecourse, Yorkshire

November

- North Wales Antiques Fair, Portmeirion,
  Wales
- Kensington Antiques Fair, London
- Olympia Antiques Fair, London
- Birmingham Antiques Fair, St. Martin's
  Market
- Melba Fairs Giant Fleamarket,
  Racecourse, Cheltenham
- Newmarket Antiques and Collectors Fair,
  Racecourse, Newmarket
- Annual Castle Howard Antiques Fair,
  Castle Howard (near York)

December

- London Decorative Arts Fair, London
- Period Fashion Fair, London
- Chiltern Antiques Fair, Racecourse,
  Windsor
- Petworth New Years Antiques Fair,
  Petworth

COUPONS & TICKETS

• • • • • • • • • • • • • • • • • • • •

I have seen advertisements in collector's magazines
that not only announce big flea markets and
fairs, but provide coupons good for discounted or
free admission. Since most fairs cost about £3 to
attend and most of you are traveling in at least a
twosome, this can offer a savings of $10 or more.
If you are planning to attend a particular event,
ask your hotel concierge if he or she has seen any
coupons.

SOMEDAY, MY LOVE MARKETS

· ·

I've rarely met a market or fair I didn't like, and if I had my druthers I'd spend almost all of my time abroad visiting them. As this isn't possible (my family would disown me), I have a short list of special events that I plan to get to sooner or later.

Alexandra Palace

I first heard about the events held in Alexandra Palace several years ago and have made a few attempts to get to London on the right date (so far, always in vain); it's on a Saturday. I've read that this fair gets 2,500 dealers but an advertisement I clipped at the time of writing claims a mere 700 stands. I hope I can cope.

Before I get too carried away with the romance of it all, I should mention that Alexandra Palace is a convention center on the outskirts of London and not a real palace. You can get there by public transportation. Events are held in the Great Hall every three to four months. For more information, call 181/883-7061.

Shepton Mallet

I'm attracted to this market for several reasons. The first two are the most important: 1) They have free shuttle bus service from the Bath Spa railroad station and 2) Shepton Mallet is the village where the Mulberry factory outlet shop is located, even though it is not within walking distance of the fair. This event has about 500 dealers—big but not overwhelming. Furthermore, there is a trade preview the day before the event begins. Admission is £3 for the public, £5 for the trade. There's free parking at the site and children under 16 are admitted for free. This is a Saturday and Sunday event; early viewing trade preview is 8 to 10am. The fair is only held a few times a year, so call 1278/792-580 or fax 1278/792-687 for details. See page 173 for more on the Mulberry factory shop.

Newark

If you're a collector, you know that a few times a year the biggest fair in England—which claims to be the biggest in the world—is held at the Newark and Nottinghamshire Showground. Who needs Robin Hood or the sheriff of Nottingham when you can spend a lifetime wandering the 2,500 to 3,500 stands? Many are tented. The fair covers 92 acres, has up to 3,500 stands, and more than 120,000 dealers and visitors.

To get there, take the train from London to Newark Northgate BR station and then hop the courtesy coach. The fair is usually held during the week because it is considered a trade fair, although the public is, of course, welcomed. Note that the fair opens at 7am on the day it is open to the public and closes at 4pm—so don't plan on a casual day in the country. You may want to spend the night nearby. The 1996 dates are: April 1 and 2, June 3 and 4, August 5 and 6, October 21 and 22, and December 9 and 10. For more information, call 1636/702-326 or fax 1636/707-923.

Ardingly

To get there, take BritRail to Haywards Heath (Brighton) and connect there to the courtesy coach. If you are driving, Haywards Heath happens to be on the way to Brighton. It is also quite near Uckfield, which is covered later in this chapter.

There is a full-day trade preview before the opening of the fair for £20 per person. This fair is run by the same promoters who do the event at Newark. For some reason, this fair does not run on a weekend, possibly because it is considered very much an insider's event and therefore for the trade. The public is admitted on the second day of the event, which is also the last day. The dates for 1996 are:

April 23 and 24, July 23 and 24, September 24 and 25, and November 5 and 6. For more information, call 1636/702-326 or fax 1636/707-923.

Stone Leigh

A promoter tipped me off to this event, which is currently only held three times a year because of the availability of the venue. It's held near Birmingham and has between 500 and 600 dealers. It's considered a comer because of its steady growth. The promoter I spoke with thinks it will become a 1,000-dealer show in the future. Because of its proximity to Birmingham, you can fly into this city's airport rather than Heathrow to get there. Venue: Royal Showground, Stone Leigh.

PACKING & SHIPPING

You may think that I'm the tackiest person alive when I admit this, but here goes. I often book my airline tickets based on the extra baggage allowance of a specific carrier and their charges and schemes for additional baggage. Because these things do change, I call around and ask before each trip. Let's face it, if there's an airfare war on and each carrier has the same ticket prices and the service is more or less the same, then the excess baggage policy becomes a major feature.

As of this writing, American Airlines allows you to check three pieces of baggage. Delta allows you to check two pieces and then charges you a combination of fees for additional luggage. The basic charge is $125 for an additional bag. If the bag is heavier than 50 pounds, you pay another $125. If it's larger than 26 inches across, you pay another $125! Delta charged me $375 for a single piece of excess baggage last year!

I usually fly British Airways for various reasons. High on my list of reasons is that it only charges a flat fee of $99 for each piece of additional baggage. Depending on the cost of excess baggage (and what it is you are transporting), you can decide exactly how you want to bring home your British bargains. If you are buying furniture or lots of items, you probably need freight information.

Charges on freight vary with the method of transport: air or surface. Surface is transported by ship and takes much longer than air but is much less expensive. There are two kinds of surface freight: groupage or buying container space outright. Groupage is when you pay by the item to share a container with others who are sending articles to your destination. It is cheaper but takes longer since you must wait for the entire order to be assembled and packed before it leaves the United Kingdom. Buying container space outright is generally more expensive, since you are paying by the size of the container, not by the item. You can, however, arrange to receive your goods faster since you do not have to wait for an entire container to be filled before it departs the United Kingdom. When making a decision about what kind of freight to choose, remember: Much freight does not go by weight of the item, but by the amount of space it takes in a container.

There's a lot to learn.

The best thing to do is get on the phone and start asking the same questions to a group of packers and shippers. Ask if packing and shipping are priced together or separately; ask the same questions about insurance. Ask if your purchases will be delivered to your door or if you need a Customs agent; ask if you have to claim your goods at your local airport or at the port of entry to the United States.

Listed below are some of the most famous and reputable packers and shippers in the trade. These people provide tons of services, everything from delivering one item to filling up the hull of a freighter. They deliver goods around the world as well as around the United Kingdom and provide booklets for you to keep notes in and all sorts of customer services to help you organize a serious buying trip.

Don't blindly pick one without calling around to at least three of them and asking a lot of questions. I like to chat on the phone to get a better feel; you can also fax your queries, however. You should be comparing prices and services rendered.

If by chance you are going on a huge buying spree around the United Kingdom and don't know what you will buy and where, ask the potential shippers if they will pick up your goods at a variety of destinations. This is a rather standard practice, so don't sweat it—most will do it gladly. Often antique shops or warehouses will arrange to gather your local goods for a shipper.

All of the firms listed below specialize in art and antiques but will handle any legal shipment. Please note that Lockson's is frequently the official shipper at an antique fair or event and that they keep a van to arrange shipping, couriers, deliveries, etc., at the two major dealers' fairs: Newark and Ardingly.

Art & Antique Shippers

- Davies Turner; local phone: 171/622-4393; fax: 171/720-3897.
- Lockson; local phone: 171/515-8600; fax: 171/515-4043.
- Gander and White; local phone: 171/381-0571; fax: 171/381-5428. New York, local phone: 718/784-8444; fax 718/784-9337. Paris, phone: (33)1.42.02.18.92; fax: 1.42.06.33.31.
- Hedley's Humpers; local phone: 181/965-8733; fax: 181/965-0249; New York, local phone: 212/219-2877; fax: 212/219-2826. Paris, phone: (33)1.48.13.01.02; fax: 1.48.13.07.08.
- The Packing Shop; local phone: 171/627-5605.
- Wingate and Johnston; local phone: 171/732-8123; fax 171/732-2631.

Chapter Seven

· · · · · · · · ·

SHOPPING LONDON

WELCOME TO LONDON

· ·

Whether this is your first trip to London or just your first this year, you can't help but be excited— even if it's raining. London has a lot of big-city spirit to it, and just being there is exciting. It's more exciting than ever since the recession lifted and money returned, however. With it has come energy and great retail.

I've traveled to London enough to know that if you are a visitor on a tight time leash, you want to pack as much into a day as possible. If you plan to spend most of your time in London, you really owe it to yourself to purchase a copy of *Born to Shop London*. This book assumes that London is only one of several destinations you plan to visit in the United Kingdom and therefore is less detailed and more streamlined in its coverage of London.

Anything that is overly reflective of the American lifestyle has been left out of these pages, despite the fact that the newest trend in British retailing is to build American-style malls or to buy from The Gap. I can't tell you how many new American shops have opened on Regent Street and Bond Street.

THE LAY OF THE LAND

The city of London is actually tiny, only one mile square. It is the business district, and you probably won't even go there. Everything else called London is in fact a different borough or city that has, over time, been incorporated into the giant whole most people think of as "London."

As a visitor, you probably won't have time to visit many of these places or to even learn the difference between, for instance, the city of Westminster and the borough of Hammersmith. And you don't need to: Many of the main shopping districts and important sights in London are congregated in nearby or adjoining areas. If you can't walk from place to place on your shopping and sightseeing list, you can certainly ride the tube. Almost everything in the city's wide web is accessible by tube and BritRail.

GETTING AROUND

As I just mentioned, you can get everywhere you need to by foot or by tube. By all means, buy a Travelcard for either the day or the week, and take advantage of it. The Travelcard, which can be bought in any tube or BritRail station, entitles you to unlimited use of tube and/or bus (and sometimes BritRail trains) for one day. For an idea of what you'll save by using this pass, here's just one example. If you use the tube alone three times in one day, you will have paid for the price of an all-day Travelcard. The Travelcard is £3.90.

Now, here's the good part. If you use Travelcards for more than three consecutive days, you have paid for the price of a weekly card. The best thing about the weekly card is that a week is defined as any consecutive seven-day period, so you can begin your week whenever you want.

To get the weekly card in London, you need a passport-type photo. You can buy Travelcards through BritRail USA, however, they do not sell the one-day Travelcard. They sell three-day, four-day, and seven-day cards. You do not need a photo.

You can get free bus and underground maps through the British Tourist Authority (BTA) before you leave America, or at many information booths in train stations in London. Please note that bus routes are different at night; don't assume anything.

BOOKING LONDON

The most essential book to London any visitor can have is an A to Z (say "A to Zed") guide, which is a book of interlocking maps that show incredible detail. You can buy them in various formats and sizes, including ones with maps in either black and white or full color, at any newsagent, kiosk, or bookstore. Mine is called *Inner London, A to Z* and it's a little bit smaller than a full-sized A to Z guide.

Time Out is the weekly guide to what's happening in the city; it has a shopping column in the back. It's not inexpensive, so if you don't need it, don't splurge. It can become your bible, but on a short trip (especially if your theater tickets have been prearranged) it might be a waste.

SLEEPING IN LONDON

If you pick a hotel that is described as "charming," its rooms can be quite small. Charming usually means old. That means that your kids might not fit into your room with you. Before you choose two charming rooms, compare the cost to that of a big American-style chain hotel where they don't even charge for kids, or won't blink at a family of five holed up in one room. Note that the average price of a good-sized luxury room in a big American chain hotel is about $300 per night, although it can be more (or less) depending on a number of variables.

American chains are all represented in central locations, good for shopping and business. **Hilton** (tel. 800/HILTONS) has a **Conrad** hotel at the more inconvenient Chelsea Harbour location, but it has a convenient promotional price (£99) that includes suites that are great for those traveling with kids.

There are other Hiltons in Mayfair; all have promotional rates based on weekends, seasons, events, or even shopping. I usually stay at the fancy **Park Lane Hilton** or the **Langham Hilton,** both in Mayfair.

Hyatt has the five-star **Hyatt Carlton Tower** in Knightsbridge, call 800/233-1234.

There is a **Sheraton** (tel. 800/325-3535) in the heart of Knightsbridge's best shopping; and a **Marriott** (tel. 800/228-9290) in Mayfair, next door to the American Embassy.

One of my favorite hotels in London is the **May Fair,** which is a member of the **Inter-Continental** chain, so check them out, too.

Forte has taken over the Meridien chain; **Le Meridien** in London has a great location at Piccadilly—and you can benefit from Forte's special program of discounts: book the room 30 days in advance and get 30% off. Call 800/543-4300.

If the dollar is weak, investigate rates that are frozen, or can be prepaid in dollars or frequent-flyer mileage (don't laugh). Never assume that a big-name chain with a family reputation has inexpensive prices; I priced the **Holiday Inn** in Mayfair and found it competitive with the Ritz! Yes, the real Ritz! Need I tell you which one is nicer?

Some of the best things about London hotel rooms are that children under the age of 18 can usually stay for free in their parents' room; many hotels will sell you a second room for the kids at a greatly reduced rate; and still other hotels have apartment suites or wings for the whole family. Also note that much of the year is out-of-season in London, so that price breaks are fairly regular.

London is always full in June and it's hard to get a deal then. July and August and November through March are off-season, so deals abound. The only exception is Christmas. Christmas in London is getting to be the "in" thing, so hotels are not as flexible as they once were about extending off-season rates throughout the Christmas and New Year's holidays. Watch newspapers and call toll-free numbers. Pretend you are Sherlock Holmes. Which reminds me, Dr. Watson told me that the cheapest five-star luxury property in London is Dukes. Check it out.

SECRET HOTEL FINDS FOR SHOPPERS

. . . .

The Athenaeum Hotel & Apartments

The lobby is small and just a little glitzy. The hotel has small but deliciously deluxe rooms (with full-sized bath amenities replenished daily) and apartments that easily sleep four. Athenaeum is a show business hotel; the insider's secret of the Beverly Hills set. Everyone in TV and many in movies stay here, because the guests and staff are quite discreet. Prices are also much lower than at places like The Dorchester. And you can get an apartment for $300 a night, which is quite a deal in London. Phone: 171/499-3464; fax: 171/493-1860. For U.S. reservations, call 800/525-4800.

Cadogan Hotel, Sloane Street

This is a small hotel with only 65 rooms, done in a series of connecting townhouses; very British and divine. You are also a sneeze from Harrods and Harvey Nichols. I know a fair number of women who routinely travel alone and like this hotel for its combination of location, price, and security. Local phone: 171/235-7141; fax: 171/245-0994. Book in the U.S. through Prima Hotels by calling 800/447-7462.

Dukes Hotel, St. James

Another veddy, veddy English hotel that is a dream
to look at (and sleep in) and possibly represents the
best luxury bargain in London. This hotel is small
and is hidden on a dead-end street next to Spencer
House (yes, that Spencer House) and around the
corner from St. James's Palace. Rooms start at about
$225 per night. Local phone: 171/491-4840; fax:
171/493-1264. In the U.S., call 800/381-4702.

SUNDAY SHOPPING

More and more shops are now open Sundays.
Covent Garden is the hot spot, but Hampstead and
Greenwich get the local crowd for those who are
looking for The Cute.

All major department stores, all major multiples,
all malls, and just about any place that wants to sell
you something is open on Sunday, usually from noon
until 5pm, but Tesco Metro, the grocery store
with the fancy address (Covent Garden, Oxford Street),
opens early in the morning and stays open most of
the day.

Department Stores

The following department stores are open Sundays
from noon until 5pm unless otherwise indicated.

BRITISH HOME STORES (BHS)
252-258 Oxford Street, W1
(Tube: Oxford Circus). Open: Monday to
Saturday, 9am to 6pm.

99-105 Kensington High Street, W8 (Tube: High
Street Kensington). Open: Monday to Saturday,
9am to 6pm.

C & A
505 Oxford Street, W1 (Tube: Oxford Circus).
Open: Monday, Tuesday, Saturday, 9:30am to
6pm; Wednesday, Thursday, Friday, 9:30am–8pm.

D. H. EVANS
318 Oxford Street, W1 (Tube: Oxford Circus).
Open: Monday to Friday, 9:30am to 6pm;
Saturday, 9am–6pm; Thursday, until 8pm.

DEBENHAMS
334-338 Oxford Circus, W1 (Tube: Bond Street).
Open: Monday to Saturday, 9:30am to 6pm;
Thursday, until 8pm.

DICKINS & JONES
224 Regent Street, W1 (Tube: Oxford Circus).
Open: Monday to Saturday, 9:30am to 6pm;
Thursday, until 7:30pm.

FORTNUM & MASON
181 Piccadilly, W1 (Tube: Piccadilly Circus).
Open: Monday to Saturday, 9am to 5:30pm.

HARRODS
Brompton Road, SW1 (Tube: Knightsbridge).
Open: Monday to Friday, 10am to 5pm;
Saturday, to 6pm; Wednesday, to 7pm.

HARVEY NICHOLS
109 Knightsbridge, SW1 (Tube: Knightsbridge).
Open: Monday to Saturday, 9:30am to 6pm;
Wednesday, to 7pm.

HOUSE OF FRASER
63 Kensington High Street, W8 (Tube: High Street
Kensington). Open: Monday to Saturday, 9am to
6pm; Thursday, to 6:30pm.

JOHN LEWIS
Oxford Street, W1 (Tube: Bond Street).
Open: Monday to Saturday, 9am to 5:30pm;
Thursday, to 8pm. Closed Sundays.

LIBERTY
*210-220 Regent Street, W1 (Tube: Oxford
Circus). Open: Monday to Saturday, 9:30am
to 6pm; Thursday, to 7pm.*

MARKS & SPENCER
*Main store, 458 Oxford Street, W1 (Tube: Bond
Street or Marble Arch). Open: Monday to
Saturday, 9am to 6pm; Thursday, to 7:30pm.*

PETER JONES
*Sloane Square, SW1 (Tube: Sloane Square).
Open: Monday to Saturday, 9am to 5:30pm.
Closed Sundays.*

SELFRIDGES
*400 Oxford Street, W1 (Tube: Bond Street or
Marble Arch). Open: Monday to Saturday,
9am to 6pm; Thursday, to 7:30pm.*

QUICKIE LONDON SHOPPING TIPS

Some of these rules are generalizations, but if you've
only got limited time, they should hold up pretty
well:

- If you've got time to go to only one department
  store in London, it should be **Liberty**, not **Harrods**.
  I'm not anti-Harrods (who could not love those
  Food Halls?), it's just think that if you have to
  choose, there is no choice.
- If you decide to go to **Harrods** (which you will, of
  course), go early. The store opens at 10am and is
  relatively uncrowded until noonish. If you are
  considering china, Harrods offers an incomparable
  selection. It also has about the fairest shipping plan
  in London.
- If you are sampling the chain stores, which the
  British call multiples, aim for the flagship store of
  any particular house—usually on **Regent Street**.

The only immediate exception I can think of is that The Scotch House in Knightsbridge is better than the one on Regent Street.

After a while, any place you shop in Britain, or in the world, all branch shops start to look alike and only the flagship store really strikes you as impressive. I call this the Laura Ashley Rule of Retailing. Only the flagship store is special. So wave the flag, and your credit cards.

A tremendous amount of British retailing is done through the multiples. See pages 67–76 for information on specific multiples or chains.

- Arrange sightseeing and shopping with some plan to save time, energy, and your sanity. If you're going back to buy wallpaper, arrange your day so that's your last stop—if you have ever schlepped four rolls of wallpaper around London for a day (I have), you'll know that it's not fun. Tour the museums of Knightsbridge before you shop, so you don't have to lug the packages with you.
- Wear something with pockets (if it's summer), or arrange your coat so that one pocket is empty— you'll get in and out of the tube that much more easily if you keep your Travelcard in your pocket so it's always available. You also might want to keep a few pounds there (if you have deep pockets) so you can use up your change—which weighs a ton—and have ready access to money for snacks, tips, and small purchases.
- Make as many purchases as possible on a credit card, preferably one with a protection plan so that if your purchase is broken, lost, or stolen within 90 days you can get a refund or a replacement for free. Aside from this added attraction, credit cards will get you a far better rate of exchange than cash or traveler's checks.
- Ask about the value-added tax (VAT) minimum in every store you go to; ask if the store has a service charge for refunds. There are huge, indeed, enormous doings on the VAT front, partly because

of the EU and partly because of various needs in differing countries. Watch this space and get a hold of the **Tax Free Europe** book *Shopping in Great Britain*. You can either pick one up from the BTA or send away for one before you leave home: Europe Tax Free Shopping, 233 South Wacker Drive, Suite 9700, Chicago, Illinois 60606. Tel. 312/382-1101; fax: 312/382-1109.

Most stores will not grant you a VAT refund on a purchase of less than £50. Many department stores carry the same luxury merchandise as London's boutiques, but have a higher requirement for a refund. Harrods has just lowered its VAT minimum to a mere £100! If *mere* strikes you as the wrong word, consider that it used to be £150! Also note that not every store has a minimum, especially outside of London. I bought a jacket for £30 and still got a refund! Rule Britannia.

Save your receipts as most stores let you pool them over a six-month period. Once they total the minimum for a refund, you qualify.

• If you are most interested in London's sales, as well you should be, it's the January sale period that is so wonderful. The July sales are okay, especially if you need summer clothes, but they also are filled with the leftovers of seasons past, and lack the pizzazz of the January sales. Do note that the dates of the sales are getting earlier each year.

Some stores begin their January Sales the day after Boxing Day (December 27) and many begin their July sales around June 27. The Harrods sale gets the most publicity, but just about every shop in London (actually, England) has a sale during the same time period. So don't just shop Harrods and think you've done it all.

Some sales don't begin until after Epiphany (January 6)—like Harrods. The sale price plus a VAT refund can make an item worth buying in London while it isn't a month later (or earlier) at regular retail. I am so enamored of the January sales that I think it is worthwhile to fly in for a long weekend. Who needs the Caribbean when you can have London on sale?

ROYAL SHOPPING

· ·

If you want to know where the royals shop, just look to the front door or pillars of a shop. Should it bear a royal coat of arms, the store has secured a royal warrant, making it an official purveyor of goods to at least one member of the royal family. (The Prince of Wales's coat of arms bears three feathers.

Royals may shop in stores that do not have royal warrants, of course (that's the fun of being royal), but the main bulk of their business goes to these firms, which may have their warrant rotated every several years (you can get a royal pink slip), or may have been in service for hundreds of years.

Many shops hold several royal warrants for their services to different members of the family.

Royal warrants are granted to jewelers, department stores, chemists, and all sorts of places. Lea and Perrins, maker of Worcestershire sauce, holds a royal warrant. It is the purveyor of Worcestershire sauce to her majesty the queen, and don't you forget it.

Most shops with royal warrants are in London, but there are many located outside the city. In fact, they are all over the United Kingdom

Also note that the royal family is in trade and uses its own coat of arms on its products. Sure you've heard of the House of Windsor gift catalogue made for Americans, and you know that there are gift shops in palaces like Hampton Court and Buckingham, but did you know that Prince Charles has many entrepreneurial projects emanating from his farm in the Cotswolds? The next king now sells two different fruit drinks made from the apples, pears, and raspberries farmed on his Sandringham estate and Cotswold Farm, Highgrove. Cost per bottle: about £2.50.

SHOPPING LONDON BY NEIGHBORHOOD

· ·

Knightsbridge (Tube: Knightsbridge)

Unlike many London areas, Knightsbridge is not a sightseeing-cum-shopping neighborhood. It is mostly a shopping and residential area. But as it does abut the main museum neighborhood—Cromwell Road—you can easily fit some culture into a day of shopping.

Of course, everyone who visits considers **Harrods** a major sight, so you can shop and sightsee at the very same time there.

The main shopping area around Knightsbridge is not too big to handle, which is gratifying and makes it the perfect destination for a half-day (or full-day) adventure.

NEIGHBORHOOD FINDS

HARRODS
Brompton Road, SW1

There are many things I don't like about Harrods, but I will not bore you with them, since essentially Harrods is a great store: It does have everything. Since everything can be daunting, I maintain that the only way to manage this amount of space and merchandise is by going for the gusto and forgetting the rest. It is imperative that you wander the Food Halls. The basement boutique where Harrods logo merchandise is sold is also a good bet.

The china department is the most extensive in England, and actually has things you won't see anywhere else: china arranged by maker in a series of salons that seem to go on forever. Shipping is arranged by the actual weight of what you buy, not the number of pieces.

The toy department is almost as extensive as **Hamley's,** and it's all on one floor.

If you are heading on to the Continent and need a business gift, something from Harrods is always welcome because its international reputation is great and it has no branch stores. Harrods has a very strict dress code; I have received mail from a reader who was barred admission because she was wearing a backpack. The rules are posted outside the store but basically it goes like this: no shorts, no bare feet, and no thongs, so torn clothing even if it is fashionably distressed is verboten. And last but not least, no backpacks.

GENEVIEVE LETHU
132 Brompton Road, SW3

This is a French designer who has literally hundreds of shops all over France but has not yet come to the United States, so this could be your only chance to shop here and begin to worship at her corner of wicker. The bad news: Only a percentage of the line comes to London and, of course, it costs more than in France. The good news: Lethu is inventive, clever, and colorful and does tabletop that is moderately priced—even at London prices.

THE SCOTCH HOUSE
2 Brompton Road, SW1

A quasi department store dedicated to the British look (despite the name) and, of course, the Scottish look as well, with one of the best selections of kilts, tartans, and Scottish fashions/supplies in the United Kingdom. Not the source for buying a new pin for your kilt, however. They carry good sweaters and fashions to help you create the upper-crust country look we all love so much.

In fact, there are many very chic items here that will mix and match with the hautest of your couture—like the shawl with the ruffle on the end, for example. Don't write off this store as a tourist trap. Its goods are not inexpensive and you may indeed find the same things for less if you search, but this is an easy source for those who need easy.

Although there are several branches of this store, this is the best one. Across the street from Harrods.

HARVEY NICHOLS
109 Knightsbridge, SW1

If you've run out of Harrods overwhelmed by its complexity and size, you'll find comfort at Harvey Nichols—a kinder and gentler department store with merchandise carefully chosen to represent only the upscale and fashionable point of view. Many designers have boutiques here; many American designers are sold here. The store has recently been renovated in order to look more like an American department store. There's a rather good food hall on the fifth floor, but it in no way compares with Harrods Food Halls. It possibly compares with Zabars or a good neighborhood deli.

I like Harvey "Nicks" for several reasons, all of which boil down to this: We seem to have the same taste. While a few too many American designers are represented, it has a fabulous hat department (first floor), and a splendid home decor floor.

PANDORA
16-22 Cheval Place, SW7

While you're in the neighborhood, I'd be cheating you if I didn't tell you that around the corner from Harrods, only one block away, is an entire street selling used designer merchandise from six or seven different shops, one right next to the other. The best of them all is Pandora. My friend Marie was horrified that I'd sent her to look at gently used anything ("The British don't know how to gently use anything," she sniffed), but she made off with a real-life gently used Hermès Kelly bag on her last visit. I've bought almost all my Chanel here.

Central London

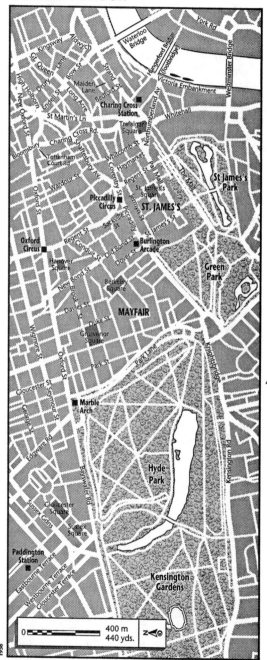

Waterloo Bridge
York Rd
Hungerford Bridge
Footbridge
Westminster Bridge

Kingsway
Aldwych
Gt. Queen St.
High Holborn
New Oxford St
Endell St
Drury Lane
Bow St.
Long Acre
Strand
Maiden Lane
Bedford St.
Victoria Embankment

Charing Cross Station

St Martin's Ln
Charing Cross Rd
Bloomsbury
Tottenham Court Rd
Trafalgar Square
Northumberland Av.
Whitehall

Oxford St
Wardour St.
Shaftesbury Av.
Whitcomb St
Coventry St
Haymarket
Regent St
Pall Mall
The Mall

St James's Park

Piccadilly Circus

ST. JAMES'S

St James's Square
Piccadilly
St James's St.

Oxford Circus

Regent St.
Conduit St
Old Bond St
Sackville St
Dover St

Burlington Arcade

Hanover Square
New Bond St
Berkeley Square

Green Park

Davies St.
Duke St.

MAYFAIR

Grosvenor Square
Park St.

Knightsbridge

Wigmore St.
Oxford St
Park Lane
Kensington Rd

Gloucester St
Seymour St.
George St

Marble Arch

Edgware Rd

Bayswater Rd

Hyde Park

Paddington Station

Sussex Gdns.
Gloucester Square
Sussex Square
Eastbourne Terrace
Westbourne Terrace
Gloucester Terrace

Kensington Gardens

0 ___ 400 m
440 yds.

N

1956

Mayfair (Tube: Bond Street)

Mayfair probably has more shopping per square foot than any other shopping district in London, if not the world. There is an amazing variety of tastes and styles in its retailing, from top-of-the-line fancy designer shops to big-time department stores (on Oxford Street and Regent Street), to teenybopper shops and even the infamous Carnaby Street. In recent years, an amazing number of stores have opened in this neighborhood and the scene is quite trendy.

As much as I adore Mayfair, I'm going to be very blunt and say that if you are on a tight schedule with a limited budget, you may not want to see it all. You have to go to Liberty and you have to go to Hamley's (if you have kids or are a kid), but you can do those two errands and move right into Soho without getting into the seriously high-rent district (see page 126 for information about Soho and Covent Garden).

There are actually several tube stops to use for this neighborhood; I've given Bond Street as the basic overall stop, to bring you right into the center of things. If there is a tube stop right outside the door of a particular shop, I've placed the closer tube stop in the actual listing. If you want to explore the whole neighborhood, you can easily walk to any of the stores listed in this section from the Bond Street tube.

Don't forget that Piccadilly is part of the Mayfair area, although you can use the Piccadilly tube to get to stores like Fortnum & Mason (page 125), the Burlington Arcade (pages 125–126), etc.

NEIGHBORHOOD FINDS

📖 LIBERTY
210-220 Regent Street, W1
(Tube: Oxford Circus)

It is possible to shop the Liberty department store sort of thoroughly and miss the good part. So pay attention, please. The stuff that dreams are made of is in the back building (the half-timbered one), which you can enter through the book department or can find if you meander along the ground floor, bearing left after you enter from Regent Street until you turn right at the back of the handbags; it's marked "Tudor Building." Once there you'll find a fair housewares department with a complete tribute to the Orient downstairs, an excellent home sewing and knitting department, and a wonderful linen and antique area, on two upper floors. Note the way the quilts are hung over the balconies, the dark old Jacobean-style woodwork, and the grace of the selling space.

I think the best buy in the store is one of the Kaffe Fassett sweater kits. You have to knit it yourself, but you get a kit for £75. The finished sweater will be worth about $500. In the fabric department and on the ground floor there are tons of famous Liberty prints in various forms of finish (there are many do-it-yourself skirts) that will suddenly seem essential to your lifestyle.

The hat department is good, but not quite as good as Harvey Nichols to my taste. The Liberty souvenirs are bountiful, but can be pricey.

Give me Liberty or give me death.

HAMLEY'S
200 Regent Street, W1
(Tube: Oxford Circus)

Although the British no longer own Hamley's, it remains an institution in British retailing. Hamley's claims to be the world's largest toy store; it is certainly a toy department store, with demonstrations and sample toys in every corner and aisle and crazy tourists (young and old) trying to determine what's a good buy and what isn't.

PAST TIMES
155 Regent Street, W1 (Tube: Piccadilly Circus)

This is a small multiple that has recently opened on Regent Street, although there has been one in

Kaffe Fassett on Picking Knits

Kaffe (rhymes with "waif") Fassett is an American artist who has lived in London for 30 years. He's become a living legend in the world of design—particularly sweaters, woolens, and needlepoint, or what the Brits call tapestry. His sense of color and whimsy have made him a best-selling author of five books published in the United States and United Kingdom. His tips:

- Don't worry about flight delays or travel hassles; just knit.
- Color brings energy, so use a minimum of 20 colors.
- You don't have to know how to knit or how to read a pattern; start simply and work your way up.
- Don't worry about lumps and bumps; go for color and texture.
- Think about design as you travel—look to your surroundings for inspiration when choosing color combinations. Nature has always had the best sense of what works together.
- Don't get caught up in how much is enough or worry what should I buy, so I can make such and such? Go with your heart and your eye. Start with a little of this and that—whatever works for you—and have enough going on so that if you run out of one color or one texture, it simply doesn't matter. Pile on the pattern.
- Buy wool while you travel so that you can take away the colors of the destination and create color combinations while you are still on the scene, then whenever you knit and wherever you knit, you'll take along your memories of that place. When you're finished, your sweater or creation will be a living souvenir.

London near Harrods for ages and there are other branches dotted around England. Because the shops are small and the brand has a low profile in America, it's my job to tell you that this is a museum store of sorts selling reproduction goods from the Middle Ages. It's truly unique and fabulous and the kids will love it. They also do mail order.

LILLYWHITE
Piccadilly Circus, SW1
(Tube: Piccadilly Circus)

Sporting enthusiasts will go mad for this department store full of toys of the sporting kind. Gear to wear and play with for men, women, and children. Price brands carefully; most items will cost less at home. The selection is unbeatable, however.

FORTNUM & MASON
181 Piccadilly, W1
(Tube: Piccadilly Circus)

Although this establishment serves the local public as a department store, to me it is a toy store of yet another sort: It's a fancy grocery store. As far as I'm concerned, you can ignore the china downstairs and the clothes upstairs. This is a good resource for gifts and foodstuffs and for lunch—there are two or three different eateries depending on the time of day. They will ship your jams and mustards. Book a hamper downstairs.

BURLINGTON ARCADE
Piccadilly, W1
(Tube: Piccadilly Circus)

This is the original mall. A stroll through the gates begins as you leave Fortnum and Mason (you must cross the street), and gets you to Savile Row or New Bond Street high fashion quite painlessly. The arcade is filled with old English retailers, many of whom sell cashmeres and sweaters and knits. The arcade is locked at nights and on Sunday, so you can't even get through for a peek. There have been a lot of vacancies lately and some new faces

(**Georgina Von Etzdorf** is a must-see), but mainly the arcade is known for sweater shops and a very good linens shop at the far end.

BROWN'S
23 South Molton Street, W1
(Tube: Bond Street)

If you know from Brown's Hotel, Molton-Brown (hairdresser), and Brown's, you are a complete Londoner. Brown's is the leading specialty store/ boutique for designer clothes in Britain; many designers were discovered by Brown's, had shops there, and went on to open their own stores. Some international designers prefer to remain exclusively at Brown's and don't even have their own shops (like **Jil Sander**, Missoni, and Sonia Rykiel). The store is a series of town houses on South Molton Street, and is the reason for the high reputation of this little shopping street. You connect from house to house as you shop, going upstairs and down and in and through walls and doors. You may actually do quite well during the sale period.

Soho–Covent Garden (Tube: Covent Garden)

Covent Garden is one of the most successful urban redevelopment plans you'll ever enjoy. Its popularity as a tourist destination and its proximity to Mayfair have made the real estate between the two and Soho more and more valuable. Once a tawdry area of sex shops and peep shows, Soho is becoming more and more gentrified. It's not postcard perfect, but within ten years this area will be devoted to the adorable; right now it's for up-and-coming designers and smart little shops.

Two recent great finds of mine are the **Ally Cappelino** shop, which gets raves from fashion editors who love expensive cutting-edge clothes, and the **Woodhouse Outlet Store**, which sells castoffs from the various ranges Woodhouse makes. I don't think the latter store is permanent, but as it's been there for a year, look for it when you're in the area, or ask at Ally's.

The best way to really see it all is to put on your walking shoes, get out at **Charing Cross** station, and move along the Strand up into Covent Garden. Walk through the **Jubilee Market** into the rest of the marketplace, until you come out on **Neal Street**. Stop for a rest at **Thomas Neal's**, a rather new mall.

NEIGHBORHOOD FINDS

COVENT GARDEN GENERAL STORE
111 Long Acre, WC2

Perhaps the best thing about the Covent Garden General Store is that it is almost always open, even when no other stores are open. So if you need a shopping fix you can always race over. It's also pretty good shopping. The store is very large, with two levels of wares ranging from junk to tabletop. There are party gifts and gags, but there are also jams, mustards, gourmet food items, giftables, souvenirs, Britgoods, and a never-ending supply of Botanic Garden dishes. A very good place for all your gift and souvenir shopping. Yes, folks: This store is open on Sunday; on weekdays, it is open until midnight.

DR. MARTENS DEPARTMENT STORE
3 King Street, WC2

This is a department store only in the sense that it sells more than shoes, but it is not a department store to anyone over the age of 22. Maybe 18. This rather large, five-story boutique pays tribute to just how far a name can take you. The first floor has bins of Doc Martens merchandise, although even at age 15 Aaron Gershman was not impressed with the nylon Dr. Martens wallet I bought him (£6). So why should you go to the store? Because you've never seen anything like it in your life. This is everything Carnaby Street was back in the good old days.

APPLE MARKET
Covent Garden, WC2

In between the buildings that comprise the stores of Covent Garden Market, there are stands for Apple Market craftspeople and vendors. Since there are three rows of buildings, they form two different alleys; so see everything, although the craftspeople all huddle in one particular area. A large percentage of the regular shops around the market are branch stores of such British multiples as **Monsoon, Bertie, Whistles, Culpeper the Herbalist,** and **Hobbs.** If the thought of more multiples makes you yawn, please don't! In fact, if you have only a few hours to shop in London, the Covent Garden area and specifically the Apple Market should be on your must-do list. No matter what shape the dollar is in, your best chance of finding fair prices and even bargains on fine merchandise lies in the stalls of the Apple Market. Nearby Jubilee Market has some cheap thrills, but Apple Market has fabulous crafts, buttons, sweaters, hats, and even ceramics at modest prices. In fact, it may just be the best one-stop shopping ground you can find.

PENHALIGON
41 Wellington Street, WC2

If you have not yet visited a branch of Penhaligon, now is the time to walk one block over and see one of England's premier fragrance houses. Designed in dark woods with the feel of a shop 100 years old, Penhaligon sells several fragrances they alone make, as they have since Queen Victoria was a young woman. There are scents for men and women, and their men's fragrances provide an excellent gift for the difficult-to-shop-for gentleman.

NATURALLY BRITISH
13 New Row, WC2

If you need gifts, or simply a good time, walk over toward Leicester Square via New Row, a tiny pedestrian street chockablock with cute shops. Naturally British sells handicrafts from all over the British Isles, including sweaters, and everything else you can think of as well. The shop has the extra ingredient of warmth—it just feels good in there.

ACADEMY SOHO
15 Newburgh Street, W1
(Tube: Piccadilly Circus or Oxford Circus)

This is a branch of Academy, which began on King's Road when King's Road was way-out and funky. The shop is fun to look at, and it gets you started on Newburgh Street, which is one of Soho's most exciting areas of reconstruction. Be prepared: We are not talking cheap goods or poorly made teen fashion. Academy, like the stores around it, sells very pricey duds. For rock stars and the like.

King's Road (Tube: Sloane Square)

Everything that's old is new again and everything I hated last year I love again now. So say hello to King's Road, which was getting a bit boring to me but sure woke me up in a hurry when I was there recently. Talk about young and kicky and fun. Who cares that there's no underground stop and you'll have to walk forever or jump on and off the bus? That's why God made feet.

You can taxi directly to the heart of King's Road or do it the old-fashioned way: I visit King's Road via Sloane Square, directly from Sloane Street and Knightsbridge, so it's a fashion walk and shopping prowl that makes sense to me if not to my feet.

The chic stuff and the antique arcades and the designer sources are all at the Sloane Square end and the trendy stuff is way in the other direction.

Because of the antique galleries here and the occasional fun shops, this is not a waste of time. It's just not "Oh, wow!" every second.

Please note that if you do this the way I do, you'll start at the very low two-digit numbers on King's Road, which is where Sloane Square is, and go up quite high—I go almost to the 600s, despite the long, dry stretches in between. There are good things all through the 300s. **Morgan,** for the teens and tweens, is at 69A . . . just to get you started. Comfortable shoes, please. Sure, Dr. Martens will be swell.

For the hip and the hot, there's **Bluebird Garage Fashion Market** (Twiggy, where are you?), **Steinberg and Tolkein** (collectable costume jewelry), **Thomas Dare** (Sloane Ranger home design par excellence and French chic), and the usual suspects like **M&S, Habitat, David Mellor, Jaeger,** etc.

For the more traditional in retail, the following two finds are located right near Sloane Square.

NEIGHBORHOOD FINDS

THE GENERAL TRADING COMPANY
144 Sloane Street, SW1

The General Trading Company, where Diana Spencer registered as a bride, is in what must have been a house or two or four; it wanders up and down and around and sells a little of everything— from inexpensive Indian imports to china, crystal, table linens, wastepaper baskets made with pressed flowers, hand-painted ties, and kids' toys. You can also eat here. Something for everyone; I've found much merchandise that I haven't seen elsewhere here.

PETER JONES
Sloane Square, SW1

This is a medium-sized department store where you could buy ordinary things if you wanted to. Luckily, you came here for the street-floor fun, which includes a china department with many choices, a fabrics department with one of the best selections of trimmings in London, and a bed linen department with sheets in solid colors that I have never, and I mean never, seen anywhere else.

BASIC LONDON RESOURCES FROM A–Z

· ·

Antique Centers

Britain may be a nation of shopkeepers, but I find it a nation of collectors. Everybody collects something; great time and attention are paid to collecting. Thus, there are antique centers all over the country, and especially in London. Most have their own personalities and attract a certain type of dealer and clientele. The fancier the address, the higher the rent, the higher the prices—an old rule of retailing in any city. About the only center with any funky feel to it is Alfie's; the rest range from really fancy to almost fancy. There are several on the King's Road, so see them all while you are there.

ALFIE'S ANTIQUE MARKET
13-25 Church Street, NW8 (Tube: Marylebone or Edgware Road). Open: Tuesday to Saturday, 10am to 6pm; 370 stalls.

ANTIQUARIUS
131-143 King's Road, SW3 (Tube: Sloane Square). Open: Monday to Saturday, 10am to 6pm; 170 stalls.

BERMONDSEY MARKET
Long Lane and Bermondsey Street, SE1 (Tube: London Bridge). Open: Friday only, 5am to 2pm; 50 dealers.

BOND STREET ANTIQUES CENTRE
124 New Bond Street, W1 (Tube: Bond Street). Open: Monday to Friday, 10am to 6pm; 30 dealers.

CAMDEN ANTIQUE MARKET
*High Street and Muck Street, Camden Town,
NW1 (Tube: Camden Town). Open: Thursday
only, 7am to 2pm; 40 dealers.*

CHELSEA ANTIQUE MARKET
*253 King's Road, SW3 (Tube: Sloane Square).
Open: Monday to Saturday, 10am to 6pm;
40 dealers.*

CHENIL GALLERIES
*181-183 King's Road, SW3 (Tube: Sloane Square).
Open: Monday to Saturday, 10am to 6pm;
70 dealers.*

GRAYS ANTIQUE MARKETS
*58 Davies Street, W1, and 1-7 Davies Mews, W1
(Tube: Bond Street). Open: Monday to Friday,
10am to 6pm; 200 dealers.*

JUBILEE MARKET
*Covent Garden, WC2 (Tube: Covent Garden).
Open: Monday only, 9am to 5pm; 25 dealers.*

KENSINGTON CHURCH STREET ANTIQUES GALLERY
*58-60 Kensington Church Street, W8 (Tube: High
Street Kensington). Open: Monday to Saturday,
10:30am to 6pm; 14 dealers.*

OLD CINEMA ANTIQUE WAREHOUSE
*157 Tower Bridge Road, SE1 (Tube: Tower
Bridge). Open: Monday to Saturday, 9:30am to
6pm. (Note, this is a warehouse not a fair. Don't
count by the number of dealers present; size is
what's important.)*

OLD CROWTHER MARKET
*282 North End Road, Fulham, SW6 (Tube:
Fulham Broadway). Open: Wednesday to Sunday,
10am to 6pm; 60 dealers.*

British Big Names

The world of British big names spans from old-
fashioned traditionalists to newfangled New Wave,

with the entire sportswear (as quasi-couture) gang thrown in. I've listed here those names I consider to be the backbone of British fashion. There are certain looks that are right in London (and the British countryside) and many of those looks work quite well in America's heartland. They are not as cutting edge as what I call New York fashion; so if you live a mainstream life, don't worry. Classics never go out of style in London.

Bargain hunters who are serious about their savings, have wheels, and don't mind a small schelpp will note that a large percentage of the names on this list have outlet stores that are located in either the London suburbs or other parts of the United Kingdom.

AQUASCUTUM
100 Regent Street, W1

LAURA ASHLEY
256-258 Regent Street, W1 (main store)

BURBERRYS
165 Regent Street, W1

🛍 ALLY CAPELLINO
95 Wardour Street, SoHo, W1

CAROLINE CHARLES
170 New Bond Street, W1

CONRAN SHOP
81 Fulham Road, SW3

JASPER CONRAN
303 Brompton Road, SW3

PAUL COSTELLOE
156 Brompton Road, SW1

ALFRED DUNHILL
30 Duke Street, SW1

🛍 NICOLE FARHI
158 New Bond Street, W1

FRENCH CONNECTION
249 Regent Street, W1

KATHARINE HAMNETT
20 Sloane Street, SW1

JAEGER
204 Regent Street, W1

JOSEPH
88 Peterborough Road, SW6

MULBERRY
40 New Bond Street, W1

NEXT
160 Regent Street, W1

BRUCE OLDFIELD
27 Beauchamp Place, SW3

MARY QUANT
3 Ives Street, SW3

AUSTIN REED
103-113 Regent Street, W1

JOHN RICHMOND
62 Neal Street, WC2

PAUL SMITH
41-44 Floral Street, WC2

VIVIENNE WESTWOOD
41 Conduit Street, W1

6 Davies Street, W1

China Shopping in London

You cannot leave England without taking advantage of the bargains in china. I think the best deals are possible in Stoke-on-Trent, if you're willing to purchase discontinued styles. If you want first-quality goods, be aware that they cost the same in London as they do in Stoke-on-Trent.

Stoke-on-Trent is for bargains of the discontinued sort; London has a better selection of current styles.

Also please note that prices do not vary much (at all) between shops. You score only if you can get someone to deal, which is quite possible on a large order. Try either **House of Chinacraft** or **Reject China Shop** if you are buying service for 12, or even six. (They are owned by the same parent company.)

The best time to buy is in January, when there are sales that will make you weep. For instance, in January, Harrods trucks in seconds from Stoke-on-Trent and sells them at Stoke-on-Trent prices.

There are two or three different shipping plans available. Some stores go strictly by weight; some go by the number of pieces; a few will offer you a flat price for the entire set. Shipping is not inexpensive; insurance should be included—ask.

It really doesn't matter where you shop, so don't make yourself crazy trying to find the best prices. It's all a matter of selection, service, and shipping. Go where you are comfortable. If you can hand-carry your purchase you'll have the greatest savings.

HOUSE OF CHINACRAFT
198 Regent Street, W1 (among many)

THOMAS GOODE
19 South Audley Street, W1

HARRODS
Brompton Road, SW1

LAWLEY'S
154 Regent Street, W1

LIBERTY
210-220 Regent Street, W1

REJECT CHINA SHOP
134 Regent Street, W1 (among many)

WEDGWOOD
66 Regent Street, W1

International Big Names

No shopping mecca is more international than London; no international resource can consider itself in the big time if it doesn't have a London address listed on a glossy shopping bag. No American firm can consider that it has gone global until it too has a London address. As a result of all these needs, London is crammed with stores, with more to open tomorrow.

There are very few bargains in international merchandise, unless you hit a big sale and can then get the VAT refund on top of the sale savings. The biggest news on the international designer and big-name scene is the changes in the key addresses:

- Regent Street (now crawling with American stores)
- Bond Street (all the international big names have taken space here)
- Sloane Street (Dead? Did I say it was dead just two years ago? Silly me!)
- Oxford Street (You don't think the addition of a major supermarket on a major shopping street is news?)

You will find most of the international big names on these four streets or in the department stores; note that British department stores are especially good resources for the cheaper bridge lines from the major makers, such as Variations by Yves Saint Laurent.

GIORGIO ARMANI
177-178 Sloane Street, SW1

EMPORIO ARMANI
112A New Bond Street, W1

187 Brompton Road, SW3

AGNÈS B.
111 Fulham Road, SW3

PIERRE CARDIN
20 Old Bond Street, W1

CÉLINE
28 New Bond Street, W1

CERRUTI 1881
76 New Bond Street, W1

CHANEL
26 Old Bond Street, W1

31 Sloane Street, SW1

ADOLFO DOMINGUEZ
57 South Molton Street, W1

ESCADA
67 New Bond Street, W1

FENDI
37 Sloane Street, SW1

LOUIS FERAUD
73 New Bond Street, W1

FERRAGAMO
24 Old Bond Street, W1

GIANFRANCO FERRÉ
20 Brook Street, W1

GENNY
19 South Molton Street, W1

GUCCI
33 Old Bond Street, W1

18 Sloane Street, SW3

HERMÈS
155 New Bond Street, W1

179 Sloane Street, SW3

ISTANTE
183 Sloane Street, SW3

CHARLES JOURDAN
39-43 Brompton Road, SW3

KENZO
15 Sloane Street, SW1

KRIZIA
18 New Bond Street, W1

CHRISTIAN LACROIX
29 Old Bond Street, W1

8 Sloane Street, SW1

KARL LAGERFELD
173 New Bond Street, W1

201 Sloane Street, SW1

LALIQUE
162 New Bond Street, W1

GUY LAROCHE
33 Brook Street, W1

LLADRO
194 Piccadilly, W1

LOEWE
130 Old Bond Street, W1

MAX MARA
153 New Bond Street, W1

32 Sloane Street, SW3

ISSEY MIYAKE
21 Sloane Street, SW1

270 Brompton Road, SW3

PRADA
44 Sloane Street, SW1

RODIER
106 Brompton Road, SW3

YVES SAINT LAURENT
137 New Bond Street, W1

33 Sloane Street, SW1

EMANUEL UNGARO
39 Sloane Street, SW1

VALENTINO
160 New Bond Street, W1

174 Sloane Street, SW3

GIANNI VERSACE
34 Old Bond Street, W1

LOUIS VUITTON
149 New Bond Street, W1

198 Sloane Street, SW3

ERMENEGILDO ZEGNA
37 New Bond Street, W1

Markets

I'll be honest with you. I've now been to so many antique fairs and markets all over England that I've been spoiled out in the countryside. You will be too. Prices are lower; people are friendlier. I've really come to ignore most of the fancy London fairs. I'm not interested in things I can't afford to even dream about, nor am I particularly interested in the see-and-be-seen social scene that surrounds antique and collectibles fairs and markets in London.

I'll pay £1 to enter a fair, but that's about where I draw the line. There are three of us in my family, and when the entrance to a fair totals £10, we think twice. I much prefer fairs and markets that are free, that cost a pittance, or that are out of town. I'll take Portobello Road (free); you can have Grovesnor House, be it the merry month of June or not.

If you happen to be in town and are looking for a fair, you'll find it posted in *Time Out*. There are regular weekly events, annual events that are held more or less the same date every year, and occasional events that you have to either see an advertisement for or get lucky to catch.

🛍 PORTOBELLO ROAD
Portobello Road, Portobello Road, London W11
(Tube: Notting Hill Gate).

There are few things (or places) in London that I think are more fun than a Saturday at Portobello Road. It's crowded, possibly dangerous (they hand out brochures warning you of the pickpockets), and rumored to have lost its competitive edge—but hey, I always find bargains and have a ball. I go back week after week without tiring of it. To me, it's the only fair in London that competes with outside-of-London prices (if you're willing to haggle).

I don't want to oversell this, or your expectations will be so high that nothing will satisfy you. Suffice it to say that the streets are teeming with people, vendors, talking parrots, fire-eaters, dancing poodles in frilly collars, and merchandise. Some of it is old, some of it is new, and some of it is new pretending to be old. If you hated the circus, this might not be your thing.

Please note that it's a little tricky to get to Portobello Road market, especially if you are a first-timer. As you exit the tube at Notting Hill, there are directions written on a board. Read them or follow the throng. Open: Saturday only, 8am to 4pm.

🛍 JUBILEE MARKET
Covent Garden, London WC2
(Tube: Charing Cross or Covent Garden).

The Jubilee Market stands at Covent Garden, closer to the Strand end, and is a full-time market open to vendors selling anything from ice cream cones to tie-dyed T-shirts. This is not the group of stalls set up in between the rows of stores in Covent Garden (that's Apple Market), and it can be confusing to someone who does not know the layout.

If you are on a first visit, you may want to wander the length of the market before you stop to shop, so you can see what's what. The quality of the merchandise sold in the Jubilee Market is not impressive; I would not insist you attend this market on any day save Monday.

Every Monday, the Jubilee Market is taken over by stall holders selling antiques, old clothes, collectibles, cigarette cards, and fun junk. It opens about 8am (when the smell of fresh bread baking is enough to drive you insane), and goes on pretty much through the day, slowing down between three and four in the afternoon, unless there is a ton of tourist traffic.

Any other day of the week, Jubilee is good for teenagers or those with limited budgets. Clothes are cheap; most are imports. There are things to buy, but they aren't classy. Open 9am to 5pm daily.

APPLE MARKET
Covent Garden, London WC2 (Tube: Charing Cross, Leicester Square, or Covent Garden).

The Apple Market is the official name of the marketplace under the rooftops of Covent Garden in the courtyard space between the brick lanes of stores. This is a rotating affair that usually houses craftspeople; antiques are sold on Monday only in order to coordinate with the antique market across the way at the Jubilee Market. It's easiest to understand what this market is in contrast to the Jubilee Market.

Jubilee is junky; Apple is classy.

The courtyard space is filled with vendors who set up little stalls and pin their wares to backdrops; sometimes boxes of loot are under the tables. The market is vetted, so the participants must apply for permission to sell and be granted an official space and day. If they show up on other days, which many do, they set up in stalls other than their regular ones. Thus you can prowl the market on two different days of the week (ignore Monday for this example) and see the same people but in different places with a few new faces interspersed. Monday is more formal because this is the sole antiques day. Any day is a good day for the Apple Market.

Many vendors take plastic; some will bargain if you buy a lot. They don't get set up before 10am and many are still setting up at 11am. Sunday is fabulous; this is one of the few places in London where Sunday retail is allowed and the energy in the entire area can sweep you away. Open: 9am to 5pm daily.

CAMDEN PASSAGE
Upper Street, Islington, London N1
(Tube: Angel).

If you want good stuff, consider Portobello Road a tad too pushy, and aren't interested in the high- or low-end aspects of antique hunting in London, you should plan your trip around a Wednesday or Saturday when you can easily get to Camden Passage in Islington.

Camden Passage is not the same as Camden Town; they are not related, are not at the same tube stop, have nothing in common (save the word *Camden* in their name), and if you are an upscale shopper, you won't like Camden Town.

The tube stop for Camden Passage is Angel. This should be an easy association because this market is heaven.

The Passage itself is sort of an interior mall or long arcade with shops and stalls that are open during the week. As on Portobello Road, on market days more vendors come out to play, so the area is overflowing with fun. This is one of the few markets where you find higher-priced, fancy junk. I don't mean the merchandise is junky, I just mean that some of it may be without provenance. The most serious business is done here early in the morning on Wednesday, when the trade buys, you will be all but ignored. You had better know your stuff, know what it's worth, and buy enough to make you a mover and shaker, if you want to get a dealer's attention.

Saturday can be a tad crowded and touristy, but you will have a ball. Open: Tuesday to Saturday, 10am to 4pm.

New Caledonian Market
Bermondsey Square, London SE1
(Tube: Tower Hill).

Because of its location in Bermondsey Square, this market is often called the Bermondsey Market. It is mainly an outdoor market, although there is an indoor market next door, on the corner of Long Lane. Bermondsey is a dealers' market, held on Friday morning only; silver and silver plate are the specialties, but all manner of items, most of them small, are sold. The most important trick we can pass on to you is to go when it is daylight. The market gets going at 5am, and regulars always bring a flashlight ("torch" in Britspeak). My trusty adviser Nancy Davis tells me that unless you know the dealers and/or are an expert at buying what you are buying, you need the safety of daylight to make sure you are not taken. For the most part, the dealers at Bermondsey have bought their goods at estate sales and auctions out of town, and are bringing them to London for a quick profit. They may not know the value of what they have, which is why dealers and pickers frequent this market. Value, in the real antique market, is based on provenance and education. These goods are sold without proof of what they are. They may not be what they seem. If you are willing to get caught up in that, you will enjoy this outdoor market with its atmosphere of camaraderie. Most of the shoppers are regulars, although some tourists do show up. If you arrive by 7am (in summer it is light at 7am), you will not have missed the fun, although the dealers may have been haggling since 5am. In winter, remember to bring a flashlight—and your common sense—for the early visit. There are a few snack booths for an early morning snack or tea (or coffee). There's also a change booth.

This market is not located in a magnificent neighborhood. I suggest a cab, especially early in the morning. If it is daylight, you can take the tube or train to London Bridge and then cab it, or use the Tower Hill tube station and then get a cab. Open: Friday morning only.

Note that the area has become "in" because it's filled with warehouses; there are fair numbers of antique and used furniture places around here that are open during the week, not just during the fair. You may want to make a day of it. Be sure to check out Old Cinema Antique Warehouse at 157 Tower Bridge Road as well.

Souvenirs

No trip is complete without a few souvenirs. Here are a few sources:

• Almost all of the department stores have not only good souvenir departments but store logo merchandise that makes good souvenirs. There is an entire Harrods boutique of Harrods merchandise—including tea towels, tote bags, and coffee mugs—on the basement level. Liberty has such an identifiable print category with its William Morris lawns that it serves as a logo gift, but watch out! Some of its stuff is incredibly expensive. I once picked up a tiny Liberty of London print beanbag frog, smaller than life size, and it cost £17! The boxer shorts, which I thought would be a cute joke present, were £30! That's not my idea of funny. On the other hand, don't get frightened off. I consider the olive green plastic raincoats I bought at Harrods for £1.95 apiece the best souvenir from anywhere in the world, let alone Britain. I only hope you don't have to use yours!

• Street vendors are cheaper than department stores and often sell the same stuff. Whatever you do, don't buy your souvenirs at Heathrow as you head home (unless they are from the duty-free): I saw a plastic bobby hat, like you would buy for a child, for £3.50 at Heathrow. It cost £1.50 in a department store and 99p from a street vendor.

- There is a chain called **Cerex** that is your basic cheap souvenir stand; there are many of them scattered all over town, and they do have what you are looking for. They are slightly higher priced than street vendors.

- There is another chain, not as big as Cerex, called **Splash**, but they have a sillier sense of humor than a grown-up can take, and while they still sell the same junk as other souvenir stands, they sell it in a crasser way that your kids will adore.

- All museums, palaces, and stately homes have souvenir shops. Even Lord Rothschild now has one in his country manor home! Some have more than one. (Hampton Court has two, the Tower of London has three, etc.) Windsor is one big souvenir city. (See page 181.) Portobello Road, on Saturdays, has tons of souvenirs.

Teens & 'Tweens

Few cities in the world offer as much of a teen scene as does London, and much of what's happening is retail related. There's really no need to worry about your kid running off to have her hair dyed bright pink—that's really passé. All they really want is to buy bootleg CDs that can't be found in the United States and hang out. Preferably at the Dr. Martens Department Store.

If your teens are old enough to take in the city on their own, you may be happier to let them roam without you. The hard-core will want to shop Kensington High Street or Camden Town, which may make some moms shutter. Others may be very happy with mom and the delights of Oxford Street.

The best compromise for all is **Carnaby Street**. The street has revived itself with the rebirth of the adjoining Soho neighborhood. Among the better features of Carnaby Street nowadays is that it is short and conveniently located.

There are a few hip designer shops; a few regular touristy shops (sweaters, kilts, and china); and a lot of shops that sell black and/or purple leather. There's also a branch of several multiples where mom and teen will be able to compromise, like **Boots** (the Chemist), **Monsoon, Karen Millen,** and **The Body Shop.** All will enjoy **Muji,** a unique Japanese package store, and **Shelly's,** the most famous shoe shop in London, which sells the latest Doc Martens as well as copies of catwalk styles in the £30 range.

Just as exciting as Carnaby Street, and right in the same neighborhood, is **Oxford Street,** stretching away from Oxford Circus toward Tottenham Court Road. In a few blocks of wonder, you have every major teen-oriented, lower-priced, high-fashion-look chain store, and some giant record stores to boot. No one, no matter what age, should miss **X** (yes, that's the name of the store), which is the teenage part of the **Next** chain. Use the Oxford Circus tube for either venue, although you can also get to Carnaby Street via Piccadilly Circus.

Assuming you've already done Carnaby and the little bit of Oxford toward Next, now you're ready to cross Regent and head across town on Oxford Street. The Teen Queens hang at **Hennes,** right on the corner of Regent Street and Oxford Circus.

Chapter Eight

. . . .

SHOPPING LONDON'S SUBURBS: GREENWICH & HAMPSTEAD

SHORT EXCURSIONS

. . . .

Greenwich and Hampstead are usually at the top of most traveler's lists (including mine) because each is actually part of greater London. To most people, this is the definition of an ideal day trip—a 20-minute journey.

GREENWICH

. . . .

It doesn't take any kind of special train ticket or rail pass or inside knowledge to get to Greenwich. You simply have to know that it's a must-do on your schedule. Greenwich is technically part of London, but there's so much to do there that it makes a perfect day out.

Someday an extension of the Jubilee line will offer a tube stop right at the edge of Greenwich. For now, take a train from **Charing Cross** station or a boat from **Westminster Pier**.

Greenwich is not a beautiful city in the classic English tradition. But it is a port city and a royal city (and it's beautiful to me).

Greenwich has several major tourist attractions: the *Cutty Sark* (a ship); the Old Royal Observatory, where a red ball is dropped every day at 1pm GMT (Greenwich mean time); and a palace or two. Greenwich was one of Henry VIII's favorite cities. It is also one of my favorites because it is filled with flea markets and crafts—in sum, whole weekends' worth of shopping glee.

The Lay of the Land

Greenwich is built on a curve that connects two ports of entry on the River Thames, and can therefore be reached by boat. The best way to see the whole city (for a shopper, anyway) is to arrive by train and walk along the high street, curving to the left where the high street becomes Greenwich Church Street, which leads directly to the pier. Along the way, you'll pass most of the shopping in town.

The downtown section of Greenwich is based around the old market square between King William Walk and Greenwich Church Street. There is shopping inside the covered arcade of the market, as well as along the side streets surrounding the square. The Arts and Crafts Market is held in the covered market area every Saturday and Sunday. Hours are from 8am to 5pm.

There's more to see and do here than one day allows, so you may have to make choices. Or come back.

Shopping Greenwich

Greenwich is so dull in the traditional shopping department that it doesn't even have its own **Boots**. Locals go to Lewisham or Black Heath to shop for basics. There are no multiples here.

However, Greenwich has several antique markets and a fabulous crafts market. Greenwich is a great place for a family visit; it is the best place in London for Sunday shopping. Prices are also better.

Greenwich

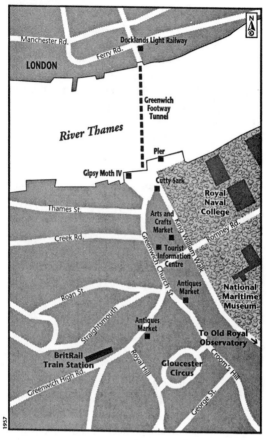

Day Tripper Tips

Your all-day Travelcard should cover your train fare to Greenwich; a BritRail pass also covers the fare. There are at least two trains per hour, sometimes more during peak times during the week. Of course, you really want to come to Greenwich on a Saturday or Sunday when there are only two trains an hour; they leave from Charing Cross station, London Bridge, and East Waterloo. If you are traveling during peak hours Monday through Friday, you might want to get on at Charing Cross to ensure that you get a seat. From London Bridge, the ride is about 10 minutes; from Charing Cross, about 20.

If you want to splurge on a nice day, consider taking the boat one way. It takes an hour, so you probably don't want to go both ways by boat. Boats leave from Westminster Pier in London and arrive in Greenwich at the Greenwich Pier, which is where the *Cutty Sark* is berthed. Boat fare is about £4 per person one way. Round trip is about £6. There is a guide on the boat who will point out historical sights. You'll want to tip him.

Coming to Greenwich for the weekend is not my personal secret, so be prepared for crowds, especially on beautiful summer days. Locals as well as tourists shop the antique fairs and crafts fair, loading up their station wagons. Antique collectors may want to come early to get the best pickings. If you are driving, be prepared to grit your teeth.

Markets

ANTIQUES MARKET
Greenwich High Road, Greenwich

The main Greenwich antique market is held in a parking lot on the high street about a block from the train station. You can't miss it. The market has about 50 dealers, sometimes more, and sells old junk of the best kind. The used-clothing dealers are more to the back. Open: Saturday and Sunday from 9am to 5pm in summer and 10am to 5pm in winter.

SOUTH LONDON ANTIQUES & BOOK CENTRE
18-19 Stockwell Street, Greenwich

This small building houses stalls selling old books and some ephemera. Adjacent to this building and outdoors (weather permitting) is the spillover from the antique market on Greenwich High Road, which is only about a block away. The vendors here sell both new and used goods. There is a van in the back where you can get a haircut; the food trolley up front sells "biegels." Could I make this up? Open: Wednesday and Thursday from 10am to 6pm, Saturday and Sunday from 9am to 5pm, and closed Monday, Tuesday, and Friday.

CANOPY ANTIQUES MARKET
Church Street entrance/Stockwell Street exit, Greenwich

This is the market where I had the fight with Ian. "You don't want to go there, it's junky," he said. Poor Ian. He'll never get the hang of my kind of shopping. I love junky markets.

There's no question that Canopy is the junkiest of the Greenwich antique markets and that they probably don't really even sell what anyone would call antiques. It's all jumble, but it's massive fun. The market sprawls in- and outdoors, through sheds, through garages (honest), and around a driveway. Vendors drive a hard bargain. There's a large number of 1950s and 1960s specialists and a lot of people selling vintage clothes. There are some new things (as well as a barbershop in a bus) in the main part of the market, but as you ramble, it gets funkier. Don't miss it. It wraps around the South London Antiques and Book Centre. Open: Saturday and Sunday, 9am to 5pm in the summer, 10am to 5pm in the winter.

ARTS AND CRAFTS MARKET
Market Square, Greenwich

I like this crafts market better than any other regular crafts market in Britain—including Apple Market. It's impossible to list all the vendors, since they are constantly changing. Vendors for the two days are somewhat different; I think Sunday is better. Open: Saturday and Sunday, 9am to 5pm.

BOSUN'S YARD
Church Street, Greenwich

If you are a touristy shopper and any old thing will amuse you, Bosun's Yard is fine. To me, it's very commercial and not nearly funky enough. The market is a poor imitation of the crafts market across the street in Market Square and sells some of the same things, although there are too many imports from India and South America for my taste. Weekend hours are from 10am to 5pm.

Finds

STITCHES & DAUGHTERS
Greenwich Market, Greenwich

A gift shop selling a nice mixture of goods from tote bags to decorative items and household gadgets, with some ready-to-wear and jewelry thrown in. It's located in the arcade part of the covered market. It's a really nice shop; kind of the fantasy place every woman hopes to open someday. Open: Saturday and Sunday.

BOOK BOAT
Cutty Sark Gardens, Greenwich

Next to the *Gipsy Moth,* which is not far from the *Cutty Sark,* is the Book Boat, which sells only children's books and is adorable. It's actually located on a small boat, and we think you'll love it whether you have kids or not. Aaron used to buy his Tintin books here. Open: everyday except Thursday, from 10am to 5pm.

HAMPSTEAD

· ·

Hampstead is inhabited by literary types, actors and actresses, and, of course, British yuppies. It's sort of quaint and perfect with a lovely feel to it. You'll find little shops, restaurants, delis, specialty food stores, and pubs all woven into one perfect urban landscape.

Sunday shopping has become the rage in Hampstead. All High Street shops open at midday. Even with Sunday shopping now legal all over the United Kingdom, Sunday in Hampstead is still a special celebration.

The Lay of the Land

If your back is to the door of the train station, the commercial part of Hampstead lies mostly to your left. You can ramble on the Heath, visit Keats's house, and see George Eliot's or Karl Marx's graves at Highgate Cemetery, across the Heath. If you came to browse and shop, you'll probably be happy simply roaming Hampstead High Street (which, ironically enough, is the lower of the two shopping streets in Hampstead).

Shopping Hampstead

Shopping Hampstead is very pleasant because few tourists come here; you can enjoy two fantasies—the architecture and the thought that you really belong here. It's not at all crowded, but you'll find that the shopping is very good. Almost all of the multiples have a branch store here, since this is a very wealthy community. There are no department stores, however. If you need to find more commercial shopping, you are only two tube stops away from Brent Cross, a huge American-style mall. There is a small amount of antique shopping in town.

Day Tripper Tips

It's hard to stretch this out into an all-day shopping trip. If you don't plan on sightseeing you might even call this simply a shopping adventure. You can shop all that Hampstead has to offer in a matter of a few hours. But it's still a very nice Saturday activity, especially if you piggyback it with a visit to some of the nearby antique markets. Sunday afternoon, most stores are open, and strolling and shopping are a social sport. Tune in for brunch and a walk on the heath as well.

Take the Edgware branch of the Northern Line. Your regular Travelcard should take care of the fare. You will need to take an elevator up from the depths of the Underground station. When you emerge at street level in front of the station, head to your left and take the downhill fork in the road. Please note that as you are standing in front of the train station in Hampstead, you will not see a thatched roof cottage or the cutest piece of Merrie Olde England you ever did see. You may think I am nuts for sending you here. It gets better in about one minute.

Hampstead Shopper's Stroll and Tour

1. Begin your tour at the intersection of Hampstead High Street and Heath Street, where you exit from the tube station.
2. Most of the good shops lie in a row on the left side as you descend Hampstead High Street. Just up from the station to the right is a shopping center with a Whistles and other multiples. I usually wander off to the left because that's the way to the Cute.
3. As you wander, some of the shops you'll pass are branches of stores you'll encounter in London. One of the reasons this is such a good shopping trip is that it offers an encapsulated version of the best of London branch stores in one handy spot. Look for Berties, Next, and so on. The Laura Ashley (37 Hampstead High Street) is rarely crowded and is a very complete store, with clothing and home furnishing lines—paints, papers, everything you need to create the English country look in your home. There are also branches of Hobbs, Monsoon, Pied à Terre (shoes), Nicole Farhi, and The Body Shop.
4. Now you can turn left on Downshire Hill for a stroll on the Heath or a visit with Keats. Or you

can head back up the hill until you see Perrin's Court, across the street. This little road cuts through to Heath Street, the other commercial lane in Hampstead.

5. Naturally, you've headed for Perrin's Court and more shopping. So you're off. On Heath Street there's **John Barry** (No. 39), which sells Escada and other upscale lines; and the **Hampstead Bazaar** (No. 30), where you'll find fabulous casual, chic, and comfy clothes—they also have stores in London in the best places.

6. Don't forget the **Hampstead Antiques Emporium** (No. 12), a collection of small dealers. The Emporium has about 20 dealers who have everything from silver to bric-a-brac to porcelain to important 18th-century furniture, and is open Tuesday to Saturday, 10am to 6pm.

Chapter Nine

. . . .

SHOPPING BATH, BRIGHTON, WINDSOR & ETON, STRATFORD-UPON-AVON & WARWICK

ABOUT LONDON DAY TRIPS

. . . .

There are day trips and there are day trips. What works best for you depends upon your personal style, curiosity, and stamina. London trains are built to haul you in and out of town on a regular basis—have train pass, will travel.

While **Stoke-on-Trent** can be reached within a day's travel from London, I have included it in the chapter that covers day trips from Manchester (see chapter 11) since Stoke is far easier to reach from that outlying city.

Stratford-upon-Avon (and the nearby village of **Warwick**) are here. Because of changes to train and bus routes, it is now a bit easier to get to Stratford on the train than previously.

Day trippers who adore flea markets should consider going to specific sale events chosen for the market, not the destination. See chapter 6 if this describes you.

BOOKING LONDON TRAINS

. . . .

If you are taking a lot of day trips in and out of London and want to be flexible, treat yourself to a copy of the *ABC Rail Guide*, which you can buy at the newsagent in any train station. This delightful paperback is worth its weight in gold; it has every train schedule in Britain and is updated frequently. This is not to be underestimated: Various other printed tourist materials may not be as up-to-date.

You only need reservations during high season on peak-service trains. Most peak-service trains run during rush hours. Many trains don't take reservations, but all InterCity routes do. If you have a first-class ticket or train pass, reservations are free.

ABOUT THOSE ADDRESSES

. . . .

The shopping in most tourist areas is located on one or two streets, usually the high street (most often named High Street) and one or two streets nearby. It's not unusual for stores not to have street numbers. Don't worry, you'll find everything you're looking for, and then some. If you have a favorite store in mind and want to go directly there, merely ask at the train station or Tourist Information Centre.

BATH

. . . .

"Bath is a charming place," wrote Jane Austen. "There are so many good shops here."

Who would have believed it? Jane Austen was born to shop! (Does Emma Thompson know?)

Bath is a wonderful combination of the necessary British multiples (chain stores), the right ratio of fun shops selling touristy items and souvenirs, original boutiques and little haunts for locals and sophisticates, and excellent antique centers. One of the antique centers in Bath is so good you may want to come to town with a van. If you are into vintage clothing, this city is a shrine.

The Lay of the Land

You get off the train at Bath Spa, which is the full name of the town, although no one calls it that. If you stay on the train after Bath Spa thinking that Bath itself is the next stop, you will very shortly find yourself in Wales.

The town of Bath sprawls up a hill, so wear comfortable walking shoes. Just about everything is within walking distance, although you may want to taxi to the top—especially if you are going to all the antique markets on a Wednesday—and work your way down. It's nice to just wander around Bath, and the lower city lends itself to particularly enjoyable walking tours.

There is also a minibus, called the Badger, which picks up people at the train station and makes the rounds.

Almost all of the stores are located back-to-back on three or four main streets, with the antique parts of town just a little higher up the hill. Don't be alarmed if stores do not have street numbers as part of their addresses; they are so densely packed that you will happen upon them automatically. Don't forget to test some of the side streets. Just wander.

Do note that the immediate scene upon arrival is neither cute nor quaint: Don't panic. It gets better.

Shopping Bath

There isn't anything to buy in Bath that you can't get anywhere else, although some of the souvenirs from the Roman baths are quite amusing, and the "Bath Sponge" is a pretty funny gift. (They also sell "Bath towels.")

The true charm of shopping in Bath is that it is so visually appealing: Bath is one of the most charming

Bath

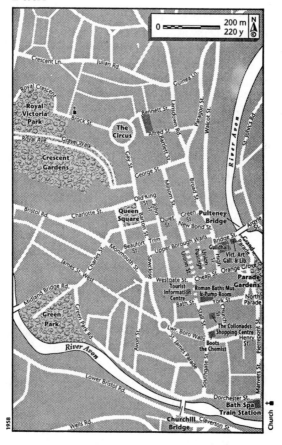

cities in England, and it is perfect for browsing. While the tourist traffic can get heavy, you'll still enjoy window- and more serious shopping.

Bath is also a great town for antiques, although it is more expensive than many true dealer sources. I've heard that many Americans come to town thinking they will undercut dealers. Few real dealers shop in Bath. Bath is too expensive for them.

The best day to go to Bath is Wednesday, since this is the biggest antique day. The antique stores and the main antique market are open on regular retail days, but there is an additional flea market held on Wednesday that you'll probably want to take in, especially if you are a collector.

There is also a flea market on Saturdays. It's fun but not as special as Wednesday's market. If you have the time, you can always stick around for both and then check out Bristol, which also has a fair number of antique shops.

Aside from antiques, Bath is a good place to buy used books—such as previously read best-sellers. A paperback novel can cost £6 in Britain if new. Visit Guildhall, with several stalls where you can stock up on used paperback novels and contemporary reading for 50p each.

Bath Design

Partly due to the antique business in town, Bath is one of the country's leading centers for interior design. There's also a large local restoration business here, which aids the trade.

Seemingly zillions of designers have set up shop and run service businesses that provide for "the look" and also sell antiques and repro items. Some of the better-known designers and studios are **No. 12 Queen Street** (12 Queen Street); **Jadis** (The Old Bank, 17 Walcot Buildings, London Road), known for pine furniture with or without fancy and faux finishes; **Martin Dodge** (16A Broad Street), a source for elegance in true English style; and **Impacto** (13 London Street), where moderne is more the rage. **Helena Hood and Co.** (3 Margaret's Buildings, Brock Street) brings Colefax and Fowler to Bath; while **Penny Philip** (5 London Street) competes for the same clients.

With English chintzes costing so much more in the United States, design-conscious Americans who have no time for showrooms in London may find that the small-town nature of Bath makes it an easier place to make choices.

The basic feeling in the design trade in Bath is that top-of-the-line, serious antiques go for top price anywhere in England and that professionals always know the good stuff, so there's no savings in Bath or anywhere else on these items. Where you save is by using design talent in Bath (so they claim) who can steer you toward the look and even to reproductions so that you can get the feel you want at a savings over London and U.S. prices.

Day Tripper Tips

Trains to Bath leave London from, and return to, Paddington Station.

The fare to Bath varies tremendously depending on the type of ticket you buy. You can pay anywhere from £25 to £50 ($40 to $80) for roughly the same trip, so beware. The least expensive way of making a day trip is to buy a "Cheap Day Return" after 9:30am. If you insist on leaving London before 9:30am, the price of a one-way, second-class ticket is about £25! If you are using a BritRail pass, there are no restrictions on use, and you can leave for Bath bright and early in the morning. This is one of the best reasons to be using a BritRail pass.

The trip lasts 1 hour and 20 minutes; there should be buffet service on the train, especially in the morning when a large number of commuters ride these rails.

You get off at **Bath Spa.**

There is a tiny tourist information desk in the station; stop here to pick up an extremely useful free map of the city. Bath isn't complicated, but it is not laid out on a grid system, so it's a good idea to have the map. You can also use the map on page 159.

Pick up the return train schedule on your arrival at the station so you can make plans accordingly. There are trains rather frequently, but your ticket (if it's not a BritRail pass) may have restrictions on it.

If you have a car, park it and walk—there's a city car park right near the Hilton in the heart of town. Also make use of a car by planning to take in some

of the surrounding area, which is especially good
for antique shopping, and the Mulberry Factory
Shop, see page 173. Bradford-on-Avon has about
six antique shops. For a list of these and others
nearby, stop by the tourist office at The Colonnades
or ask for a free brochure in any of the antique shops
in Bath. Or write: Bath and Bradford-on-Avon
Antiques Dealers Association, P.O. Box 694, Bath
BA1 2JX, Avon, England. There is a small antique
fair–cum–flea market in Bradford-on-Avon every
Tuesday from 10am to 4pm at St. Margaret's
Hall. Bradford-on-Avon also has **Bertie Golightly,**
a shop that sells designer samples and gently worn
designer clothing, 12–13 Market Street. The designer
I am thinking of is Chanel, not St. Michael. It's about
15 minutes from Bath. Once you're out and about,
don't miss Castle Combe, only 12 miles from Bath,
which is one of the little villages you came to England to see.

Be flexible about lunch plans and decide how
important lunch is to you as you plan your day. I
wanted to take Pat for a perfect lunch at a cute place,
or even the Pump Room in the Roman Baths, but
we were so carried away with our shopping and our
own schedule that we decided to forget about the
fancy lunch and we grabbed toasted cheese sandwiches from a little no-name cafeteria that we just
happened upon. Some people need the experience
of fine dining to help define a destination; others
don't. Plan accordingly.

Bath-in-a-Day Shopper's Tour

Exit from the train station, turn left, and walk one
block. You'll pass the bus station and the Badger
stop and get to a **Boots the Chemist.** (This is an
excellent Boots, by the way.) At Boots, turn right
and head up the Mall. You'll be making an enormous U-turn so you can take in all the main shopping areas (consult a map if this is unclear):

1. Turn right at the Mall and walk one block, then zig left to Southgate, which soon becomes Stall Street.
2. Stall Street becomes Union Street; just keep shopping as you walk uphill. Union Street then becomes Milsom Street. Concentrate on one side of the street only. You'll have a chance at the other street on the way back down.
3. Turn right on George Street. Shop up one side of the Paragon then down the other.
4. Cut over from Paragon and continue to Walcot, making sure to hit **Walcot Reclamation**. Then walk down toward town on Walcot until it becomes High Street.
5. Go uptown on High Street until you get to New Bond Street. The streets are lined with the most famous British multiples. Shop for one block until you get to Milsom, then turn around and cut downhill on Union Street. More multiples. Shop till you drop.
6. Partway down, Union Street becomes Stall Street, then Stall Street becomes Southgate. More multiples, right until you get to **Boots**, which is right before you get to the train station.
7. Follow Southgate until it dead-ends. Turn left, walk one block to the train station. Return to London!

Finds

THE COLONNADES
Bath Street, Bath

This is a shopping center in the quasi-American style—rather small and swank and tony. There are several designer boutiques here, mostly international big names (**Alexon**) or famous London names (**Pied à Terre**). It's located slightly off the main walking route, across from the side entrance to the Pump Room, just off Stall Street. The tourist office moved in recently.

MEMENTOS OF BATH
Stall Street, Bath

Okay, so it's a tourist trap, but all tourist traps should be this attractive. It's attached to the Roman baths and the Pump Room; buy your souvenirs for the kids, including Roman coins, here.

THE MAGGIE WHITE SHOP
9 Saracen Street, Bath

One of England's best shops for bold and bright hand-knit sweaters, coats, hats, gloves, and accessories. This small shop is off on a side street but is near the Hilton and not difficult to find. Prices may seem high until you realize the quality of what you are buying—then a few hundred dollars for a piece of art no longer seems outrageous.

WALCOT RECLAMATION
108 Walcot Street, Bath

Although the general atmosphere on Walcot Street—which has the potential to offer fantastic retail—is declining, and there aren't as many fun shops here as there used to be, it's all worthwhile if you are into salvage. In fact, Walcot Reclamation is almost the Disneyland of salvage lots.

The first time I visited, I kept gasping, "Oh, my!" The second time, I came with a camera. It's laid out rather like a small village and you wander around looking at heaps of everything.

Portable items include bathroom taps, doorknobs, letter-box trim, brass hardware, and so on.

They also have tiles, floor planks, doors, and the like, although the airline probably will not check a door through with your luggage. There is a catalogue.

The bathroom is a little hard to find but it's clean and they are friendly about letting you use the facilities.

No trip to Bath is complete without a visit here.

THE GENERAL TRADING COMPANY
10 Argyll Street, Bath

The first branch store out of town, if you missed
it in London (see page 130). Great for gifts,
browsing, fun, and ideas. This shop is just a little to
the side of most of the main action, but not off the
beaten path at all—Pultney Bridge becomes Argyll
Street.

Bath Resources from A–Z

AMERICAN CHAIN STORES

Thankfully, there aren't too many of them in town,
but there is The Gap (18 Old Bond Street) and
Gap Kids (17 Milson Street), and then there's
High and Mighty, for tall and large men (1 Saracen
Street).

ANTIQUE MARKETS

The main reason serious shoppers go to Bath is for
its antiques. Dealers abound, and regulars with sharp
eyes feel that the prices are considerably (20% to
25%) lower than in London. Naturally, London
dealers are on top of the situation, and have friends
who call them, and good stuff moves fast, but you
can still find some good buys and have a lot of fun
in the meantime. If you have an awful lot of money
to spend and are dead serious about all this, you
should perhaps plan to stay for a few days. I could
fill a shipping container in a matter of hours, if I
were shopping for shipping.

Day trippers, please note: Wednesday is considered antiques day, and there is a lot of special-day
traffic. Serious shoppers, please note: Most of the
Wednesday markets are in collectibles and small
knickknacks; if you are buying top-of-the-line fine
furnishings, we don't think the day of the week will
matter much. There is little in the hoity-toity arena
that is available at the Wednesday fair.

If you are in Bath just for antiques, you may want to begin your day with a taxi ride to the Guinea Lane Market, which is open only on Wednesday and is the farthest point uptown that you will be visiting. You'll be walking downhill toward the train station, so you'll get to see plenty of town. It advertises itself as the Portobello Road of the West, but we think it makes Portobello Road look swank. There are several floors of dealers. Some 85 stall sellers set up shop starting at 7am. It's a very in crowd—most of the shoppers and the stall holders are dealers, and they gossip about each other and about American dealers who come over to see them. You will be competing with dealers (many of them American), so be sharp.

After Guinea Lane, you'll work your way downhill (on foot). Be sure to take in:

PARAGON ANTIQUES MARKET
3 Bladud Buildings, Bath

Open on Wednesday only, this market has improved dramatically and is now good, junky fun. Don't miss the stairs to the right, which lead to more dealers. It's tag sale time, but you can't ignore this one.

BARTLETT STREET

If you have time to visit only one street in Bath, this is the one. There are two great antique markets on this street (Great Western Antiques Centre and Bartlett Street Antiques Centre) as well as a few other dealers. There's more in the next block that leads to Alfred Street—and then you are next to the Costume Museum. Perfect planning. The Great Western is one of the best antique markets I've ever seen—it's indoors in a nice building, and each stall is housed in bright green wooden booths with the name of the shop and the stall number in large black letters.

On Wednesday there is a market downstairs that is more like a tag sale, but it is a pretty good addition.

The Wednesday market opens at 7:30am. The everyday market opens at 9:30am six days a week.

The Guildhall Market does have a few dealers in it, but this is mostly a fruits and vegetables market. This resource is best for used paperback books. You can also buy picnic fixings at food stalls. If this is your first stop (which it may be if you are working your way up the hill), it does get better.

BARTLETT STREET ANTIQUES CENTRE
7-10 Bartlett Street, Bath

This clean, well-lighted market offers about 50 dealers. Stalls do not have names or numbers but are called "The Linen and Lace Stall," or something like that. Every type of antique is sold here. Open: Monday, Tuesday, Thursday to Saturday, 9:30am to 5pm; Wednesday, 8am to 5pm. Excellent.

BATH WEDNESDAY ANTIQUES MARKET
Guinea Lane, Bath

For true believers and dealers. Open: Wednesday only, 6:30am to 2:30pm.

BATH SATURDAY ANTIQUES MARKET
Walcot Street, Bath

What else would you do on a Saturday? This isn't a huge market but it is right near the Hilton and completely within the central, downtown area and core of Bath, so there's no reason to miss it or believe anyone who tells you that it's Wednesdays you're thinking of, dearie. (Two different dealers once told me it didn't exist and one cabdriver had no idea what I was talking about.)

The market itself is in a barnlike garage, with some spill outdoors. There is no admission charge. It's a jumble market, which is the kind of market I like, and prices seemed rather good on my last visit. My friend Pat and I both fell in love with a dealer who was selling oleographs—reproductions of serious works of art applied to board or canvas—from a heap on the floor. His prices were in the £5 to £7 per item range, depending on size. As we bought more, we bargained more, and the vendor was the sort who was willing to give and take on the exchange.

Pat was so taken with the oleographs that she did more research on them while in London and found them for sale at Bermondsey Market (in London, Fridays only) for about £20 per unit. I found them advertised in one of my favorite British home and garden magazines for £39 each! Open: Saturday only, 7am to 5pm.

GREAT WESTERN ANTIQUES CENTRE
Bartlett Street, Bath

Sixty stall holders during the week, more than 100 on Wednesday. It's clean, well organized, easy to shop, has a restaurant and cafe, and is very much worth the cost of the trip. Clean bathrooms downstairs offer the perfect pit stop. Open: Monday, Tuesday, Thursday to Saturday, 9:30am to 5pm; Wednesday, 7:30am to 4:30pm, in basement.

PARAGON ANTIQUES MARKET
3 Bladud Buildings, Bath

One block down the hill from Guinea Lane, this rather ordinary market handles the overflow from that market. Convenient to Landsdown Hill. Open: Wednesday only, 7am to 4pm.

Information on neighborhood markets and special sales is posted on a bulletin board at the Guinea Lane Market, at the entrance to the main doorway. The neighboring towns in Avon have markets, fairs, and antique dealers.

ANTIQUE SHOPS

JOHN KEIL ANTIQUES
Quiet Street, Bath

On a quiet street called Quiet Street, where there are a few other shops to browse as well, this one is a heavy hitter. Veddy formal. While you're here, also poke into **Quiet Street Antiques.**

ANDREW DANDO
4 Wood Street, Queen Square, Bath

Some furniture, but with this much Staffordshire on hand, we know you china freaks will be at the door, panting.

G. A. BAINES
15 John Street, Bath

Very fancy 18th- and early 19th-century furniture; mostly dark woods. For the extraordinarily serious who know their stuff and don't look at price tags but patina. By appointment only. Call local phone: 01225/332-566.

ANN KING
38 Belvedere, Landsdowne Road, Bath

Period clothing and textiles as befits a dealer in a town with a famous costume museum. Hours are a tad erratic; shop opens at noon on Wednesdays so the owner can go to the markets herself. Otherwise, it's 10am to 4pm. Don't let the address throw you, this is simply around the corner from the Guinea Lane market.

GRAYLOW
Bartlett Street, Bath

Homey-feeling shop for not-so-formal and borderline country looks; high quality but not too hoity-toity.

SUSANNAH
142 Walcot Street, Bath

Textiles and more.

ANTIQUE BEDS
3 Litfield Place, Bath

It's near the suspension bridge; an appointment is advised (local phone: 01272/735-134) so you can see the enormous selection of fancy beds. Prices range from about £1,000 to £5,000, but all your dreams will come true.

BOOKSTORES

There is a branch of **Waterstones** (4 Milsom Street) and a **W. H. Smith** (6-7 Union Street), the newsagent that runs all the bookshops in train stations and airports in Britain.

CHINA & KITCHENWARE

THE KITCHEN SHOP
495 Quiet Street, Bath

This shop is filled with all types of kitchen supplies, many of a quality suitable for professionals. Aside from the tons of cookbooks and heavy-duty pots and pans, there are all sorts of decorating items, molds, and fun items you'll want to have; there is also a section for inexpensive china and restaurant supplies.

ROSSITER
38-41 Broad Street, Bath

A department store or a rambling house—actually, it's both—filled with household goods and lots of china and dishes and gift items. You'll find much merchandise that you won't see elsewhere. In its Walcot Street shop (No. 13-15), Rossiter sells British and Continental reproduction furniture.

DEPARTMENT STORES

BOOTS THE CHEMIST
Southgate Street, Bath

I chose to list this branch of Boots, the British drugstore chain, here even though it isn't officially a department store because this Boots is a particularly good one.

JOLLY'S
13 Milsom Street, Bath

This is the local department store of choice. It has everything you might need if you lived here, including a wide range of cosmetics and a bridal registry. Since the high street multiples bring their London merchandise to the streets of Bath, this store finds its niche with an odd assortment of daily needs. It has a small cafeteria downstairs and clean bathrooms. Not for the Giorgio Armani customer but a fine pit stop nonetheless.

LIBERTY
12 New Bond Street, Bath

If you've been to the London flagship, this will feel small. It's really more of a specialty shop, but not to worry, it has the fabulous Liberty fabrics as well as clothing for men and women and a large selection of home decor.

LITTLEWOODS
19 Stall Street, Bath

A real-people department store for imported low-end goods and personal needs; it's across from Marks & Spencer.

MARKS & SPENCER
16-18 Stall Street, Bath

Here's my day tripper's trick. Marks & Spencer (M&S) is not too far from the train station. On my way back to London, I pop into the M&S grocery store and buy dinner to eat on the train back.

HOUSEWARES & FOODSTUFFS

While this really is a city for seeing the sights, getting into antiques or vintage clothing, or just enjoying the browsing, there are a fair amount of housewares to be found within easy reach. **Jolly's**, the department store, has an excellent china department; there's a big spiffy **Habitat** on Broad Street across from the mall, **The Podium**; and in the mall, **Second Best** sells off-price linens from international big names, although £40 for a Sheraton duvet cover didn't strike me as dirt cheap.

There's a **Marks & Spencer**, with its large grocery store, and a newer **Waitrose** supermarket in The Podium—both sell all the goodies you could dream of for a wonderful picnic or dinner for the train ride home.

WATER

Bath Spa got its name because it has been a spa town for centuries—there's the Roman Baths, a major tourist attraction, and the famous Bath Spa Water—which you can taste for free and buy at the Pump Room. I like to eat lunch in the Pump Room because it's centrally located and it's fun, but as for the taste of Bath's famous water, well, in a word: Yuck.

BEYOND BATH

. . . .

Antique shoppers will enjoy both **Bradford-upon-Avon** and **Bristol**; real bargain hunters might want to scurry off to the Mulberry factory shop (see listing below). You can also get to **Salisbury** and head back into London from the back route, so to speak. Check a map. For the culturally inclined, there are a number of excellent museums nearby, as well as **Longleat**.

While distinctly uninspired in design, the Hilton Hotel in Bath has a convenient in-town location for those who want to stick around for a bit longer.

🛍 MULBERRY CO. FACTORY SHOP
Kilver Court, Shepton Mallet

Mulberry is a high-priced British design firm that offers leather goods, accessories, and men's and women's clothing in a country look. Their goods are status items in the United Kingdom. If you prefer to buy last year's stock or seconds, hightail it to their factory shop.

A 7,500-square foot space, the factory shop comes complete with a tea room. There is also some full-priced merchandise here, so ask questions or watch what you fall in love with.

Please note this is a new factory shop and it's only a matter of miles from the old factory shop in Chilcompton. From Bath, take A36 south to A37. From Bristol, just head south on A37. Once in Shepton Mallet, you are looking for Kilver Court. If you get to the footbridge, you've gone too far. The journey time between the old shop and the new one is about 10 minutes; the drive time from Bath center or Bristol is about 45 minutes.

If you need more specific directions or a map, call Mulberry directly at local phone: 01749/ 340-500. This is King Arthur country and nearby is the Glastonbury Tower where Arthur rescued Guinevere. He probably heard she was about to spend a king's ransom at the Mulberry factory shop and got her out of there as fast as possible.

BRIGHTON
. . . .

If you are thinking of Brighton as a fantasy of white wicker, Victorian splendor, and old England by the sea, you can forget it right now. If you are thinking of Brighton as tacky beyond belief and funnier than Atlantic City, you can forget that too. Well, keep it in the back of your mind.

Brighton has a lot of personality, but you have to leave your expectations at home in order to really appreciate it. Brighton is best as a day trip for those who want to see a little something outside London, don't want to go too far, and want to hit an antique fair or two and maybe some antique shops. I will not send you to Brighton as a high-priority visit or as a visit to the Seriously Cute.

The city is quite large; you'll be surprised by the urban sprawl you spy as the train gets closer to the sea. The main tourist area is downtown and offers something for everyone—there's an antique street, a street of funky fun boutiques, and an area of restored cottages and houses and meandering little medieval lanes. And there's a boardwalk and a pier. And cotton candy.

But don't worry about wearing your white flannels and straw boater; no one here cares. Come to see Brighton as it really is; have a day's outing and do some shopping. But don't come for what might have been here 100 years ago. Because it's not here anymore.

The Lay of the Land

Downtown Brighton stretches from the sea up a small rise where the train station is located. To get into town, you simply walk downhill.

Downtown has traditional high street shopping, but most of the multiples aren't there! In one of the few cities where British retail dares to be different, the multiples are beside the high street in the quaintest part of town—the Lanes.

The high street stuff of the downtown area is on Western Road, where there's a 1960s-style shopping complex with everything from **Dunnes** (like Marks & Spencer) to **Habitat, BHS, Mothercare, Miss Selfridge, W. H. Smith,** and then some. Phones and toilets are also here. **Marks & Spencer (M&S)** is directly on Western Road across the street from the shopping complex. If your back is to M&S and the shopping center is in front of you, everything you want to see (except the Upper North Street antique area) is to your left.

Western Road becomes North Street at the clock tower.

In just a block or two you'll hit The Lanes. If the medieval tangle of shops (pedestrians only) is just too sweet for you, walk directly north back toward the train station to the North Lanes, where all the up-and-coming stores are located. Please note that The Lanes look great in pictures. Truth is, The Lanes aren't that impressive in person, either as a visual treat or as a shopping treat. They aren't uncute but they lack subtext. No serious charm for the sophisticated traveler; trust me.

Shopping Brighton

Shopping in Brighton is downright strange. The city has no apparent glow to it, no energy, no temptations to lead you on. Then you discover the North Lanes, and the place is alive with the sound of music and shopping. You have to go hunting for the good stuff, but it exists, if you're willing to prowl. In addition to the great buys in used merchandise, there are a few hot boutiques owned by designers who aren't ready for London rents.

There are maybe a dozen antique shops spread out along Ship Street, Union Street, and Middle Street, many of which are quite fancy. On the other hand, there are many tourist traps here, and they aren't particularly fun or interesting.

As for regular retail, most of the British multiples have branch stores in downtown Brighton (except Laura Ashley Home, which is located in the Marina, a few miles away), and there are a few shops. A number of them sell South American imports; one sells Spanish tiles and pottery. So much for the traditional English look of the seaside.

Dukes Lane, a small pedestrian street at the edge of The Lanes, is known to locals as Designer Row. This is where the more modern fashions thrive. This might interest a store buyer, or a tween to 20-something with a good eye. For the average

American tourist or the person who has only a short amount of time to hit the cute and keep on running, Brighton is lacking in obvious delights. You can work Brighton, but it takes time and energy and, uh, work.

Antique Shopping in Brighton

Most of my readers who are going to Brighton are going for the antiques, which, in all honesty, are so-so. If you latch onto a big fair or so, you'll have fun—but if this is your one big outing for bargain antiques, forget it. The real antique bargains are up north; the real charm is in Bath on a Wednesday! But Brighton is just an hour south of London on the train and is easy to do if you're up for something simple. If you have a car and really want to get into the prowl after you've "done" Brighton, take in the nearby town of Hove (where Ian was born) and then drive along the sea across the bottom of East Sussex toward Kent and stop in villages like Seaford, Eastbourne, Bexhill, and St. Leonards on the Sea. Finish up with your own personal battle at Hastings. There's got to be some antique there worth fighting for.

Antique shoppers just going to Brighton should check for fairs and flea markets through the tourist office or one of the all-England fair guides. There is a flea market held every Sunday next to the train station that easily justifies the one-hour trip to Brighton. Besides this weekly venue, check with the tourist office for dates of special-event markets, which are usually held once a month—you might get lucky.

There are a few antique shops in The Lanes; there are many more in the North Lanes that offer more funky and fun stuff. A third area to explore is Upper North Street. These three areas alone should keep you pretty busy if you come during the week when all the antique shops are open. It is pleasant, but not heartthrobbing.

Don't be surprised if many buildings, especially in the Lanes, are not marked with a street address. Often an address is just "The Lanes."

Day Tripper Tips

Trains for Brighton leave London from Victoria, London Bridge, or Blackfriars stations; Victoria station offers the most choices in departure times. There are usually two trains an hour. There's always a train every hour in either direction.

The trip takes a little more than an hour. Some trains are express and take exactly an hour; local runs are a tad slower and have more stops, which add about 15 to 30 minutes to the ride.

A cheap day return, second class, should cost under £10; you can buy tickets from a machine at Victoria, saving you from having to wait in line at the ticket window.

There is a shuttle bus into town if you don't want to walk. It drops you off at the Old Steine, at the end of The Lanes and a block from the pier, which is where the tourist office is located. There is an information booth at the train station, but since they also give out train information, there is usually a long line here.

Saturday is not a great day to visit because many of the antique shops are closed. Sunday is fun because of the big flea market, but many of the regular stores are not open. The Pavilion Shop is an exception. There is a flea market in the North Lanes on Saturday, but it is not much more than a big tag sale. During the week the city has fewer visitors from out of town, and may be better for serious shoppers.

Brighton-in-a-Day Shopper's Tour

1. Taxi from Brighton station to Upper North Street because it's time to go antique shopping in an out-of-the-way nook of Brighton. This is walkable (and downhill, mostly), but I know you're saving your strength and it's a cheap fare—less than £3. I assume you've arrived after 10:30am, when the stores are open.

2. The antique shops—and there are about a dozen of them—run chockablock from No. 33 to No. 53. Most have a casual atmosphere, so you will enjoy poking in and chatting up the owners. When you finish exploring, walk on Upper North until it hits Dyke Road, which will angle right into the Clock Tower. Pass the tower while walking on North Street, which is the main downtown street. If you go right at the clock, you'll be on Western Road.

3. Where North Street meets The Lanes you'll see the Royal Pavilion to your left, on East Street. Visit the Pavilion quickly (you must be starving by now), shop at the Pavilion Shop, then cross the street and enter The Lanes, where you can find any number of pubs for lunch. There are many around Brighton Square. If you can wait a bit for lunch, you can enter The Lanes through **Hanningtons'** blue department stores.

4. After lunch, explore The Lanes at your leisure, coming out on Union Street so you pass the **Palmers'** shop for antiques, and hit Duke's Lane so you can see the young designer shops. Then get back on North Street again, or walk back through The Lanes until you get to the junction of North Street and Bond Street, where you begin the walk uphill.

5. Shop Bond Street, then Gardner Street (which is a continuation of Bond Street), then take a quick right and a fast left onto Kensington Gardens, where the best of the fun and funky shops are.

6. Top it off at Trafalgar Street, which leads to the train station to your left, or cut back down the street that runs parallel to Kensington Gardens (Gardner Street), and explore the shops on Gloucester Road as well. Follow Gloucester to Queen's Road, turn right, and you are a few feet from the train station. You'll be out of breath from the hike up the hill and the weight of all your goodies. But you will have seen the best

of Brighton. Don't miss **Kollect-O-Mania,** 25 Trafalgar Street, a small antique mall (10 dealers) with quasi-junk, but it's fun.

Finds

THE PAVILION SHOP
The Royal Pavilion, East Street, Brighton

One of the best stores in Brighton, the Pavilion Shop is the gift shop next door to The Royal Pavilion. The Royal Pavilion was commissioned by George IV, and is a crazy hodgepodge of Oriental-style fantasy architecture. The shop is not such a hodge-podge, limiting itself to stippled walls and faux marble finishes in wood grain. It offers many gift and home-furnishings items inspired by the design schools associated with the Pavilion, which range from Regency to Victorian. Great stencil kits and otherwise good souvenirs such as books, jams, needlepoint kits, little paperbound notebooks and pencils, etc. Open: Seven days a week, 10am to 5pm.

FARNSWORTH
130 Queen's Road, Brighton

A general store offering gifts and sweaters and other fun ideas—from dried flowers to cute soaps to toys to sweatshirts—displayed in a nice country store.

HANNINGTONS
North Street, The Lanes, Brighton

A row of blue town houses joined together to make a sort of department store with many different entrances. It sells a little of everything. Check out its excellent china department, which stretches across several different buildings. It will ship. Its toy department is in still another store. The whole family can have fun in this maze of shops. There is even a cafe where you can grab a quick bite.

LOUIS POTTS
24 Bond Street, Brighton

The sign says "China Dealer," and this simple shop has stacks of china all over, some of it from big names, some not. Very fair prices. Nothing fancy, but if you're adding on to your blue and white transfer set, you may score.

APPENDAGE
36 Kensington Gardens, Brighton

One of the more exciting stores in town in terms of interesting design of both shop and merchandise. Note the crushed mirror glass set into the pavement at the front door. The graphics on T-shirts, scarves, and hand-printed fabrics are sensational.

NIPPER
25 Kensington Gardens, Brighton

This adorable kids' shop carries a line that I think could sell anywhere in the world. Open one of these shops in your local mall and get rich as you watch these brightly colored pull-on clothes walk out the door.

LEOPARD TEXTILES
35 Kensington Gardens, Brighton

This shop carries one of the best selections I've ever seen of old linens and white work, as well as some costumes. Prices are competitive, but there are no steals.

BRIGHTON ARCHITECTURAL SALVAGE
33-34 Gloucester Road, Brighton

I've become addicted to British salvage yards—and Scottish ones, too—and this is one of my most favorite. If you're looking for a door or any other large piece for a home renovation job, this is the place.

Open: Weekdays from 9:30am to 5pm and Saturdays from 10am to 4pm.

WINDSOR & ETON

· ·

When you hear talk of the world's great twin cities, you rarely hear discussion of Windsor and Eton. Windsor gets tons of press, yet it's Eton that's really charming, and it's only a bridge away from Windsor. Furthermore, Eton is a school town (Eton was founded in 1440, 200 years before Harvard) where you can frequently see young men in striped blazers or black gowns, making you think you've walked onto a movie set. Yes, Prince Wills is an Eton man these days.

Windsor is great fun, but it is so commercial that it could be accurately described as crass. I love it, but it is a tourist trap that rivals some sort of a theme park. What else would people do on a Sunday if they couldn't go to Windsor and maybe see Prince Charles play polo?

The Lay of the Land

Once upon a time there was the River Thames. And on its banks grew many a village. A few of them even grew up to have castles. So it is that Windsor, on one bank, hosts Windsor Castle, summer home of the queen. On the other bank, a less royal village developed and became host to a castle of the mind: Eton.

Both cities are one-street towns, although the principal action in Windsor revolves around the castle, which is right in the middle of town. Despite the recent fire at Windsor and the restoration work now in progress, little has changed in town and the castle is still accessible.

Eton is actually just an extension of Windsor's high street. Simply cross the little bridge at the far end of town and you'll be in heaven. Walk the high street right through town; it's all antique shops on both sides of the street. Every now and then you'll pass a group of students or a marvelous piece of architecture and sigh, "Oh, to be in England."

Day Tripper Tips

Windsor and Eton are served by two different train stations, so pay attention. The stations are relatively close to each other (within easy walking distance), so you will choose the station of arrival according to your departure from London.

If you'd rather be closer to Eton than to Windsor, go to Riverside station, which is right at the bridge leading to Eton. Windsor's central station is up the hill a little bit, and is directly across the street from Windsor Castle. You may arrive at one station and depart from the other.

Now then, if you want to leave London and get to Windsor and Eton without changing trains, you should leave from Waterloo station in London and proceed directly to Riverside station (where you will be closer to Eton). If you go from Paddington station in London, you must change trains in Slough, where they have a very lovely Victorian station and where you will switch to another track for a commuter train to Windsor central. The second train ride takes about 10 minutes.

Fares are identical no matter which method you choose; a cheap day return is about £5.

There are bus connections to Windsor Safari Park (an amusement park) from central station, if this should interest you as a family activity. If you want to go out to the polo grounds, you'll need a car or a taxi.

The Windsor Airport Trick

If you are laying over at London Heathrow you should know that Windsor is actually closer than downtown London and makes a fabulous day

Windsor

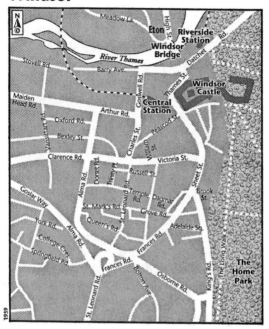

trip, half-day trip, or overnight. You can book a hotel room by the night or half day. The hotel will also arrange transportation to and from the airport.

Sleeping in Windsor

THE CASTLE HOTEL
High Street, Windsor

The Castle Hotel is right on High Street and one block from Windsor Castle. It's in the heart of the main street shopping and is one of those old-fashioned grande dame hotels that make you want to curtsy for the queen. You can't do much better in terms of location. Try to book the old part of the hotel, which has been renovated in the country charm style we all so much appreciate; there is a nice restaurant for full English breakfast if you have just arrived from the airport or are day tripping.

This is the perfect place to begin a country tour of Great Britain. Or a visit to Windsor and Eton. A Forte Grand hotel. If you arrange it ahead of time, they will pick you up at the airport or make a deal with a local taxi service for you at a reduced fare.

Rooms normally cost about $200 a night but will be higher or lower depending upon the season and availability. Local phone: 1753/851-011; fax: 1753/830-244. For U.S. reservations, dial 800/225-5843.

Shopping Windsor & Eton

Windsor serves several purposes for the shopping visitor. There's something to be gained from its commercialism: The shops are wide open on Sunday.

There are several gift shops right on the premises of the castle. Please note that when the queen is in residence tourists are limited as to what parts of the castle they may explore, but that the gift shops remain open. It costs a princely £8 to enter the castle (and the gift shops)! You may not shop the gift shops without paying admission.

While a good number of the multiples do have branch stores in Windsor, and there's even a **Reject China Shop** right on the high street, Windsor is not one of those British cities that has been completely overrun with look-alike stores.

Most of the serious mutliples are decorously set back from the Castle, on Peascod Street, so that the high street has a local feel to it. You have to know where **Boots** and **M&S** are in order to find them. There's also real-people shopping on Peascod, such as one-hour photo processing shops and the like.

The high street is more devoted to tourist traps than to multiples; I don't think I've ever seen so many tourist shops. I did get a very precious duchess of York spoon in a tourist trap in Windsor long after Fergie split, so you never know what you'll find in those stores. Look for my favorite souvenir stand right near the train station outside the Windsor

Story—a little historical theme park—in the alley there.

FINDS

WOODS OF WINDSOR
Queen Charlotte Street, Windsor

At first glance you might think of this as the poor person's Crabtree & Evelyn, yet this adorable little blue shop was established in 1770. Woods of Windsor offers soaps, shampoos, and various scented products with old-fashioned packaging and pretty colors galore.

ASQUITH'S TEDDY BEAR SHOP
31 High Street, Eton

One of the few non-antique stores in Eton's main shopping area, this small shop sells teddy bears and teddy fashions as well as bear designs. Your kids will love it; the best bear prices we've found anywhere in the world. There's another branch in Windsor on the way to the bridge for Eton.

THE TOKEN HOUSE
High Street, Windsor

The biggest and brightest store in the area, the Token House is a multiroom china shop with gifts and souvenirs, commemoratives and mugs, full place settings and teapots, figurines, and everything else you can imagine. A small percentage of its wares are sold for less across the street at the Reject China Shop, but its selection is so vast that it can't be compared to anything else in town.

BILLINGS & EDMONDS
132 High Street, Eton

This is one of those *Goodbye Mr. Chips*–style retail stores in Eton; they also have a branch in Harrow.

Obviously, they are the purveyors of school goods; everything here is so authentic you could almost get a costume for Halloween, or impress Central Casting with your English schoolboy looks. The clothes, jackets, gowns, and accessories are not inexpensive, but do make a fine fashion statement and a good souvenir. They will educate you in the shop so that you don't make a social faux pas with your selection. A genuine straw boater is £13; it's a hat none of us should be without.

STRATFORD-UPON-AVON

Considering that the place is virtually overrun with tourists from all nations (especially in season), it's a miracle that the town is in such good shape. Stratford is indeed cute; it's just that there's a subtext of planned cute that has no authentic old English ring to it.

If you're a theater buff and you've come to see Shakespeare performed in the evening, spend your day strolling around town. See the museums and possibly a few stores or the antique center, and you'll feel pleased with the day—exhausted but pleased. Do not come to Stratford just for the shopping.

But wait, if you've come to Stratford-upon-Avon for the shopping and find there is little to behold, you may want to flip to page 3. You are just a half-hour drive from Bicester Village, the American-style factory outlet mall where you can have more fun than even Shakespeare could imagine.

Now then, if you are going on your own from London to Stratford-upon-Avon and you are looking at a map of Britain, please note that Stratford-upon-Avon is not Stafford. I mention this because they are in more or less the same place on maps, and Stafford is usually set in larger type than Stratford-upon-Avon.

The Lay of the Land

Stratford is located on the banks of the River Avon, hence the name. When you cross the bridge, you will know you are there. Actually, when you see all the traffic, the coaches, the tourists, the flags flying in the breeze from the RST, you will also know you are there.

This is not a one-high-street town, and while it's not complicated, it's not that simple, either.

The main high street where the multiples are located is Bridge Street. There's a new, modern Covent Garden–style mall right after you cross the bridge onto Bridge Street and before you get to the heartland multiples.

The main street where multiples such as **Laura Ashley** (as well as the tourist traps) can be found is Henley Street, which branches off to the right if you are on Bridge Street and the Royal Shakespeare Theatre is to your rear. It's very touristy.

There is a market square with shops around it that aren't quite so touristy.

Henley Street is paved for pedestrians; it's very modern and feels like your local mall. The Shakespeare museum is right there on the outdoor mall. Like I said, this is a tourist town.

But the architecture, especially in the most touristy parts, is adorable, and in season there are flowers everywhere and the town smiles.

Shopping Stratford

I expected to find some marvelous kitsch in Stratford—you know, Shakespearean refrigerator magnets or "Neither a Borrower Nor a Lender Be" T-shirts—something.

Nothing. Despite there being a million tourist traps in Stratford-upon-Avon, they are seriously lacking in kitsch. There is a cattle market on Tuesdays, and a street market on Fridays, however.

FINDS

GILMERS
Henley Street, Stratford-upon-Avon

I can't say this is a great find in any sense of the word, but it is my favorite of the many tourist traps on Henley Street. It's heavily into dolls and looks like the cover of *Victoria* magazine.

THE TRADING POST
1 High Street, Stratford-upon-Avon

This is Judith Shakespeare's home turned retail establishment. And for those of you who did not brush up your Shakespeare before the trip, Judith was his daughter.

SUPER DRUG
Bridge Street, Stratford-upon-Avon

This is where you go to buy anything you need— from film to health and beauty aids to snacks.

ANTIQUES CENTRE
Ely Street, Stratford-upon-Avon

This isn't the greatest antique center in all of England, but at least it's not as touristy as the rest of town. About 60 dealers. Local phone: 1789/ 204-180. Open: 10am to 5pm every day.

WARWICK

. . . .

Warwick is a village and a castle, and the castle is not in the center of the village, so don't get confused and think they are one and the same. Warwick Castle is the most visited castle in England and since it's just a few miles from Stratford-upon-Avon, the two are frequently seen in the same day or as part of the same visit. Fortunately, most tourists don't know about the beauties of the village of Warwick,

Warwick

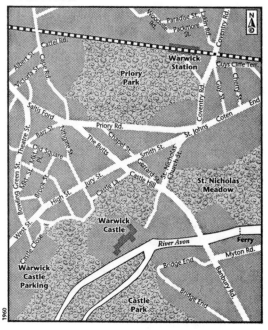

so it's rather unspoiled and perfect. And filled with antique shops.

But before I go any further, some important advice: Say "War-ick," not "Warwick."

The Lay of the Land

The village of Warwick is built in a small square center unit; there's not just a high street dotted with multiples. They are very few multiples, but there is a branch of **Oxfam**, the charity shop.

The streets do tend to change their names, but if you keep following the signs to "centre," you'll be fine. While there are a few ugly modern buildings, about half the town is half-timbered. There are antique shops in the downtown center as well as in a row at the edge of town on West Street, where you first entered town.

Indeed, you can do a complete loop from West Street along Bowling Green around to the pretty church with the spires and the clock tower (St. Mary's) and then back to West Street with all the tiny antique shops. Along the way, you'll take in the **Doll Museum**, the pedestrian walk, Castle Street, **Warwick Antiques Centre**, and Lord Leycester Hospital.

STOKE-ON-TRENT

. . . .

In case you have never heard of Stoke-on-Trent (called Stoke by most), and think that all my ramblings are curious but crazy, here's a quickie: Stoke is the capital of a group of small towns called The Potteries. Guess what they make in The Potteries! How did you ever guess? It's pottery. There are some 30 outlet stores dotted around Stoke and The Potteries, through factories, malls, highways, and byways. Make that buy-ways.

Stoke in a Day

If you've got a BritRail train pass, this trip is a cinch. If you are buying a single destination ticket, you will have to pay top price because in order to get to Stoke and back in the same day, you're going to have to be on an early train (the most expensive). You may end up paying £70 ($100) for your round-trip, one-day ticket, depending on the strength of the dollar and whatever promotions you may latch onto. Unless you are planning on buying a lot, the price of the ticket may stop you dead right there.

During January and June and July sales at china shops in London, as well as in the china departments of big department stores (Harrods), it is customary to truck in seconds from the factories in Stoke. There is no reason to go to Stoke during one of these sale periods; prices on seconds are the same. Of course, there are other choices in Stoke and various sale promotions there too—but do understand what's going on and don't think you can beat

Harrods's January sale price by sneaking off to Stoke.

If you are planning on buying a lot (the only reason to go to Stoke in the first place), consider bringing those airline carts with wheels or a giant, nylon, strong tote sack. Some outlets will pack your purchases in boxes for you. I find that most of my Stoke shopping is a few small pieces at each outlet, so I end up with lots of shopping bags and no overall organizational method. Last trip to Stoke, I got on the train with 17 shopping bags. Honest. Someone had to help me on the train and then off again.

Do not plan an elaborate evening in London on the day of your Stoke day trip. A hot bath and room service may be all you can handle.

Chapter Ten

. . . .

SHOPPING THE COTSWOLDS

The Cotswolds offer visitors the perfect combination of riches:

- A location not too distant from London, but readily accessible from not only London's international airports but from the new international gateway at Birmingham.
- Gorgeous hills, valleys, vistas, flora and fauna, and picture perfect villages, and waiting for you around every bend.
- Stores, stores, stores—many of them selling antiques—and each village usually has an antique center, too.

The Cotswolds are a small group of hills and valleys located mostly in Gloucestershire, but also in Oxfordshire. The many villages in the area are collectively called the Cotswolds. There seem to be core Cotswolds cities that everyone wants to see, fringe Cotswolds cities that sometimes get overlooked for lack of time or adventure, and then fringe Cotswold areas that may not even be in the Cotswolds. But don't worry, I'll give your regards to Broadway, because Broadway happens to be one of the key Cotswolds villages.

This is sheep country: a land of rolling green hills, limestone buildings, and ditches called "ha-has."

But she who shops for antiques gets the last laugh, because prices are less than those in London. More importantly, shopping is part of what you do when you come to the Cotswolds, even if you are just browsing.

If you're really trying to make a kill, don't miss the car boot sales. They may not have the golden glow of limestone about them, but when you can buy an all-leather suitcase from the 1960s (perfect condition) for £2, well, you'll quickly grasp the beauty of the Wolds. The Wolds are alive with the sound of shopping, no doubt about it.

GETTING THERE
. . . .
From the U.S.

You can either fly to Heathrow (not Gatwick) and pick up a rental car at the airport or take the bus directly from the airport to Oxford; if you insist, you can also go into London, catch the train to Oxford from Paddington station, and head right back out from whence you came.

Or you can get smart. You can fly nonstop from the United States (either New York or Chicago) into Birmingham. British Airways has opened up the Birmingham airport to nonstop service from New York; American Airlines offers nonstop service from Chicago. Birmingham is closer to Gloucestershire than London and also offers easy access to Wales and one of my favorite cities, Stoke-on-Trent.

If you are driving anyway, and want to save yourself a good bit of aggravation, you may want to try the Birmingham option. Needless to say, getting in and out of the Birmingham International Airport is like singing a song—there are no lines, there are no hassles, there are only simple realities. It's almost as easy as flying into Manchester.

From London

Essentially, the Cotswolds start in Oxford, so if you are doing this from London and don't really want to rent a car in London proper (who would want to?), you can jump on the train at Paddington station and head for Oxford. Oxford is a walking town, so you can do a day or so there and then pick up your rental car in Oxford and head out.

GETTING AROUND

There isn't any public transportation to speak of in the Cotswolds. There are car rental agencies at the airports and on the outskirts of Oxford. If you are afraid to drive on the "wrong" side of the road, remember my mantra: Right shoulder to the center of the road. If that doesn't do it for you, consider a tour, a private car and driver, or even taking taxis for a day or two. Taxi drivers will often cut a deal for a flat rate of day's driving.

There are two kinds of taxis in the Oxford area: legal and illegal. There is a huge business in ferrying tourists to various little villages and then charging them an arm and a leg. Make sure your taxi has a licensed number on the outside.

THE LAY OF THE LAND

Located about an hour and a half from London, the Cotswolds boast a few stately homes (like Blenheim Palace), several manor homes of note (the prince of Wales's home, Highgrove), villages with names like Upper Slaughter (and Lower Slaughter), a few touristy attractions from zoos to antique motor car collections, and scads of antique shops.

While summer in the Cotswolds seems to attract an equal mix of British and foreign tourists, all doing the sights and some shopping, from October through Boxing Day the crowd tends to be made up of those in the know—including serious antique hunters and dealers all keenly looking for the last, best bargain in Britain.

Inns and manor homes offer special weekend package prices; shopkeepers realize they are dealing with more serious customers; weekend schedules are jammed with antique fairs, flea markets, jumble sales (church bazaars), car boot sales, and the usual pre-Christmas excitement. Spending Christmas week at the perfect country house/hotel is a major local sport; many houses are booked from year to year by regulars. June is not considered early when it comes to booking the place of your choice for Christmas week.

The villages of the area have distinct personalities; strangers must discover for themselves the ins and outs. Insiders already know: Bourton-on-the-Water is a tourist trap that takes the motor-coach crowd; Tetbury is one of the most charming little towns in the area and one of the best for antiques; and Stow-on-the-Wold wins, hands down, for Village with the Best Antique Shops in the category of villages that have more than one street. (Tetbury has one street.) Summer Sundays may find villages crammed with tourists who clog the roads while licking ice cream cones and pointing to the sheep. Baa!

ANTIQUING IN THE COTSWOLDS

If you are the type who must know every single shop in the area, in order to properly do it all, please write for a free booklet with that lists all the local dealers: Secretary, Cotswold Antiques Dealers' Association, Barcheston Manor, Shipston-on-Stour, Warwickshire, England; or call local phone: 1608/661-268.

SLEEPING IN THE COTSWOLDS

There are two methods to attacking the area: Stay several nights in one lodging and drive 20 to 60 miles a day; or move to a new hotel in a slightly different location every night. Everything is pretty close to everything else, so pick a B&B or a manor house and plunk yourself down. I can't stand one-night stands myself. Besides, if you find a great country hotel, dig in; the next one might not be so good.

WYCK HILL HOUSE
Stow-on-the-Wold

I almost hate to share this secret because I don't want this hotel to be discovered. Yet I am compelled to shout: This is the manor house/hotel of your dreams. Furthermore, the location, price, kitchen, and décor create that incredible blend that must be called sublime. Here's the best part: You can actually book a room for two here for £90 a night! And what a room. I've seen many a hotel in my time and I promise this is one of the nicest I have *ever* stayed in. Considering that this is a mansion hotel, dripping with charm, tapestries, croquet, and even bunny rabbits on the lawn (real bunny rabbits), well, you may not find a better deal in all of England.

There are numerous breaks packages (promotions), including Breakaway, which is offered for any two consecutive nights and includes accommodation, three-course dinner, full English breakfast, morning newspaper, and VAT. All for £150 per person! To put that into dollars and good sense, you're looking at about $500 for a luxury hotel for two nights (a more than $500 value right there) with dinners that may make you swoon—valued at about $400 for the two nights for two people. I mean, really.

The chef, Ian Smith, is quite famous, and you will be most pleased with your meals here. The nearest Cotswold village is Stow, by far the cutest of them all. This is the most perfect choice you will ever make. For reservations, call local phone: 01451/831-936.

THE LYGON ARMS
Broadway

If nothing but a big-name status hotel will do the trick, go ahead and spring for the Lygon Arms in Broadway. Doubles begin at £130. You can book through Leading Hotels of the World. In the United States, call 800/223-6800. The hotel is filled with yesteryear English charm of the most luxurious sort.

If you don't stay here, go out of your way to eat a meal or have tea or coffee. Lunch for two on the fixed-price luncheon menu will cost about £50.

On my last visit, Carolyn and I stopped here for afternoon coffee: total bill, all of £4. It was pure delight: We got out of a bright sunny day and sank into stuffed chairs in front of the silent fireplace. We used the lovely ladies' room (upstairs); we sopped up the luxury. We gossiped about everyone we know and had a fine time for next to nothing in terms of cash outlay. Local phone: 1386/820-243.

LORDS OF THE MANOR
Upper Slaughter

This is a grand manor house that has been nicely remodeled into a hotel. It is rather similar to Wyck Hill House. It's located in the middle of the Slaughters in a sensational setting. Various promotional price breaks, fall and winter weekend rates, and Christmas festivities. Member Small Luxury Hotels of the World. Call 800/525-4800 in the United States. Local phone: 1451/820-243.

OXFORD
. . . .
Oxford is one of England's most visited cities outside of London, and with good reason: It has that good old-fashioned feel to it, and yet it's only an hour from London.

Oxford is quite different from Cambridge. If you are choosing between the two and just want a perfect university town without access to the Cotswolds, then Cambridge is more perfect than Oxford. Oxford is much more commercial than Cambridge; the university has beautiful parts to it and there are moments when you can lose yourself in time and space, but Oxford has a hustle and bustle to it that Cambridge does not share. And if you have the transportation, Oxford can also offer factory outlets.

The outlets are on the far side of the town of Oxford away from the Cotswolds, to the east. The biggest and best are the Bicester (say "Bista") Factory Outlet stores, a mere 15 miles away.

The Lay of the Land

Oxford is a pretty big city, and the main shopping-cum-university area at its heart is spread out just enough that you'll have to study a map in order to get the immediate picture. This is not a one-street town nor is it as intimate as Cambridge. If you arrive by bus, be prepared to study a map to get your bearings. The train station is also at the edge of town.

The River Thames serves as one town boundary and the River Cherwell as the other. The main downtown shopping area is in the center between these two rivers, making a sort of H formation. Street names change frequently, often after only a block or two, so you can get lost without ever moving, although if you pay no attention at all to street names you'll be fine. The joy of Oxford is that everywhere you roam you find something else interesting. Just look up at the architecture; look out at the people; look aside at the shops.

The main shopping streets are Cornmarket Street (which is called St. Aldate's at one end and Magdalen Street at the other) and High Street, which runs

Oxford

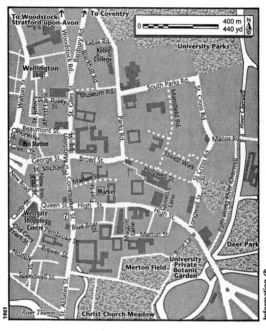

perpendicular to Cornmarket Street and will eventually take you out of town over the Magdalen Bridge. Please note that if you are used to traditional English village format, High Street is not this town's high street. Go figure. Cornmarket is really the high street.

There are several shopping streets branching off Cornmarket that can't be ignored, especially Broad Street with its many bookstores (and the Bodleian Library!) and Market Street with the city's fabulous covered market. The nugget of real estate between Broad Street and High Street including Cornmarket Street is the best area for the shopper. But there is also shopping directly behind Cornmarket, with an American-style mall or two. And then, if you walk the distance between the malls and the train station, you'll come across the Oxford Antiques Centre.

Getting There

The best way to get to Oxford directly is to take the bus to Oxford from Heathrow. Buses stop every hour right in front of Terminal Four. It cost £8 for the one-way ticket to Oxford.

Note that because of the terrible design of the new bus station at Gloucester Green, there is no direct access to the taxi stand from it. Furthermore, there are no trolleys and no porters there, so you must be able to manage your own luggage for this travel option to work smoothly for you.

If you're coming from London, the train takes about an hour; the Oxford rail station is slightly outside town but conveniently across the street from the Antiques Centre. You will at least be able to get a taxi easily from here.

If you drive to Oxford, you may want to park at the edge of town; there are park-and-ride lots that provide a bus shuttle into town.

Sleeping in Oxford

THE RANDOLPH HOTEL
Beaumont Street, Oxford

Owned by Forte, the Randolph has always been the grande dame of Oxford. If you don't stay here, stop by for tea in the traditional parlor. It's conveniently located right among the main shopping streets.

I booked a half-day rate last time I was in town. My British Airways overnight flight arrived at Heathrow at 7am; I caught the 8am bus to Oxford and was in my room at the Randolph by 10am for room service breakfast and a bath in the old-fashioned tub in the William Morris tiled bathroom. It was the most delicious way to get over jet lag and to start off my weekend in the Cotswolds.

By 5pm, I had walked around town, been to the Bodleian, eaten lunch, and had a nap in my adorable room. When I checked out at 5pm, I was fully refreshed and ready to conquer the rest of the

Cotswolds. You can't do better. In the United States, call 800/225-5843. Local phone: 1865/247-481; fax: 1865/791-678.

Shopping Oxford

With the great population of students and tourists in Oxford, there are all sorts of shopping opportunities. Most of the multiples have shops here; there are very good department stores as well. Debenhams—your basic all-purpose department store—is right in the thick of things on the main street, taking up about a block of space in front of St. Mary's. There's a very good **Marks & Spencer**. There are tons of bookstores and a fair number of antique shops, and the covered market is absolutely adorable. Yet most of the shopping in Oxford is geared toward the locals, so that unless you are into the town-and-gown scene or want university souvenirs, you won't find that much here that can't be found elsewhere.

Do consider, though, that Oxford is the official start of the Cotswolds, which you must understand is Antique Heaven. The local antique center is pretty good. It's not as attractive as those in some other cities, but the prices are pretty good, and compared to those in the more touristy Cotswolds cities this center is a solid find. You can choose from a mix of old carpets, royal memorabilia, books, costumes, china, and knickknacks (see "Oxford Resources from A to Z," below).

Day Tripper Tips

Trains to Oxford from London leave from Paddington station at least every hour. During peak times they run more frequently. The schedule is different on weekends. A cheap day return for the one-hour trip is about £12, which is also the amount of the one-way fare if you just happen to jump aboard and buy a ticket or travel at peak times.

Oxford-in-a-Day Shopper's Tour

1. After you arrive at the train station, walk to your right (where everyone is walking) and hit Park End Street, which leads into town. You could catch a cab (and should, if it's raining), but otherwise, enjoy the walk.

2. In less than a block you are at the Oxford Antiques Centre on Park End Street. Give yourself more than a half hour to browse, then continue into town on New Road, going right at Castle Street, which will take you to the Westgate Centre, where you can browse as you walk through to the other side. There's not a lot here to keep you, but there's usually a crowd, and you begin to get into the shopping spirit of the city.

3. Once out of Westgate, continue on St. Ebbe's to Queen Street, where you'll find the big **Marks & Spencer** as well as many of the real people multiples from **Next** to **The Gap** and then **Crabtree and Evelyn**. In just one block you'll be at Cornmarket Street, and right in the thick of things. Note that if you go to the right, Cornmarket Street is less busy and becomes St. Aldate's, where you'll find **Alice's Shop**. The tourist information office is also on this street (before Alice's), and you can stop here for lists of antique stores and booksellers if you want to make your own tour. You'll know the corner of Cornmarket Street and Queen Street by the Carfax Tower; head toward it on Cornmarket Street.

4. Finish your tour on St. Aldate's and reverse on the other side of the street so you are now walking back the way you came and toward Magdelen on Cornmarket Street, which is the main shopping street. Don't miss the exterior of the **Laura Ashley** shop.

5. Turn right when you get to Broad Street (shortly after you pass Laura Ashley), where all the most famous bookstores are, take some time for the Bodleian Library (which has a very good gift shop, natch), and then head out via Turl Street.

6. Shop Turl for some of its university stores, then hit High Street, coming around on High to that entrance of the **Covered Market**.
7. After you've done a complete tour of the market, come back out on High Street so that you can finish your shopping there. If you duck out the back end of the market onto Market Street, you'll have missed a block of fun.
8. If you have any energy left (or time), head to the Randolph Hotel for tea. Otherwise, it's time to tote those books back to London on the train.

Finds

LAURA ASHLEY
Ship Street at 26 Cornmarket Street, Oxford

You can probably find a Laura Ashley store in England on your own. But the architecture of this particular branch store is so wonderful that you have to at least stare. I took pictures. The inside of the store is rather normal, but still adorable.

OXFORD CAMPUS STORE
126 High Street, Oxford

This is a tourist trap, I admit that, but it's a slick one. And it has a sister tourist trap inside the Covered Market. But one of the things you came to Oxford to buy was university souvenir merchandise, so you might as well go to the best tourist trap in town. There are student stores; this is a tourist store. Sweatshirts start at £15; there's notebooks and pads and pens and mugs and even some unusual items.

BOSWELL'S
Broad Street and Cornmarket Street, Oxford

A very strange store but worthwhile if you need anything or hate touristy stores. It's a department store, a supermarket, a drugstore, and a variety store; it offers absolutely everything for sale. The display is terrible, but there's so much here that you have to take stock. There's a good selection of souvenirs and a good china department.

THE COVERED MARKET
Market Avenue, Oxford

Taking up just about a whole city block, with entrances from different roads and at different places (some marked in different colors), this is a fine example of what happens when an old-fashioned market is revitalized without being overdone. There are fruit, vegetable, and flower dealers, butchers, eateries, bakers, candlestick makers, and then vendors of arts and crafts and cute T-shirts. Find home-made sausages, a saddlery, a little card shop, etc. I even bought a designer hat here—I'd seen it in *Vogue* magazine and it was £5 cheaper than in London.

WALTERS
10 Turl Street, Oxford

The place for the university souvenirs—check out the long woolen scarves in various college colors. (There are 30 colleges here.) For £60 ($100) you can get a university sweater with embroidered logo. The shop doesn't feel old-fashioned preppy, but it has the goods and the gowns.

SHEPHERD AND WOODWARD
109-114 High Street, Oxford

A tad more traditional and preppy, but selling much the same stuff as Walters—good for souvenirs or for locals. They have been dressing university men for more than 100 years.

ALICE'S SHOP
83 St. Aldate's, Oxford

This entire shop is devoted to Alice in Wonderland merchandise. You'll find everything from teapots to tea towels and tote bags, etc. The storefront itself was the Old Sheep Shop in several Lewis Carroll tales; there is more Alice merchandise here than anywhere else in England. And a very happy unbirthday to you too.

Oxford Resources from A–Z

ANTIQUES

If you are specifically interested in antique shopping, stop by the tourist information office and ask for the latest list of dealers.

The Oxford Antiques Centre (opposite the train station at 27 Park End Street) is open Tuesday through Saturday, 10am to 5pm, as well as the first Sunday of each month, 11:30am to 5pm.

BOOKS

As much as Oxford has going for it—and it has *many* things going for it—perhaps it is best remembered as a great city for buying books.

Blackwell's is the Alice's Restaurant of bookshops in Oxford. You can get anything you want at no fewer than 11 shops in Oxford—five of them on Broad Street alone. In addition to the main store (48–51 Broad Street), there is a map and travel shop next door (No. 53), a paperback shop (No. 23–25), an art and poster store (No. 27), and, across the street, a children's specialty store (No. 8). The music shop is just half a block east (38 Holywell Street), and there are branches at the Museum of Modern Art Bookshop, near the Westgate Shopping Centre, and in Beaver House on Hythe Bridge Street. Finally, there's a medical bookshop near the John Radcliffe Hospital and a polytechnic bookshop at the corner of London Road and Gipsy Lane. Blackwell's Rare Books is located in a 15th-century prayer chapel 8 miles away in Fyfield (Fyfield Manor, Fyfield, Oxon OX13 5LR; tel. 865/ 390-692). Or call Blackwell's in town, tel. 865/ 792-792, for directions to Fyfield.

In addition to the 200,000 titles you'll find on the shelves, the music shop stocks sheet music, cassettes, and CDs, the art store has posters and calendars, and the children's shop sells small toys and stationery. If you can't visit in person, the firm offers free delivery in Oxford and accepts Visa, Access, and American Express for out-of-town delivery. If you're going to spend some time in Oxford, Blackwell's frequently schedules author readings, literary lunches and dinners, and illustrated lectures. The main shop is open Monday through Saturday, 9am to 6pm.

In addition to Blackwell's, Oxford has numerous antiquarian and secondhand book dealers (the Tourist Information Centre provides a list). Waterfield's (36 Park End Street, near the railroad station) has one of the largest stocks of antiquarian books—four floors of them—and regularly issues catalogues of 17th- and 18th-century English books. Open Monday through Saturday, 9:30am to 5:30pm.

A smaller shop, but one noted for the helpfulness of its proprietors, is Titles (15 Turl Street). Ralph and Gillian Stone are particularly knowledgeable about agriculture, travel, and natural history.

On Fridays, used books are sold at the Northgate Book Market right on the main drag at St. Mary's, across from Kentucky Fried Chicken. There's a handwritten sign out front to show the way. Great good fun.

There are a few bargain book stores where overruns and remainders are sold. They don't have that good bookstore feeling to them, but they sell books for kids, cheap reads, and usually postcards. Booksale on Cornmarket is in the thick of your everyday shopping.

DEPARTMENT STORES

BHS
St. Ebbe's

C&A
Westgate Centre, Oxford

DEBENHAMS
Magdalen Street, Oxford

LEWIS'S
Westgate Centre, Oxford

LITTLEWOODS
52-53 Cornmarket Street, Oxford

LIBERTY
115 High Street, Oxford

MARKS & SPENCER
Queen Street, Oxford

SHOPPING CENTERS

CLARENDON CENTRE
Cornmarket Street, Oxford

Right on Cornmarket Street, this glitzy American-style mall is recognizable by the blue tubes that decorate it and try to grab your attention. Many of the multiples have branch stores here, right in the heart of town. Serviceable, not charming.

WESTGATE CENTRE
Westgate, Oxford

This American-style mall is set back a little from the main area at Cornmarket and reaches almost halfway to the train station. There is a Sainsburys grocery store and a few department stores attached to it. The individual smaller tenants are more like local mom-and-pop shops than big multiples.

TETBURY & CIRENCESTER
· ·

While Oxford may be the heart of the Cotswolds and the jumping-off point for many visitors, few get to the far side of the Cotswolds where Tetbury and Cirencester are waiting, with open arms. Actually, Tetbury is filled with bobbies and royal helicopters because that's where Prince Charles lives, but still, both villages are near each other and somewhat off the main tourist path, which makes them ideal.

Tetbury

This village is storybook perfect, with its one main street crammed with shops, its open-sided medieval market building, and its air of confident superiority without snobbery. The beauty of Tetbury is that it is in the opposite direction from the rest of the Cotswold villages, so you have to go purposefully out of your way to get here; this assures that you are safely off the dreaded motor-coach trail. Since many Americans don't know about Tetbury in the first place, they don't know that this is a detour worth making, and leave the village for those clever enough to pounce.

THE LAY OF THE LAND

The main street is called Long Street, and stretches only one long block from the London Road to the marketplace. The town seems to exist merely as a location for antique shops, although there are one or two highfalutin fashion shops and then the usual little village butchers and bakers.

If you drive out of town away from the London Road, you'll pass Prince Charles's home, which you cannot see. But there's a bobby in the driveway, and no one else in the neighborhood has a bobby in his driveway.

SHOPPING TETBURY

There are about 20 antique shops here as well as a newish 30-stall antique center. Most dealers specialize in high-quality country furniture, most often in dark woods and much of it in the thousands-of-pounds price range. However, there are affordable smalls.

There is a wide degree of difference in the quality and prices of the goods from shop to shop. One store is full of the fun/junk type of stuff; there are several stores in country homes, where you wander from room to room looking at the goods. Then there are a few shops that sell new antiques and the look we love on a scale for real people rather than museum collectors. No other village is so densely packed with such a collection of serious furniture from the 18th and 19th centuries. Although Stow is the perfect Cotswold village (and everyone knows it), Tetbury and its shopping scene offer the perfect hidden Cotswold fantasy shopping trip.

There is an antique market every Wednesday (9am to 4pm), upstairs in the Market Hall; the new antique center is called **The Antiques Emporium**, it's open daily, including Sunday afternoons (10am to 5pm weekdays and Saturdays, 1 to 5pm Sundays).

Finds

COUNTRY HOMES
61 Long Street, Tetbury

A winner right off the bat! This shop specializes in pine and has a selection of plank tables, armoires, benches, and dressers that would go well in an American country home. The owners have also recently opened a 30-stall antique store called **The Antiques Emporium** in the Old Chaper on Long Street. Open: Monday through Saturday from 10am to 5pm and on Sundays from 1 to 5pm.

GASTRELL HOUSE
33 Long Street, Tetbury

This is one of the more formal shops, and looks like a museum for period furniture, with room after room of pieces. The tags not only have the prices, but also a short history of each piece. Serious stuff.

ANTIQUE INTERIORS
35 Long Street, Tetbury

This nice little shop sells Designer's Guild and other
lines of fabric needed for the English look, as well
as little lampshades in paisley prints and tole work.

OLD GEORGE ANTIQUES
3 The Chipping, Tetbury

Mahogany and Regency and serious about it. Decorative arts also. Near the Snooty Fox inn.

RUDGE ANTICS
46 Long Street, Tetbury

Looks like a little shack (of the cutest kind, of course)
and has a wonderful mix of new sheets from the
British firm Dorma and pine furniture, potpourri,
and Victorian country furniture galore—all in the
repro market.

OLD MILL MARKET SHOP
12 Church Street, Tetbury

The only low-end antique shop in Tetbury, filled with
clutter plus a big, fat white cat that sleeps in the
window.

Cirencester

Cirencester (pronounced "Sar-ens-ter" and dating
from the second century, when the Romans called it
Corinium) is hardly a village, rather a town; much
of the downtown is modern, but not too modern to
have an outdoor market in front of the cathedral.
Despite the fact that the downtown represents a
newer and more modern England, there's a special
feel to Cirencester that makes it worth visiting. Plus,
it has some good shopping and is the gateway to
Tetbury.

THE LAY OF THE LAND

Cirencester is big enough to have a Ring Road. You'll have to ignore most of it and just concentrate on the older part of town for the sights and shopping treats you came to enjoy. There is a big church in the center of town, and you can use its spire as your guide. The regular shopping is on streets around the church; the antique shopping is concentrated in the area before you get to the church, on a street appropriately named Dollar Street.

The main shopping street is called Market Place directly in front of the church, and becomes Castle Street at its other end, as it moves toward the Tesco store, away from the church. Running perpendicular is Dollar Street, which becomes Gosditch Street and then Cricklade Street, all in a matter of three blocks.

SHOPPING CIRENCESTER

The market square is packed with the tents and stalls of vendors three days a week. But on Friday, the best day to visit, an antique market is held in Corn Hall (across from the market area). Monday, Wednesday, and Friday from 9am to 3pm.

Cirencester's antique street stretches to the edge of downtown—an easy walk. Here, on Dollar Street, you'll find a handful of tony shops, each selling almost museum-quality furniture in the higher price ranges. It's all arranged in shops set up like homes; it's enough to make you drool all over the patina.

Cirencester is also a good pit stop if you need groceries or the comforts of the more modern world. There are some branch stores of the multiples, of course, but better yet, there is a Tesco.

Finds

RANKINE TAYLOR ANTIQUES
34 Dollar Street, Cirencester

One of the best shops in the Cotswolds in terms of ambience and visual pleasure. The layout and display in this store just make you want to move in—both formal and country looks in furniture, bedding, and tabletop are sold. The store specializes in 18th-century oak, mahogany, and fruitwood furniture—there are smalls here, as well as antique beds, carved breakfronts, highboys, and lowboys. Mrs. Taylor lists opening hours on a card in the front window: "9ish to 5:30pm." Closed on Sundays.

WILLIAM H. STOKES
6-8 Dollar Street, Cirencester

Tons of good furniture, including Jacobean country pieces dating from the 17th century.

BREWERY ARTS
Brewery Court, Cricklade Street, Cirencester

In a building that is part rehab, off Cricklade Street and right behind Castle Street, is a fabulous crafts center with some workshops and a gallery. If you've been here before, you may remember that this shop was named the Cirencester Craft Centre. You'll see high-quality work and find many gift items; prices begin at £1! All items have been selected and vetted by the crafts council. They also provide special exhibits, courses, and lectures.

BURFORD & BROADWAY

Burford and Broadway are two of the most perfect of the Cotswolds villages and are located on opposite ends of one of the main roads, A424. By driving just on this one road and progressing, in either direction, between Burford and Broadway, you get to the heart of the Cotswolds and the best of the region.

Burford

It just could be that Burford is my favorite of the Cotswold villages. It's got everything: a high street crammed with pleasant shops, a wonderful church and churchyard, a river, and, of course, an antique center. It's also a bit different from the others: While it has a charming village feel, there's something more wide-open (without being Roman, as in Moreton-in-Marsh) that gives the town extra energy so that while the village is cute, it doesn't have that crammed-together small medieval village feel.

If you forced me, I just might be able to make it home.

THE LAY OF THE LAND

Burford is bigger than some of the teenier towns, with a main street several blocks long with just store after store; in traditional medieval fashion this is called High Street. The village has a lot more hustle and bustle to it than most, but it's not too touristy. Just slightly touristy. At the edge of town (move the car) there's a traffic circle and two antique markets—one good, the other worth a pass. But don't just do the stores and call it quits; this town begs for a wander. Visit the local church, walk by the river.

SHOPPING BURFORD

The high street has a nice mix of real-people stores where the local gentry gets its riding and shooting and country clothes, to a small church that houses antique markets on and off, to a gas station that doesn't even look like a gas station. There are some antique stores, but there are other things to look at here—from the hand-knit sweater store of local designer Maggie White to a multiple or two (**Jumpers**) to several fancy tourist traps. One of the most welcome sights in Burford is the handmade sign attached to the fence in front of the church on the high street: "Fair Today." The antique fairs, held on most Saturdays, charge a small admission fee—50p, I think (Methodist Hall, High Street). For dates or other specifics, call 1993/822-780.

Also note that one of the charms of shopping the high street is that you come to these little alleys that lead to courtyards where there are shops—these are usually incredibly touristy, but at first glance you'll find them charming.

Burford is located on a hill, so be sure to hike up to the top of the high street and then shop your way down. Photo op from up top.

Tea for Two

Hit the **Priory Tea Room** (also a B&B with a few rooms upstairs; I've never peeked inside the rooms, though) right on the High Street. Cream tea is an affordable £5.

Finds

MAGGIE WHITE
High Street, Burford

Maggie White is so popular that her knits are knocked off all over the United Kingdom; she has her original store in Burford where cotton and woolen sweaters and coats (hats, too) are sold. The White look is a special blend of color and geometric pattern; there are also some ethnic clothes and simple silks sold in the shop.

BURFORD WOODROOMS
High Street, Burford

This shop sells reproduction pine furniture and new country looks in the too-perfect-to-be-true vein; fun for browsing, or small gift items, hats, candles, tole, cards, etc. At the lower end of the high street, where you will either start or finish your exploration of the main shopping area.

THE BURFORD NEEDLECRAFT SHOP
High Street, Burford

At the opposite end of the high street, therefore marking your top note if you choose to walk downhill into the town, this needlecraft shop is small and crowded with kits by the English tapestry masters.

ZENE WALKER
High Street, Burford

This antique shop, located next to Walker's Garden statuary, is one of the most picturesque addresses in town, with the front sidewalk loaded down with statuary. The antique shop has a lot of blue and white and all the stuff you want to see and touch.

Antique Centers

On the edge of town, and not really within walking distance from High Street, are two antique centers across the street from each other. The **Cotswold Gateway Antique Centre** is a newish complex of six to eight dealers in space built to look old and located next to the Cotswold Gateway Hotel, where you can also stop for a tea break. There's more than 4,000 square feet of space here, inhabited by dealers who have a little bit of everything—it's very worth doing.

Across the street is the **Burford Antiques Centre at the Roundabout**, a giant space that is filled to overflowing but has such high prices on such ordinary merchandise that you may want to run out of there screaming. The discount fabric store in this unit sells low-end goods not particularly worth more than a quick browse at best.

Broadway

Give my regards to Broadway, I'll be buying in Burford. It's not that there's anything wrong with

Broadway, it's just that it's too perfect for me. There's something incredibly fake about the strip of the high street that is developed with its perfect tourist stores and perfect ice cream vendors (wearing costumes, no less) and its perfect hotel (one of the most perfect hotels, I might add). I just find it annoying for anything to be this perfect. Shop up one side of the street and down the other or just go for tea at the **Lygon Arms** (see page 197) and call it a day.

MORETON-IN-MARSH & STOW-ON-THE-WOLD

· ·

These are the two most academically interesting Cotswolds towns: Stow because it is perfect and Moreton-in-Marsh because it is so dramatically different from all the others. Also note that Moreton-in-Marsh is the gateway to the Slaughters, two different villages (Upper and Lower) that aren't much on shopping but offer photo ops galore.

Moreton-in-Marsh

Moreton-in-Marsh feels different. It's not touristy and crass—don't panic—but something about it tells you immediately that this village of all of three blocks is not like the rest. Just as Cirencester doesn't fit into the mold in its own way, Moreton-in-Marsh differs simply because of the way it is built. MiM (my abbreviation, not theirs) has a very, very long shopping street—you may even want to move the car. There's tons to see here and you will enjoy the feel of this town, which bustles like a town, not a village. It's particularly jammed on Saturdays in summer.

THE LAY OF THE LAND

The main street was built in the Roman style, which means it is very, very wide and makes the proportions of the entire town feel strange without your actually knowing why. It is this width that unsettles you. The length is also extraordinary; don't be discouraged, since the points at the farther end of town have some of the best antique shops; put on your walking shoes and do it all.

Except for the wide streets, Moreton-in-Marsh is not different from its sister villages. Never mind, just do as the Romans did: *veni, vidi, Visa* (I came, I saw, I shopped). There are no multiples, but the high street has several little tea shops, fruit shops, markets, and cafeterias.

SHOPPING MORETON-IN-MARSH

Moreton-in-Marsh has antique shops at both ends of town, as well as a small antique center right in the middle (**Antiques Centre,** London House, High Street). Sometimes there is an antique fair in the market hall, located in the broad median that now serves as parking space but was once part of the Roman design. You may also use the toilets in the market hall. You pay a small admission to the flea market; the toilets are free.

The main street is called High Street; most shops do not have numbers. Stores are closed on Sundays. We timed one of our shopping days so that we ended up in Moreton for lunch; we were very happy at **St. James,** a restaurant and patisserie on the high street.

Finds

SIMON BRETT
Creswyke House, High Street, Moreton-in-Marsh

This is one of the most unusual stores in the area (and one of the best). Along with the formal furniture that is dated and catalogued on the price tag, you can also find antique fishing gear, including antique poles, and fishing collectibles. Fishing lures, you may have noticed, are a very hot collectible.

Something is certainly fishy here. Although Mr. Brett's fish stories are not inexpensive, this is definitely the place to come for a gift for your fisherman or for finishing touches to a man's study. His carved wooden fish models are legend. Member British Antiques Dealers Association.

CHANDLERS ANTIQUES
Chandlers Cottage, High Street,
Moreton-in-Marsh

Specialists in porcelain, pottery, glass, silver, and other small gift items. One of the more fun shops for rummaging around and touching everything and peering at the jewelry in the front case and asking questions and just poking about and enjoying yourself.

PETER ROBERTS
High Street, Moreton-in-Marsh

Beds, furniture, mirrors, and objects, 17th to 19th century.

Stow-on-the-Wold

Stow-on-the-Wold (or just Stow) is probably the most satisfying of the Cotswold villages because it is bigger than most, has several nice hotels and pubs, has more than one shopping street, and while it boasts far too many tourists in the summertime, it has just the right mixture of uptown happenings, quaint shops, and antique stores.

THE LAY OF THE LAND

Stow is built on a crossroads and therefore has two main streets: Sheep Street and High Street. A market town since the Middle Ages, it has a very large market square attesting to its former wealth as a sheep market; the original town stocks still stand in a small green—there are several antique shops right around the green.

The back streets and side streets, like Digbeth Street and Church Street, which connect from Sheep Street to the market square, are filled with antique shops. The addresses for shops located around the market square (most of which is parking space now) usually read simply: The Square. Lining the square are limestone houses that have been converted to shops (many of them have names, not addresses). The cobblestone streets, the low doors, and the wood-beam ceilings all contribute to the aura of this authentic little Cotswold village.

There aren't too many low-end or junky kinds of stores in Stow. Across from the better antique stores on the square are a few tourist traps selling the usual teddy bears and overly cute gift items.

SHOPPING STOW

Because of its size and ambience, Stow is the kind of place where you can let your hair down and enjoy browsing for many hours, or days. There are no multiples, and most of the shops sell antiques, but the town feels like it has more shopping substance to it than most of the others, and it's easy to feel inclined to do more shopping here. It's also incredibly charming.

One of the best things about shopping in Stow is that you don't really need a guide—just keep walking. Almost every house is a store; there are more than a dozen very fine antique shops here. It's impossible to tell you about every great shop or to edit out the losers; everything here has some merit, although there are reproductions and imports at some of the stores. Almost all of the good antique shops are on the expensive side; look for the BADA seal.

All of the big, good dealers can arrange shipping.

Finds

COTSWOLDS ANTIQUES CENTRE
Market Square, Stow

A small and narrow building with all the wares in neat pine showcases—not much like any other antique centers you are used to because there is no clutter or jumble. This one is really fancy, and a little bit cold. There just aren't mounds of goods laid about in stalls; it's all lined up in showcases. Oh, well, you can still stare at it.

HUNTINGTON ANTIQUES LTD.
The Old Forge, Church Street, Stow

The entire building (a former forge) is filled, room after room, with complete sets of room furnishings spanning the ages from medieval to Queen Anne. There are a lot of ecclesiastical pieces thrown in, and several tapestries here and there for wall covering. From Market Square, take that little side street near the Antiques Centre.

KEITH HOCKIN
Market Square, Stow

Another picture-perfect, drop-dead fancy resource, right near where the stocks stand on the little green. Put your husband in the stocks and take his wallet. The house specialty is 17th- and 18th-century oaks; they also have metalware of the same time period. Don't be put off by the need to ring to enter. It's worth the trouble, even if you are just browsing—this is one of the best dealers in town and in the entire Cotswolds. Prices to match.

STOW ANTIQUES
Market Square, Stow

Central Casting's version of the perfect little antique shop on the green, you enter through a little latticed enclosure at the front door. Stow Antiques is one of the small group of good antique shops clustered right near the stocks; they have a large assortment of English country furniture—much of it from Ireland and Wales. Closed Fridays.

LITTLE ELMS
Market Square, Stow

Little Elms specializes in country furniture as well as antiques.

PARK HOUSE
Sheep Street, Stow

At last, you are rewarded with a jumble type of shop crammed with fun stuff and satisfying to your need to rummage. This very deep shop has several salons packed with stuff, selling old teddies (bears, not lingerie) and various collectibles and knickknacks, as well as china and furniture. This is one of the town's few informal venues.

Chapter Eleven

· · · · · · · · ·

SHOPPING MANCHESTER

You think you know about Manchester. You think it's industrial and ugly and not your cup of tea, and you're already skimming this chapter to find York or Chester.

Have I got news for you: Everything you think you know about Manchester is wrong.

Manchester is where dealers and serious antiquers go for the real buys. Manchester is the gateway to Wales. Manchester is the perfect base for exploring neighboring parts of country England, from the Lake District to the Yorkshire Dales, from Stoke-on-Trent to York. It's easier to get to York as a day trip from Manchester than it is from London. And yes, Scotland is close, too.

I feel like Manchester and London aren't even in the same country. Manchester is the capital of the real England. I'm not knocking London, but I actually find it shocking that you can be in Britain and survive quite nicely, thank you, without even going to London.

Manchester is the home of what is thought to be the first department store in the United Kingdom. It has the second largest **Marks & Spencer** in Britain and, get this one, there are scads of **M&S outlet stores** scattered here and there and nearby. Because of Manchester's industrial heritage, this town is home to mills and mill shops and factory outlets galore. Within an hour's drive (or less), you can be shopping at outlet stores selling **Liberty of London, Marks & Spencer, Laura Ashley,** and other name-brand goods at discount.

And did I mention the warehouses of antiques?

My guess is that once you discover how much is going on in Manchester and the area, you won't even have time for London.

MY MANCHESTER

. . . .

As you read this, I'm off humming a few bars from the musical *Hair*, you know the part: "Manchester, England, England, across the Atlantic Sea and I'm a genius-genius . . ."

Well I am a genius-genius, because I have put together a total Manchester of my own imagining that gives you so much of the north country experience that you may not mind that my geography is a little bit off. I put Chester—a mere 40 miles from Manchester—into the Wales chapter. But Stoke-on-Trent and York are here because it's easier to get to both from Manchester.

This chapter is meant to represent *my* Manchester and to me, Manchester is a nice city, but it's a *great* destination. Sure, I want you to come to Manchester to shop and to visit and, hey, why not take in the culture (great science museum, good theater, big university town)—but what impresses me the most about this town is the way it draws you in and surrounds you with all the country experiences you ever wanted to have.

Getting to know Manchester means:

- Antiquing in the string of villages right outside the city proper.
- Hitting the giant car boot sale in Trafford Park on the waterfront.
- Getting into the big-name outlet stores.

- Catching the views of hill and dale as you drive to sources and resources.
- Shopping the jumble markets at Tommyfields or joining the daily market carnival at Ashton-under-Lyne.
- Buying antiques from real insider's sources.
- Checking out the brand-new American-style factory outlet mall that has become one of the new hot spots in Britain.
- Day tripping to the honey-pot cities of Harrogate, Chester, or York.
- Finishing up your triumphant shop-a-thon with a day or two in The Potteries, home to more than 30 outlet stores selling discounted dishes!

Yes, I am a genius, because now I understand the difference between London and the rest of England.

THE LAY OF THE LAND

Manchester sits on almost on the western coast of England. The major port city today is neighboring Liverpool, yet years ago, in the industrial heyday, Manchester had enough access to the sea that its docks competed with those in Liverpool. Because of its location in northern England, where the island is at a more narrow part, Manchester is not that far from what are considered eastern parts of England, like York.

Manchester proper is sort of like Los Angeles: There's scads of little cities out there on the fringe, each with its own personality, and each only a few minutes away. It behooves you to study a map or learn some of the basic suburbs, because if you look up something in the phone book or get driving directions from someone, they will undoubtedly mention these various little towns. The lay of the land here takes some learning, so memorize the map on page 225. We'll have a pop quiz next Thursday.

Manchester

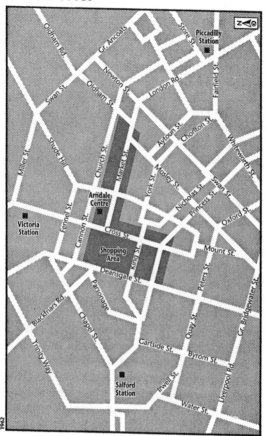

GETTING THERE

. . . .

By Plane

Since Manchester has one of the snazziest airports in the United Kingdom, it's pretty easy to get there. The airport services a population base of some 27 million people, so don't think you're flying into any dinky airport or a second-rate country facility.

As in London, **British Airways** has one terminal that is almost exclusively devoted to it. There is a second terminal for all the other carriers that serve Manchester. I mention this because 75 other airlines serve Manchester, so you can see the immediate benefit of picking the airline with its own terminal. American Airlines is making a big move on Manchester and is advertising heavily; even Continental Airlines now flies to Manchester. There are also Chicago-to-Manchester nonstops and a bevy of other gateway plans.

If you insist, there is also hourly shuttle service from London via BA, so you can connect through any of the London area airports. There is also frequent service between EU capital cities, so you can avoid London and segue right into Manchester.

Please note that most airlines will allow you to fly into one U.K. airport and out of another at no additional charge.

By Train

You can indeed get to Manchester from London, or just about anyplace else via the train. There is now Eurostar connection service directly through Waterloo's International Terminal so that you can make the trip to Paris in about six hours.

Also note that Manchester has several train stations, so do pay attention to what station you need in order to get to where you're going.

GETTING AROUND
. . . .
By Foot

Downtown Manchester proper is walkable. Allow more than one day to fully explore it.

By Car

There are car rental agencies galore at the Manchester airport as well as in downtown Manchester and in some of the villages that dot the city's perimeter.

Driving Times from Manchester to Nearby Cities

City	Time (minutes)
Chester	45
Conwy, North Wales	90
Harrogate	70
Liverpool	60
London	4 hours
Stoke-on-Trent	55
York	90

Hertz (tel. 161/872-8667) is located at the Piccadilly train station in Manchester; it sells BritRail train and drive packages that include your car rental. **Avis** (tel. 161/872-9020) can also provide on-the-spot relief.

Don't forget about **Kemwel**, which you must book before you arrive in the United Kingdom. You can arrange a rental over the phone or via fax for incredibly low rates. Kemwel uses local representatives, so it only has airport offices in Manchester. Kemwel rents cars by multiday plans, so you can get a three-day plan, a seven-day plan, and so on. I recently priced a seven-day rental with a midsized car in peak season for $345.69 with automatic transmission or $259.26 with manual transmission (minus collision insurance in both cases). There is a two-day request period for automatic transmission. Call 800/678-0678 in the United States for reservations. There are assorted promotion plans, benefits, lease programs, and deals, so ask for information on all of them. There is no extra drop-off charge if you return the car to a different location than the one from which you picked it up, as long as the location is within Great Britain.

By Car Service

Power Executive Transport is an executive car service owned by Roy Power that provides chauffeurs and guides. You can have them together and in uniform at one price, or you can get a driver (sans uniform) to drive a less fancy car or your rental car. To reserve, call 161/339-0724 or fax 161/343-1505.

You might want to try **Heritage Driver's Club,** an official black taxi service that rents out at £48 for four hours and £100 for eight. For reservations, call local phone 161/834-7751.

There are also car agencies that sell but also *rent* cars for a day or a week. They offer free pick up and delivery, cars, vans, and chauffeurs, and will provide "meet and greet" service at the airport. Make sure that rates include VAT; you don't want any 17.5% surprises later on. Two good ones that my friend Liz recommends are: **Airport Executive Cars,** contact Karen McLean (161/499-3322), and **Woods Car Rental** (161/437-1080).

By Taxi

To order a taxi in Manchester, call **Mantax** at 161/236-5133.

SLEEPING IN MANCHESTER

Manchester has city center hotels for businesspeople, but also a number of hotels located so far out of the city proper that they are practically in the burbs. Because Manchester is striving to make it on its own with Americans, its hotels have recently begun connecting with U.S. booking agents. There is a booking agency in New Jersey called **Alexander and Richardson** (tel. 800/773-5454), which represents many hotels in the Manchester spread—my name for the area around Manchester International Airport. Some of the hotels listed below are members of this booking group.

ETROP GRANGE
Outwood Lane at Manchester Airport, Manchester

I'm not quite sure how progress didn't destroy this property, but the hotel was built as a manor house in 1780 and is virtually unchanged to this day, with the exceptional roar of an occasional plane. There are about 40 rooms and a handful of suites; rooms are small but decorated to the nines with old-fashioned big beds (some with canopies) and antique furnishings.

Entering the house is like taking a step back into history—a rather bizarre notion if you consider that you are within walking distance of the airport. The kitchen is famous locally. Best yet, the weekend rates are laughably low and even weekday, peak season rates are sensational: A suite with spa and living room goes for £135 weekday; £99.50 on a weekend. A four-poster room is about £110 peak; £89.50 on weekends. And these prices include VAT! For reservations from the U.S., call 800/462-2748; or local phone: 161/499-0500.

VICTORIA & ALBERT HOTEL
Water Street, Manchester

If you prefer an in-town location and a totally different kind of charm, then only the V&A will do. This hotel is built into a rehabbed warehouse on a canal across the street from Granada Studios. If that's not good enough, consider the fact that some of the rooms are named and decorated to the theme of some of Granada's big-time TV productions.

The standard rooms still have warehouse details and exposed pipes and bricks as befitting a Victorian warehouse. The decor is certainly unusual and entertaining, but wait till you get a look at the prices and promotions. The regular rack rate is about £125, but there are seasonal promotional rates of £65 to £80 a night, which can include free entry into nearby Granada Studios.

Children under the age of 16 can have their own room for 50% off rack rate or share their parents' room for free. Many *Coronation Street* tours are booked through the hotel; don't miss Sunday breakfast overlooking the canal. For reservations, call local phone: 161/832-1188.

HOLIDAY INN CROWNE PLAZA
Peter Street, Manchester

I'm not going to tell you that this is one of the nicest Holiday Inn Crowne Plazas in the world or that I am crazy for this hotel. But it's a rehab of the most famous hotel in town and it's got a great location. The hallways are rather sterile and the lobby is a crime, but the concierge is superb and the breakfast buffet is the place to do business in downtown Manchester. This is the former Midland Hotel; the outside structure is to die for—too bad about the circa 1970 lobby. Some locals still call this The Midland, so beware.

This is a five-star hotel, but I prefer the cozy nature of the other choices. It's up to you. There are some promotions but the rate can be over £100 per night. For reservations from the United States, call 800/HOLIDAY; or dial local phone: 161/236-3333.

THE COACH HOUSE
Westerhill, Ashton-under-Lyne

This is a self-catered apartment in the outskirts of Manchester; you must have a car to get here. If you are American you must also have an adventuresome spirit because this is an apartment, not a five-star hotel. The washing machine is outside in the back. The dishwasher is in the big, fully equipped kitchen. You have a big bedroom, a small bedroom, and a den with a sofa bed, so you can easily sleep five in the apartment. It's rented by the week; the cost is approximately £300. Call local phone: 161/343-7100 or fax: 161/343-7030 for reservations.

BEECH TREE HOUSE
2 Park Road, Hale

Staying at Beech Tree House in Cheshire is like being
a guest at the retreat of a country artist who occa-
sionally has a few friends in to spend the night.

A Victorian home that has been redecorated and
hand painted (even the furniture) by artist-in-residence
Barbara Wilde-Reynolds, this bed-and-breakfast's
location gives you better access to southern parts of
Manchester, Wales, and Chester.

They do not have a fax machine and have no
intention of getting one. They are also appalled by
the thought of using a U.S. hotel booking agent.
"We're very old-fashioned people, you can write us
a letter," they suggest. Therefore, please either write
to them c/o 2 Park Road, Hale, Cheshire, WA 15 9
NJ, or phone for reservations. Local phone: 161/
927-7027. They provide free airport or train station transfers.

SHRIGLEY HALL HOTEL & GOLF COUNTRY CLUB
Macclesfield

For those who want to stay on the Chesire side of
Manchester and don't particularly want to stay in a
bed-and-breakfast, a Regency manor house set into
about 300 acres of lush English countryside should
probably do the trick. For reservations, please call
local phone: 1625/575-757; fax: 1625/573-323.

NUNSMERE HALL
Tarporley Road, Sandiway

This is also in Cheshire and is perhaps my favorite
property in the whole area, a drop-dead fantasy
manor house hotel. If you can't afford to sleep here
(rooms are approximately £150 per night), do come
for dinner or at least tea and croquet. Simply splendid, my dear. For reservations, call local phone:
1606/889-100; fax: 1606/889-055.

KILHEY COURT HOTEL
Chorely Road, Wigan

This is a smallish hotel that gives you all the amenities of a four-star lodging while still being in the Lancashire part of town. For reservations, call local phone: 1257/472-100; fax: 1257/422-401.

SHOPPING MANCHESTER

· ·

The beauty of shopping in Manchester is what you buy in all the nearby towns. (I told you to study that map.)

If you've ever traveled to London and taken day trips to Bath and Brighton to search for antiques and shopping bargains, only to find none, then you'll appreciate shopping in Manchester and the Manchester vicinity. Manchester and its nearby towns are the last home of the bargain.

Shopping in Manchester is fabulous because it's funky. Sure, there's modern malls and English multiples and you can buy designer clothes and even buy Giorgio Armani. To me, this kind of shopping misses the point. Manchester shopping is for the person who

Manchester & More

I did a special project for the city of Manchester called **Born to Shop: Manchester & More**, which is a full-color folding brochure that works sort of like a map and is loaded with information and pictures that really make Manchester come alive. (Ian took the pictures, of course.) This guide is given away at BTA offices in the U.S. but costs £3 in Manchester, where it is sold at Tourist Information Centres and all major bookstores. This is a nonprofit project and we're very proud of it; if one picture is worth a thousand words, when you see the 50 pictures in this guide you will flip!

wants to wear casual clothes, get in the car and on the road, and seek out jumble and junk. Manchester is one of the last bastions of antique stores that offer real finds; of tiles and fireplaces and rain gutters from Victorian homes that are ready to be shipped to your home back in the United States. Manchester is what separates dedicated shoppers from neophytes.

Manchester is not a fancy town. Don't get me wrong, it's a huge business center and people aren't out in the streets wearing wooden clogs. But you choose to go to Manchester as a tourist and as a shopper because you want fresh insight into country looks, you want to get out of town and mix with real people and see real sheep, you want a casual and comfortable prowl through mills and dusty junk and someone else's castoffs. If you want to dress up and take high tea, go to London. If you want to get back to nature, to get back to basics and bargains and shopping as an adventure, then Manchester is for you and yours. And you can still have tea, honest.

Shopping Downtown

Central Manchester is a compact area but it does has a few neighborhoods that can shift moods quickly, even within a few blocks. The core of the downtown area can easily be walked and shopped in a day. Because Manchester is a big city, the downtown shopping is mostly real-people retail for businesspeople and includes the usual English multiples and big modern shopping malls. Since I don't send you to Manchester to go to a shopping mall, I'll point you to a few areas but concentrate on what I think may be special to either American or British visitors.

The architecture of much of downtown Manchester is spectacular: Please keep your eyes peeled upward. The new modern malls are boxy and ugly, true, but there is cute interspersed accordingly. There is no "cute" center core, like in York or some of the honey-pot villages, but each corner you round can take your breath away with the drama of the buildings. Be sure to walk into the town hall with a package of masking tape—you'll need it to hold your jaw together when you see the glamour of the first-floor space.

The main shopping street, which is one of the pedestrian streets, is King Street, which hosts most of the upscale multiples. If you need to have your hair done, there's a branch of **Vidal Sassoon** at 19-21 King. If you just want to shop the best of Britain, most of it is laid out in a few blocks of easy outdoor shopping. Other multiples here include the usual suspects; see pages 242–243 for a listing.

But don't misjudge Manchester as a one-trick pony or as the kind of place that has only one main street or one shopping area. There's a core that spreads around a little bit and takes in quite a wealth of British retail.

Market Street, one block over from King, also has a fair number of the kinds of places you, or your teens, will want to check out. The inimitable **Shelly's**, the shoe shop of all shoe shops, is located on Market Street (No. 42) as is the far more upscale and subdued **Nicole Farhi** (No. 6).

Arndale Centre is the big downtown mall a few blocks away: It takes up an entire city block. It has several hundred stores and a food court. Any kind of real-people shopping you may need is here, as are branches of most multiples including **Boots, The Body Shop, Knickerbox, Miss Selfridge, Mothercare, Principles, Richards, Wallis, HMV,** and an enormous **W. H. Smith,** the bookseller and newsagent. If you've done King Street, you probably don't need a trip to the mall. If it's raining, you may prefer the mall.

Marks & Spencer is in a huge store across the street from Arndale Centre; this is the largest M&S after the Marble Arch flagship store in London.

The immediate area around King Street, particularly St. Ann Street, has a big square (with a taxi stand at the end) and a few narrow streets with stores, arcades, and a few secondhand agencies.

Police Street is more of an alley than a real street, but it's packed with cute stores. Because of the large university population, Manchester has several stores that feature young, hip, cutting-edge clothes.

Take a look at Deansgate, the main shopping street where the House of Fraser–owned local department store Kendals hosts the basics (including a small food hall that sells some Harrods brands foodstuffs). Kendals also sells theater tickets now and has a personal shopping service à la the big American department stores.

T. Hayward & Sons is owned by Lawley's, the big London china shop; find it at 62-66 Deansgate. Rumor has it that Harvey Nichols (see page 120 in London) will come to town in the near future. But people have been gossiping about Harvey Nichols' expansion plans for years. John Lewis has indeed just opened up in the burbs.

King Street, the main pedestrian shopping street, leads away from the St. Ann's area and into the financial district when it crosses Cross Street. This far end of King Street hosts a few interesting shops including a free-standing Emporio, Giorgio Armani's tribute to yuppies the world over. Yes, they even have yuppies in Manchester.

Finds

WILLOUGHBY'S
53 Cross Street, Manchester

At first glance this looks like simply an old-fashioned wine store—old, yes, but not unusual. Well, step right in folks and get past the wine to the back of the store where management prides itself on the selection of single-malt whiskies. They post world-renowned beer and malt whisky expert Michael Jackson's rating system (see page 327) and will mail to any address in the United Kingdom. Prices (and selection) are exactly the same as in Scotland!

ROYAL EXCHANGE
Cross Street, Manchester

This is sort of a rehab and minimall that doesn't warrant a lot of attention, but there is an antique arcade on the lower level basement that will give you a nice browse.

I fell in love with one particular dealer, **The Antiques Fireplace,** because of the selection of Victorian tiles. There were two or three other dealers who specialized in Dinky and Corgi as well as old train sets. My favorite dealer of all sells embroidered slogans from World War I—these are hard to explain, but the dealer knows me and will show you what I'm talking about.

ELITE DRESS AGENCY
35 King Street West, Manchester

Be still, my heart. You won't believe this, but there are times when I look in my closet, discover I have nothing to wear, and consider flying to Manchester just to be able to shop at Elite. Elite sells gently worn designer clothes at not London prices: My Louis Feraud dress at £90 was the steal of the century. How did I let the cream silk Armani (£100) get past me?

I found a twin set in yellow and white angora, circa 1960, that was worthy of a trip to Graceland, but the asking price of £39 did not strike me as a real bargain. I guess I was feeling tight that day. Regret is my middle name.

There's another part to the store across the alley; there's also menswear. Like all of these kinds of stores, it is a matter of hit or miss. But I have really scored some hits lately. There are a few branch stores in the burbs, by the way, but the mother shop is right downtown and should be your first stop in Manchester.

AFFLECKS PALACE
52 Church Street, Manchester

Another source for secondhand clothes, this one is totally different in feeling from Elite. Afflecks Palace is a run-down building that is currently inhabited by a bunch of stalls of either young, hip design students from the university or vintage clothing dealers. Much of the vintage is sublime. Although the building is a little bit funky, don't be put off. This is fabulous fun.

MANCHESTER CRAFT CENTRE
17 Oak Street, Manchester

This is slightly off the beaten path downtown, but not far, and easily within walking distance if you know where you are going. It's easiest to hop a cab and then take a card from the taxi firm so you can call for a pick-up if you so desire.

The center is sensational and well worth the adventure of going slightly out of your way. The barn-style building has two floors of workshops; you just shop your way up and down and around. This isn't one of those cute artsy places; many of the stalls are held by very serious designers who could break in to the biggest stores. I've bought clothing and even hats here, so don't think we're talking raku and resin.

QUARRY BANK MILL
Styal, Manchester

Quarry Bank Mill is part of the rehab at Styal Country Park, one of those Williamsburg-type of preservation historical sights. This happens to be one of the best of the type I've ever been to; the mill itself has a fabulous tour with waterwheel and gift shop. In the shop you can buy Styal souvenirs and booklets, local souvenirs, and yard goods from the mill that makes fabrics for National Historic Trust. There's also a calico range of printed fabrics.

MANCHESTER RESOURCES FROM A–Z

. . . .

American Chain Stores

As in other British cities, American retail is climbing the walls and overrunning the high streets. It's not enough to watch out for McDonald's, now there's The Gap, Disney Store, and Warner Brothers Studio Store, to name a few. Talbot's has just joined the fray.

Antiques

The entire area surrounding Manchester is fabulous for antiquing. If you want to get technical about it, once you are out of metropolitan Manchester, you may be in any number of counties as you seek the best antiques ... Lancashire, Cheshire, Yorkshire, etc.

There are a variety of types of stores, from dusty attic style to warehouses filled with staircases and chimneys. One of the things I like is that there aren't that many hoity-toity shops; you stand a much better chance of finding real country looks at affordable prices. On the other hand, you have to be the kind of person who likes to look. This type of shopping is for someone who thinks the thrill of the chase is half the fun.

Also please compare the mill shop list with the antique shop list. There are some areas or little villages that are chockablock with antique shops; other times you're more looking at a drive in the country and three or four big stops in a day including a combination of antique stores and mill shops. Is there a more perfect day?

Before I get into specific listings, let talk about a few general notions:

• **Chester.** Chester is about 45 minutes away from Manchester; you can get there by car, bus, or train. Chester has a long-standing reputation as a honeypot city and an antique shop paradise. Be sure to make a stop in **Boughton,** a suburb of Chester, where antique shops line Christleton Road. Do not get confused with Broughton, which is right across the Welsh border from Chester.

Also remember that Chester's antique center is a little out from the main touristy part of town. If you come via BritRail, you may want to spring for a few taxi rides to get to some of these neighborhoods for a more complete look at the antique picture in Chester. Downtown Chester has lost a lot of its antique stores during the recession; you'll need to branch out. Boughton offers the time of your life.

- **Royal Exchange.** The Royal Exchange is right in downtown Manchester, across from Marks & Sparks. I've listed it on page 236. The basement has an antique arcade.
- **Car Boot Sales.** They're everywhere; they're mostly on weekends. Read local papers. See page 247 for my favorite in the Manchester area at Trafford Park on Sunday.
- **Charnock Richard.** I have a listing on this venue on page 241. It makes for a nice Sunday in the country. Combine this with an early morning visit to the car boot sale in **Trafford Park,** a little Sunday in Manchester retail therapy and dinner in Manchester's Chinatown and you've got paradise.
- **Stockport and Levenshulme.** These are two separate burbs known for their junk stores. They are not far apart, but you do need a car and some patience. You will not spend hours here but you will find some good shops.
- **Liverpool.** I've been to Liverpool but haven't gotten into the antique warehouses that are supposedly numerous. My friend Ruth and I have it on our agendas for next year. There are antique shippers and trade-only resources in the Smithdown Road/Lark Lane area. There is a regular car boot sale every Sunday on Dock Road.
- **Prestwich.** Prestwich is 3 miles out from Manchester city center. Travel on Bury New Road where

the shops all line one side of the street. You park on the pavement outside the stores. Or take Metrolink and walk five minutes. A fine half-day adventure for a string of small shops with affordable finds.

NOSTALGIA
61 Shaw Heath, Stockport

This is my favorite antique shop in the Manchester area, possibly because I am a total freak for Victorian tiles. If you're looking for furniture, this isn't the place. If you want a sink, a tub, a fireplace, a surround, some faucets, or tiles, step this way. The street level is small; upstairs there's a few small salons and then a giant attic crammed with big pieces—almost an architectural salvage kind of a place. The pieces are all original; they'll tell you if something is repro or rebuilt. They're so incredible that anyone with a period home, in the United States or the United Kingdom, should shop here for the toilet, tub, and faucets of your dreams.

Speaking of faucets, I priced brand-new repro models in the United States and they cost more than originals at Nostalgia. And you can pack faucets in your luggage.

Downstairs, on the street level, the shop is filled with fireplaces, surrounds, and tiles on boards. They do sell reproduction Victorian tiles, which happen to be more expensive than the real thing. Prices marked on the tiles represent an installed price, so if you are taking tiles home with you—get a new price. Tiles are priced according to condition, to the number in the set (they are most frequently sold in lots), and the quality of the workmanship. I bought 12 tiles for £24; they wrapped them for me and I packed them right in my suitcase—no problem, no breakage. I made a sideboard with a tile inset; come over anytime and see it.

THE ANTIQUES VILLAGE
Stockport Road, Levenshulme

Located in Levenshulme in a block of ticky-tacky antique shops that are just the kind you want to browse if you can tell the good, the bad, and the ugly apart. It's in a funny old building—with sensational tiles in the lobby—and then a few other little shops.

CHARNOCK RICHARD
Chorley

This is a professional flea market and super Sunday outing that everyone knows about—this is no secret little market where you might happen upon a bargain from an unsuspecting dealer who never heard of Clarice Cliff. Charnock Richard is near an amusement park called Camelot next to the Park Hall Hotel Conference Centre. For a day in the country, it's looking very developed. Don't freak.

You pay £1 to enter and find yourself in a big hall (ladies room to the right as you enter); on either side of this main hall is another hall. You're talking three good-sized rooms with tables laid to form aisles, each table laden with collectibles. This is good stuff sold from knowledgeable dealers. I found the two side rooms to be a little more flexible.

If you come here directly from the car boot sale in Trafford Park, you will have a hard time adjusting to real prices. After everything costs £3 in a car boot sale (£10 tops), it's hard to look at a blue and white Staffordshire platter for £30. Actually, £30 is a rather fair price, but you may have some psychological setbacks if you aren't prepared.

There is a small cafe in the back part of one of the side halls (the one to your right if the front door is to your back when you enter).

ANDY THORNTON ARCHITECTURAL ANTIQUES
Elland, West Yorkshire

Mr. Thornton thinks he is the Disneyland of the antique business. If Bygone Times lacks authenticity—

as a venue, I'm not talking about the merchandise—well, Thornton's warehouse must rank as an attraction built in the English countryside to lure American and Japanese tourists who are suckers for Cute.

Thornton's property, officially called **Victoria Mills** by some, claims to have the largest stock of architectural antiques in the United Kingdom. They admit that a lot of their goods are repro. The two are mixed together.

This is the kind of place where you can buy the wood panels for walls for your library, an entire bar, some flooring or beams, and doors, steeples, and smaller accessories for home or barn. Much of the stuff is magnificent; much of it is overpriced. If money is not an object and you enjoy waltzing around the English countryside buying containers full of furniture, you may enjoy shopping here. Open: 8:30am to 5pm Monday through Friday; Saturdays 9am to 5pm; Sundays 10am to 5pm.

PRECINCT JEWELERS
20 Mercian Way, Ashton-under-Lyne

This small jewelry shop happens to be owned by my friend Raymond who sells very good real jewelry. But he has a personal interest in antique timepieces and also has a collection of cameos. The store is closed on Tuesday (traditional mill closing day).

Big Names

These are branch stores of well-known multiples or internationally famous designers who have shops in the downtown Manchester area. Various malls through the area also have an array of multiples as well as specialty shops that carry an assortment of designer labels. Anything you might need is in central Manchester's downtown district, including King Street—which has a pedestrian mall walking street down one portion of it—Market Street, St. Ann's Square, and Deansgate. One look at the map will show you how these streets all connect.

THE BODY SHOP
Royal Exchange, Manchester
Manchester Airport

EMPORIO ARMANI
84 King Street, Manchester

NICOLE FARHI
6 Market Street, Manchester

FRENCH CONNECTION
6 Market Street, Manchester

HABITAT
14 John Dalton Street, Manchester

LIBERTY
30 King Street, Manchester

KAREN MILLEN
48 King Street, Manchester

MONSOON
13 King Street, Manchester

PAST TIMES
6 St. Ann's Square, Manchester

THORNTON'S
Arndale Centre, Manchester
Manchester Airport

Books

DILLONS
2-4 St. Ann's Square, Manchester
124 Market Street, Piccadilly, Manchester

Branches of the big chain; St. Ann's is right in the heart of town. Can't miss it; don't miss it.

WATERSTONES
17 St. Ann's Square, Manchester
91 Deansgate, Manchester

Ditto the above.

Department Stores

BHS
Arndale Centre, Manchester

Lower to moderate price range department store with goods for the entire family as well as the home. Don't let the name (BHS stands for British Home Stores) mislead you into thinking they only sell home furnishings.

DEBENHAMS
Market Street, Manchester

It's Macy's.

KENDALS
Deansgate, Manchester

The original Manchester department store and perhaps the first in Britain, this is an old-fashioned department store—the kind that takes up almost a whole city block.

LEWIS'S
Market Street, Manchester

A local department store. Not to be confused with John Lewis, one of Britain's leading department stores, which is opening at Cheadle in Stockport.

LITTLEWOOD'S
Arndale Centre, Manchester

A low-end department store for the masses.

MARKS & SPENCER
St. Ann's Square, Manchester

Located at the far side of St. Ann's Square—the main downtown square—with the Arndale Centre across the street, this Marks & Spencer branch takes up just about an entire city block.

Designer Clothing

Manchester has a branch of **Armani's Emporio** but lacks the free-standing designer stores and big names you find in London and even in Glasgow. Instead, the local tradition—as it is in Italy and many French towns, etc.—is for a handful of very fancy dress shops to carry exclusive rights to specific designers.

RICHARD CREME
Barton Arcade, Manchester

Barton Arcade is a rehab, an incredible frosting of architectural bliss right in the heart of downtown Manchester that has been converted to a mall. From the outside, the building gives pure delight. I've never found the inside very satisfying, but Richard Creme is famous to locals as the place where rock stars buy their rags and where big-name designers of cutting-edge chic, like **Gaultier** and Moschino, can be bought. Right off St. Ann's Square.

DE LA MODE
24 Deansgate, Manchester

In the shadow of the department store Kendels, this boutique specializes in British designers whose names carry cult proportions in London and in the Filofaxes of the international-style Mafia, but who can't make it on their own in smaller towns, or even Paris. Check out work by **Sara Sturgeon, John Rocha, Ally Capellino,** etc.

LISA STIRLING
17-19 St. Ann's Street

This isn't a very large shop, sort of a double small boutique, but it's packed with mostly Italian designers and is one of the best stores in town for fashionable big names, including **Dolce & Gabbana, Max Mara, Moschino,** etc.

Factory Outlets

I've divided this into two parts since I think of factory outlets as an Americanized concept, often associated with outlet malls. Mill shops are the real British version of an outlet. Original local talent is listed under "Mill Shops," whereas here I'll just mention **Cheshire Oaks**, an American-style outlet mall with stores for Principles, Richards, Viyella, Scotch House, Paul Costelloe, Wallis, and assorted American names from their U.K. divisions: Timberland, Liz Claiborne, and Nike. Cheshire Oaks has been developed in two phases of approximately 30 stores, each built in a triangle shape. There is a McDonald's.

Cheshire Oaks is at Junction 10 of the M53. Hours are Monday through Saturday from 10am to 6pm and Sunday 10am to 4pm.

Markets

Because Manchester is made up of a series of many villages, you can still enjoy the old-fashioned practice of shopping market day. Every day is market day someplace—or many places. Several of these markets have a jumble day in which at least part of the market is a flea market.

A word of warning about these markets: These are real markets, not used to many tourists and seldom visited by American tourists. Mostly they cater to local trade and generations of mill workers. Dress down. All markets are served by public transportation.

Please note that these markets are so completely genuine that you may not find anything that interests you. On regular market days, there's food and dry goods—a few stalls may sell seconds from the mills. Prices are pretty low in that the customers just don't have much money; on the other hand, you are not talking Portobello Road here. Markets are more a lesson in fun: Eat homemade donuts while you browse fruit and flower stalls, sample local cheeses, admire the food halls, and find a few things you may not find elsewhere.

When it comes to "antiques," well, you have to get lucky; you have to have a good eye. These markets are for "pickers," those people who have the ability to look at a mound of junk and ferret out the few really good pieces that deserve to be collected or resold.

The two most famous markets are **Tommyfields** and **Ashton-under-Lyne**. Tommyfields has a flea market on Wednesdays; you need to go early in the morning (8am) for the best look; the market begins to pack up around 2pm. The stalls are outdoors. The market is in front of an indoor market of real-people goods (boring) that's in front of a modern mall (boring). With about 300 stalls, the Wednesday flea market is probably the biggest and best in the area.

Ashton-under-Lyne has an enormous outdoor market as well as a cute, old-fashioned market hall with traditional food halls. There is an open market every day except Sunday (Saturday is almost a carnival day), but the flea market for jumble is on Tuesdays. There are about 200 dealers at the flea market; I did spot a pair of very fine 1930s hand-painted pitchers, but the vendor refused to bargain with me and then packed up the pitchers and put them away. The indoor market is closed on Tuesdays.

My favorite Sunday market for pure junky fun is the car boot sale at **Trafford Park**. Trafford Park is an industrial estate on the water, not too far from central Manchester. Like most English car boot sales, this one includes some new merchandise and goods sold at more or less the regular discount price in town and then a host of secondhand dealers who sell from their cars. Other Manchester area flea market days include:

- Farnworth: Monday
- Grey Mare Lane, Bradford: Friday
- Denhill Road, Moss Side: Monday

- Church Lane, Harpurhey: Thursday
- Gortoncross Street, Gorton: Monday
- Oldham General Market: Wednesday
- 33 Market Street, Rochdale: Tuesday
- Wood Street, Middleton: Tuesday
- Salford Market, Salford: Thursday
- Pendlebury Market, Pendlebury: Wednesday
- Market Place, Stockport: Tuesday
- Market Square, Ashton-under-Lyne: Tuesday
- Market Street, Denton: Thursday
- Tommyfields Market, Oldham: Wednesday

Mill Shops

A mill shop is what an American might call a factory outlet. Since the industrial north is dotted with mills and there are very few developed factory outlet malls as in America (there is one on the east coast of England past York in Hull), the mills themselves have little stores for workers and sometimes the public.

There are booklets and brochures, some free, some for sale, in bookstores that will guide you to mill after mill.

LIBERTY MILL SHOP
Widow Hill Road, Heasandford Industrial Estate, Burnley

Our visit to Liberty remains one of my personal triumphs because we had a ball there and it was worth the struggle. Furthermore, I know that had I asked a man (like my husband or Ian) to drive me here, we would not be speaking today. Only another woman—and a shopping maven at that—would go this far for a look-see and be able to laugh over it.

The Liberty mill shop is in the middle of nowhere in an industrial park that is not quaint. Even getting to the right part of the car park is difficult.

When we wandered in it just so happened to be during a sale period, so there were two parts to shop—the normal store and a room upstairs in the offices that was filled with bins of goodies. This is where we bought the silk ties for £3 each.

The normal part of the mill shop had lots of nice merchandise with a good selection of fabrics at the far end. Prices were lower than regular London retail, but some items seemed to be a steal and others only moderately discounted. I bought a handsome wash kit for £8, which costs £17 in the store; I saw it myself. I bought a little notebook with a notepad and a miniature flask in it for £10—the world's best gift item. I saw a fabric tote bag for $100 that was well worth that price, but I wasn't feeling that flush.

If you are heading out this way, you might want to call for directions (local phone: 1282/424-600) or a divorce attorney. Note that because this listing is in an industrial estate, they are not open on weekends. Furthermore, they close at 4pm on weekdays. They do take credit cards and allow you to file for a VAT refund.

A. SANDERSON & SONS
2 Pollard Street, Ancoats, Manchester

The store is medium sized by British standards and has grocery store–style carts, don't ask me why. Most of the stock is fabric, although there are little niches for pillows, bed linens, wallpaper, etc. There are also travel kits (called "wash bags" by the British) and little shoeshine kits and various items made of quilted Sandersons fabrics that are delicious and well priced. They make for great gifts.

For those of you who aren't quite on the varsity decorating team, Sanderson is one of the most famous names in English printed fabrics. The outlet store has rows and rows of bolts of fabric, although when I asked if I'd be able to do 33 yards in the same dye lot, I got a big no. Fret not. There were so many patterns I would kill for that I got a headache. I spent a very long time here and came away with a few things I love, at £5 per yard, so I can't complain. But I did not redo my entire home.

Besides chintz there were silks, damasks, and wools; nothing cost more than £7 per yard. Some of these fabrics are worth £50 per yard. Also gift items (possibly the best in town) for £5 and less.

I also bought a king-sized duvet cover in a fabulous Sanderson print for about $40. This was not as cheap (I mean, inexpensive) as the one at Musbury (see below) for $25, but it's of an entirely different design and surely beats the $150 I would have paid for a similar item in the United States.

You can get here via bus or taxi; it's not that far from downtown. Don't miss it.

MUSBURY FABRICS
Park Mill, Holcombe Road, Helmshore, Rossendale, Lancashire

While they sell fabrics off the bolt at Musbury, they are ugly fabrics, and I do not trot you out for ugly fabrics. It's the other stuff that Musbury has that's glorious: towels, duvet covers, sheets, pillows, even dishes. The rather large space is crammed with bins and tables and racks of goods. It's also crammed with shoppers. Musbury manufactures for several brand names, so you may recognize some of the labels. In Britspeak, the term "famous chain store" means Marks & Spencer.

I bought a yellow and white striped all-cotton duvet cover, king size, for £13. Why didn't I buy two? Or three?

Please note that Musbury is in a teeny tiny town where there's another small mill shop and a cute tourist trap pine store, etc. It's in a beautiful part of the countryside. They take credit cards and are open seven days a week, from 9am to 5pm.

MARKS
149 Holland Street, Denton, Tameside

Well, you can't get much plainer than that, can you? This is one of several Marks & Spencer outlet stores in the immediate Manchester area. It also has goods from a few other makers. The store sells grade-A seconds, which means you won't find the damages; clothes are half the store price. The store specializes in women's work clothes and dressier fashions. Other M&S outlets are less fancy and less expensive.

CHAINSTORE FACTORY SHOP
72 Richmond Street, Ashton-under-Lyne, Tameside

Love the clever name, huh? This store is near where Carolyn stables her horse (Nimbus), so we go by quite frequently. This is another Marks outlet, but this one is not dressy and has menswear and children's clothing. I bought a man's wool blazer—absolutely gorgeous—for £25. No cashmere sweaters.

TRENCHERFIELD MILL
Wigan Pier, Wigan

I didn't like Trencherfield Mill that much and wouldn't even mention it except it's located at a fabulous place that does make for a wonderful stop and a total destination with only a little peek into the mill shop.

Trencherfield Mill is next door to Wigan Pier, which is this whole show (complete with trip on a river bus) about industrial life in England. You have to pay for the whole tour but you can go to the Wigan Pier gift shop and the mill shop for free.

There's a pretty good gift shop; then, across the river (see that little bridge?), you get to walk to the real mill (which has a cafeteria, snacks, and clean bathrooms) and pop into the mill shop. It sells mostly bedding and I admit that I saw a duvet cover I thought I would kill for, but it didn't go with anything in my house.

Locals come from miles around to snatch up the bargains on sheets and towels. Closed Fridays but open every other day of the week, including Sunday, from 11am to 5pm.

BOUNDARY MILL
Burnley Road, Colne, Lancashire

Boundary is a giant space broken down into a few rooms on the far side, but mostly just divided up by makers. There are signs, some of which won't mean anything to American shoppers who may not be familiar with English brand names. Certainly, Laura Ashley and Rodier will catch your attention. Alexon is another upmarket British brand.

The clothes are new but they are at least a year old.

There's clothing for every member of the family, shoes, bed linens, and even raincoats. Open from 10am to 6pm Monday through Friday; 10am to 5pm Saturday and Sunday. I got lost in the hills around here and it was spectacularly gorgeous.

BROADSTONE HOUSE
Broadstone Road, Reddish, Stockport

The mill finishes and processes garments for Marks & Spencer. What it sells didn't pass M&S muster and is therefore one-half the regular retail price— bargains galore!

Ian bought corduroy trousers (£16.99) and cotton shirts (£9.99); I bought a fabulous polyester dress-up, see-through blouse (with camisole) for £15.99. I admit that sometimes you can get silk for that price, but polyester is great for travel because you can wash it out on the road.

The factory does make the famous St. Michael brand underwear, which they also sell. Open: Monday through Thursday from 9:30am to 4pm; Friday 9:30am to 3pm; Saturday 9am to 1pm. Closed Sunday.

BEANS OF BRADFORD
203 Westgate, Bradford, Yorkshire

A dressy version of Boundary Mill, with men's, women's, and home furnishing items spread out over three floors crammed with last year's merchandise and a few classics. The crowd is very well dressed and some of the brand names are England's most famous. Please try on all garments, as fit is geared to an English body, which may be a little shorter and a little rounder than a standard-issue American body. Cashmere sweaters cost £99. There is a mail-order catalogue.

JAEGER FACTORY SHOP
Gomersal, Cleckheaton, Yorkshire

Not far from Beans of Bradford when you're driving the hills, but light-years away in terms of style, the Jaeger factory outlet is indeed right inside the factory that makes the goods. While men's and women's styles are available at reasonable prices, the write-home-about big news is cashmere sweaters for £39! Furthermore, Americans will get a VAT refund on all purchases. Please note the outside of the factory reads Thomas Burnley, but the Jaeger shop has its own small sign.

Open: Monday 12:30 to 4:30pm; Tuesday through Friday 9:30am to 4:30pm; Saturday 9am to 12:30pm. Closed Sundays.

Menswear

SLATER MENSWEAR
7 Dale Street, Manchester

The main store is in Glasgow; Manchester is the branch store. Famous-maker name brands are sold at prices considered 25% to 50% less than on the high streets of English towns, including London. Men's suits begin at £69; there are more than 10,000 in stock. Besides suits, there's casual clothes, sweaters, outerwear, and just about everything you may need.

Sizes go up to 54! I guess this is when I should tell you that I bought my husband a designer tuxedo shirt on sale for £5. Please note that Slater opens at 8am for those of you suffering from jet lag or craving a bit of early morning shopping.

Museum Shops

Manchester is filled with museums and I'm not talking about Granada Studios. The **Museum of Science and Industry** is stunning, fabulous, fantastic, and possessed of an excellent gift shop. Almost all the museums have gift shops, even the **Manchester United** football team museum has a gift shop in the tour center.

Teens & 'Tweens

Because of the enormous student population in Manchester, teens will have no trouble finding the look they crave. **Afflecks Palace** is the best place to start (pages 236–237), but **Arndale Centre** has branches of many of the multiples including ones with low price but high fashion gear. **Red or Dead** has a store in the Royal Exchange; **Shelly's**—the shoe store for Doc Martens and more—is on Market Street.

Vintage Clothing

Any city with this much selection in terms of antiques is also going to have a lot of resources for vintage clothing. All markets sell some used and/or vintage clothing (I got a great jacket from the sixties for £1 at Tommyfields); the very best resource is **Afflecks Palace**, right in downtown Manchester.

Chapter Twelve

. . . .

SHOPPING YORK, HARROGATE & STOKE-ON-TRENT

DAY TRIPS FROM MANCHESTER

. . . .

One of the reasons I am so enthusiastic about Manchester is because of its proximity to various all-but-perfect English towns that offer a combination of culture and shopping. To some of us, Manchester is the center of the English world. Within an hour or two of Manchester, you can visit:

- Stoke (Stoke-on-Trent): Cradle of The Potteries; home to a number of English china and pottery outlet stores.
- Harrogate: Yuppie village with expensive antique shops made famous by James Herriot books (*All Creatures Great and Small*, and so on).
- York: One of the most famous cities in England known for its cathedral and medieval streets crammed with shops.

You can also go to Chester and Boughton on a day trip (see chapter 14 for details). Or you may want to visit the Lake District, renowned for its vistas, and not yet widely known for its village of mill shops. I am dreaming of Lakeland Plastics as you read this.

YORK

. . . .

York is one of the most visited of all the English cities; few question why. The city center is almost picture-perfect, and is even more beautiful in winter or on less-than-blue-sky days when tourists are scarce. When York is jammed with an international parade of tourists, it is not at its best. But it's hard not to like this proper combination of medieval charm placed within walls that boast a castle, a cathedral, and more adorable stores than you can count. York offers the kind of day trip that every visitor to England wants to make.

The Lay of the Land

The River Ouse runs right alongside the city center of York, making it one of the dividing lines between the tourist center and the rest of the real-people world. When you walk across a bridge inlaid with iron white roses (for York; remember the War of the Roses?), you have arrived at an area thick with neighborhoods for shopping and exploring. (It's the Lendel Bridge.)

The far side of this bridge, across town, is the Minster, York's famous cathedral, which sits on the edge of the tourist part of town. There are clusters of shops around the Minster in the Deangate region, around the square where Lendel comes to Davygate (St. Helen's Square), and then more shops—like shoe repairs and photo processing places at St. Sampson's Square, where Parliament Street meets Market Street.

Between Parliament Street and The Shambles there are many teeny-tiny lanes crammed with wonderful stores. Piccadilly Street leads away from the center and has some vestiges of the remaining shopping.

Depending on how much shopping you want to do, and how much sightseeing (there are scads of museums), York can be more than a three-hour town. Could be a three-day town.

York

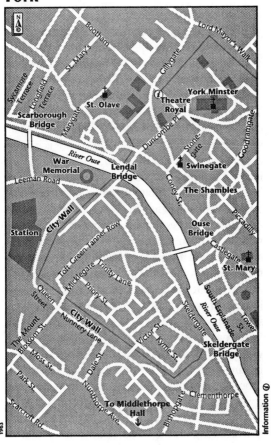

Getting There

York is essentially halfway between London and Edinburgh. Even on the fast train, it's a good 2½ to 3 hours from London—a bit much for a day trip. If you come from Manchester, you're a little bit closer to York although you are on the other side of England. The trip across the Pennines is beautiful; the train ride is a little less than two hours.

Please note that the York train station is large and has several platforms with bridges and tunnels. If you have cumbersome luggage, you need to allow extra time to get to the proper platform. I did not

find a porter and had a very hard time finding the
elevator (there is one) and getting to my platform
in time for my train.

Getting Around

York is a big city with lots of suburbs. Even the
downtown has lots of streets and different parts to
it. This surely is not a one-street town, nor is it one
of those cities that you walk into and get your bearings within seconds. A good bit of how you get your
bearings depends on how you arrive, since the train
station is at the far end of the city center.

Many of the best hotels are not within the city
walls. If you don't have a car, you will need a taxi
to get back and forth. Once in the center, you won't
want a car. If you're looking for parking, good luck.
It may help to get across the river to the slightly
less touristy portion of downtown where there are
some public car parks.

If you have arrived via train and don't have
wheels, you can still see the countryside by booking any number of coach tours that do Yorkshire
Moors or Yorkshire Dales and even Brontë country (as they call it). Tours usually go the whole day
and leave York around 9am. Check with your
hotel concierge or the tourist information center.

Sleeping in York

The first time I visited York, I insisted on a hotel
within the city walls, a cute B&B for people coming via train and wanting two days of village per-
fection. I mention this for several reasons: The
hotel the British Tourist Authority recommended
was horrible (so I won't name it).

The best way to visit York, I have since discovered, is to stay in one of the fabulous country home
hotels outside of town. I have listed only one in-
town hotel, in case you don't have a car. I did call
the Holiday Inn from the United States, thinking it

would have a good low price and make my life convenient. They quoted me £100 a night (for me alone); I thought I would die laughing. You can have the hotel of your dreams for less than that.

MIDDLETHORPE HALL
Bishopthorpe Road, York

If you trust me at all, even if you haven't got a car and are doing this trip via BritRail, this is the hotel for you. Forget about the city walls, forget about the cute little B&B. Middlethorpe Hall is a country manor house five minutes by taxi from the York train station; you could actually walk to town but then you'd be too tired to shop.

To tell you that Middlethorpe is gorgeous, to die for, has gardens and public rooms that you will never forget, and a fixed-price dinner that you will write home about is to only begin to tell the tale. The hotel is modestly priced.

The three-course, fixed-price gourmet dinner was £25 a person. The kitchen is quite famous, so you must book ahead for dinner, even as a guest. (Book dinner when you make your reservations.) If you are staying elsewhere, be sure to book one night's dinner here. Jacket and tie for the gents.

My room, all antiques and chintz and a view to the garden, was £83; a four-poster bedroom is £159; courtyard cottages cost £165. There are promotional prices for any two consecutive nights with dinner and breakfast included. Children over eight are welcome.

There are rooms in the manor house and in the attached portions of the house in what must have been stables, workrooms, and servants quarters. There's a formal English garden for wandering after dinner and an herb garden. For reservations, call local phone: 1904/641-241; fax: 1904/620-176. There is no U.S. booking agent but there is a toll-free fax service within America for reservations: 800/260-8338.

DEAN COURT
Duncombe Place, York

Dean Court is a three-star hotel of the small country inn type, right across the street from the Minster. It's slightly formal rather than country funky; the restaurant is pleasant and you'll be quite happy here. Rates begin at about £100 per night and include full English breakfast. Local phone: 1904/625-082; fax: 1904/620-305. In the U.S. call 800/528-1234.

GRANGE HOTEL
Clifton, York

This hotel is not in the center of York but it isn't too far afield. Approximately ten minutes by foot from downtown York, it is considered a must-do by many foodies who appreciate the famous kitchen, The Ivy. The hotel is in a Victorian house and features all creature comforts and fantasies. Even if you don't sleep here, you may well want to come for dinner. Book dinner reservations as far ahead as possible. Local phone: 1904/644-744; fax: 1904/612-453.

Shopping York

York is the shopping capital of middle England, partly because of location and partly because it attracts so many tourists.

Because of its size, even the center of York in the core of the tourist area has a few different neighborhoods offering different types of shopping. **The Shambles** is one narrow street that has the bulk of the touristy shops—although a lot of these stores are tourist traps. In the next ring of shops surrounding The Shambles, there's representatives from England's major multiples as well as a few stores that you may not have seen before. Even I found new stores to explore. Past this double inner core of stores, there's a third layer of real-people stores on the outskirts of the center—you've got two **Marks & Spencer** stores, among others. There's a small outdoor market where antiques are sold some days; last time I was there I found a dealer selling seconds from Stoke.

If antiques are your main quest, the town has a reputation for secondhand and antiquarian bookstores and a few small antique centers, but prices aren't particularly low. Carolyn poked into a few jewelry shops selling antique jewelry and pronounced the prices fair, which isn't bad for a town whose major trade is tourists. Ask about the weekend flea market at the racetrack.

The best way to go shopping in York is to spend a few minutes studying a map to get your bearings and then dive in and wander. As you cover ground, you'll automatically happen upon the cute little stores, the scads of tourist traps (especially in The Shambles), the famous London department stores, the multiples, and the open-air market. Street names are difficult to even find; addresses are almost impossible.

If you've got kids with you, there's a **Toymaster** store across from the Minster at King's Square, a Pizzaland nearby, and a Baskin-Robbins. There's also Jim Garrahy's Fudge Kitchen, where the lemonade is very sweet but the fudge may tempt.

If you're looking for the basics of English retail, you'll find everything from **Culpeper the Herbalist, Next, Laura Ashley, Jumpers, Poundstretchers, Boots, Marks & Spencer, Liberty,** and **Crabtree and Evelyn. Mulberry,** one of my favorite British resources for clothes and accessories, has even opened on Swinegate Court.

Tea for Two

BETTY'S
St. Helen's Square, York

You have to be from northern England to be in on it, but Betty's is the kind of landmark that every local knows about. There are about four branches of Betty's in the area; many will tell you that the whole point to a day trip to either York or Harrogate is to have lunch or tea at Betty's.

In York, Betty's is nestled in the heart of the shopping, right near the Shambles. The store sells coffees, cakes, candies, and some takeout eats; you may eat a full meal upstairs or downstairs. Upstairs is popular because the entire wall is glass and you look out at the square and see the world pass by. They are open seven days a week from 9am to 9pm.

Finds

TAYLORS
Stonegate, York

Once you become a Betty's devotee, you may want to buy Betty's products from the tea room or by mail. You may also want to stop by this totally separate shop in Stonegate, where coffees are sold in an old-fashioned store that looks like a movie set. The coffee firm is owned by Betty's, or vice versa.

ANNIE HALL
Stonegate, York

Nothing to do with the movie or even the droopy look. Annie Hall makes sweaters that are very similar to some of the other big-name English sweater designers like Maggie White and Bill Baber. Prices are over £60 ($100), but not wildly expensive considering the workmanship.

THE LANGUAGE OF FLOWERS
Stonegate, York

The two other listings are next door, so while you're in the neighborhood, stop in to a tiny two-salon shop owned by Penhaligon that sells home scents, fragrances, and products with pictures of flowers on them in an old-timey Victorian setting; there's bed linen, tea sets, stationery, and just yummy home decorating items.

SARAH COGGLES
Low Petergate, York

Surely the hippest store in York, this two-story clothing shop has fresh fashion looks that are wearable but still cutting edge. Some items on sale upstairs. Sophisticated color palette in suits and separates.

LAKELAND
Low Petergate, York

Lakeland is a plastics company not unlike Tupperware that makes a million different kitchen and cooking gadgets and has a gigantic and famous catalogue business. This is one of its few freestanding stores. An absolute must for anyone who enjoys cooking or is looking for unique gifts to bring home. Get the catalogue for mail orders.

TAKE SECONDS
Low Petergate, York

There's another one of these stores in Harrogate, and while they aren't wildly exciting, they will do the trick if you can't get into any mills or mill shops on your trip. They sell famous-maker (not M&S) cotton and wool sweaters: About £15 for a cotton jumper is a pretty good deal.

HARROGATE

After you've been doing some down-and-dirty bargain shopping in the Manchester area, Harrogate's shopping will seem like the antithesis of Manchester's. There are no bargains in Harrogate.

Visit Harrogate with the understanding that it's not funky, that it's not as touristy as Stratford-upon-Avon, but that the environment here is geared to yuppies—American, British, and international. Harrogate is the perfect day trip for people who don't like to get their hands dirty in antique shops.

The Lay of the Land

Harrogate is by no means a one-street town and can be a little confusing. Looking at a map helps only if you realize how the spread of retail flowers across the city toward Parliament Street and then beyond, down the hill.

In fact, Parliament Street is the connecting mid-point between the real-people part of the town, lying between the train station, and Montpelier, where the mostly antique stores part of town is based. This antique neighborhood is sometimes referred to as "Low Harrogate."

The city center is almost divided into two equal parts, which are not at all obvious from the train station. Nor is this one of those cities where you alight from the train and know which direction to take. (When you leave the train station, walk along James Street toward Cambridge Crescent.)

Getting There

To get to Harrogate by train from Manchester, you switch trains in Leeds and get on this little local commuter train. The view on the second ride is spectacular. It takes about two hours if you count the time spent changing trains, etc. You can drive it in about 1½ hours.

If you are driving, be sure to include the village of Knaresborough (on the A59) in your tour. It's an adorable Edwardian town that still has a town crier. There's an outdoor market as well. You can also take the commuter train to Knaresborough. Please note that the antique stores in Knaresborough are closed on Thursdays.

Getting Around

Walk.

Shopping Harrogate

Harrogate has a brand-new modern mall in nouveau hotshot architectural style (the mall even houses the market downstairs). It has multiples and plenty of upscale shops because the clientele are well-off locals and tourists. People come here to shop for a total experience—tea at Betty's, toffee from John Farrah. They stroll the streets and look at antiques and then go home. There is a branch of **Take Seconds,** a shop that sells sweaters at mill prices; there's also places like **Monsoon** and **Jaeger,** which are on the far side of the cute at the roundabout. There's a street of multiples (James Street) where stores include **Laura Ashley, Next, Susan Woolf, Alexon, Richards,** and **Principles. Hammicks** is a very good local bookstore with a section on regional publications and postcards.

On Station Parade, going away from the station and the cute parts of town, there's a strip of stores including a **Habitat. Porcelana,** in the next block, is a good pottery shop.

If you've come to town solely for the purpose of looking at the antique shops, you might want to drive right to that part of town or taxi to the Ginnel. There's a small hillside dotted with store after store. Most of the shops are very fancy—some forbiddingly so. Check out addresses on Montpelier Parade, where every storefront is an antique shop; on Montpelier Gardens (ditto), Montpelier Mews, etc. Don't forget Royal Parade, where the stores also line the road.

The entire village of Knaresborough is also made up of antique shops.

Tea for Two

🛍 Betty's
1 Parliament Street, Harrogate

If you haven't heard of Betty's, then you just have to trust me. You cannot go to Harrogate and not stop by Betty's. It's the law. I must also tell you that I've heard the lines were very bad at Betty's, so I went for lunch at 11:30am—and I stood in a line. It moved quickly because most people were waiting for tables with view or for smoking. I took a table downstairs in nonsmoking and was happy with my quiche and salad and their great coffee.

Betty's menu and prices are identical to those in York (and other Betty's). You may also get its mail-order catalogue for fruitcakes, Easter treats, and other Christmas specialties—it ships all over the world. Betty's famous fruitcake comes in a tin and costs £10.50. You can order by printed form, by mail, or by fax (0423/565-191). Packing and postage within the United Kingdom is an additional £5.20; they will quote you an overseas mail price.

Betty's is open seven days a week from 9am to 9pm.

Antique Centers

THE GINNEL ANTIQUES CENTRE
Off Parliament Street, Harrogate

A nice antique center that's jammed with merchandise, much of it put away in glass cases and not that touchable. The dealers all hobnob together; you can eavesdrop on their conversations at tea tables on the second floor. Prices aren't low but the atmosphere is fun. Tons of dealers selling blue and white, but we're looking at starting prices of £250 for a platter. Closed Sundays. Monday through Saturday from 9:30am to 5:30pm. Sometimes the address is written as "Harrogate Antiques Centre, The Ginnel."

MONTPELIER MEWS
Montpelier Street, Harrogate

A very cute, tiny antique center, very nice and very upscale, with 16 stands, sort of tucked behind the antique part of town. Open Monday through Saturday from 9:30am to 5:30pm.

STOKE-ON-TRENT

· ·

Stoke-on-Trent, how do I love thee? Let me count the ways. Service for eight, service for ten, make that service for twelve.

Stoke-on-Trent is the china and crystal bargain capital of England, and if your patterns are English, be prepared to stock up on seconds, overruns, soup tureens, plates, and all the goodies you've coveted.

Stoke-on-Trent is the center of The Potteries, the name for the area comprised of the six towns (Hanley, Burslem, Tunstall, Fenton, Longton, and Stoke) where most of England's dishes are made. All of the big-name pottery makers have their factories—and their factory outlet shops—in this little area.

The Lay of the Land

Stoke is just one of the cities you will be visiting. It is where you get off the train (from either London or Manchester), but it is not your final destination. If this sounds confusing, don't panic: The place-name Stoke has become synonymous for an entire region.

The Potteries encompass a daisy chain of communities; if you come back to Stoke as often as I do, you get to learn the individual personality of some of the villages; you get to know the places that are a little farther away from the core shopping (like Wedgwood). The honest truth is that you needn't learn anything; if you take the China Link bus, you'll be deposited at the doorstep. If you drive, you'll come to recognize the landmarks. I feared it would be impossible to drive in The Potteries. When I actually did it, it turned out to be incredibly easy; each outlet will give you directions to your next stop. There are free maps aplenty.

Getting There
FROM LONDON

If you don't have a BritRail pass and want to save your money for shopping the stores, you might want to consider taking the bus from London. Buses via National Express leave and return to Victoria station and will take you right into Hanley. If you leave London on the 9:30am bus, you'll be in Hanley at 1:40pm. Which is not bad if you consider that round-trip bus fare is about £16. Fares vary with season and promotional rates, but you're looking at a possible expenditure of $125 on the train (since a cheap-day return won't do the trick from London) and less than $25 on the bus. The difference will more than pay for a bed-and-breakfast—and dinner—should you decide to stay the night.

One of the best reasons to have a BritRail pass is that it includes peak travel on pricey runs such as the one to Stoke (which is actually the fast train to Manchester; it just stops in Stoke). If you're planning on buying such a pass or need convincing, this is your excuse.

FROM MANCHESTER

There are trains to Stoke every hour; more during rush hours. Train fare for a return ticket is a low £9. You may also take the bus if you prefer to go right into Hanley.

Driving from Manchester is a brilliant idea— it's a short drive on a motorway (less than one hour) and then you have wheels for local transport as well as plenty of space for all your purchases. You can rent a car on a one-day basis for as little as £35 in Stoke. If you want to splurge, you can hire a car and driver or a van to carry all your packages.

Getting Around

The city of Stoke offers "The China Link," a bus from the train station to most of the pottery shops and factory outlets. You just hop on and off the bus; you don't even need to pay attention to what city you are actually in. The Rover ticket allows unlimited stops for almost £4; there is a family rover pass for two adults and two children.

The problem with the China Link is a basic one; it comes around just once an hour. You have to be on a schedule and stick to it in order to not get stranded.

Since no one can possibly go to all of the outlets in one day, just decide which ones you want to visit and use the bus accordingly. It makes continuous loops and will take you back to the train station. You can also call taxis, or you can drive.

Sleeping in Stoke-on-Trent

HAYDON HOUSE HOTEL
Haydon Street, Basford

Haydon House became famous for its restaurant. When the apartments across the street became available, the restaurant bought them up and turned them into rooms and suites. You can even get an entire apartment with a kitchen (and start using your new china right away) in a converted Victorian townhouse.

Everything is decorated in period style circa 1880, with collector's ceramics displayed here and there. There is a special weekend promotional rate that includes dinner. You certainly don't want to be in this area and miss a dinner here.

If you think the decor is something, wait until you eat dinner. Ian and I drove all the way back from Wales one night just to have another dinner at Haydon House. To book a room or make dinner reservations, call local phone: 1782/711-311.

MOAT HOUSE
Festival Way, Stoke-on-Trent

I'd be a bad reporter if I didn't tell you this spanking new, modern hotel was in town, right next door to Josiah Wedgwood's first factory at Etruria Hall. Businessmen like its modern conveniences.

THE NORTH STAFFORD
Station Road, Stoke-on-Trent

Since I've been ruined by Haydon House, I can only tell you that the North Stafford has more charm than the Moat House but isn't a five-star hotel dripping with luxury or finesse. It has a great location, directly across the street from the Stoke train station, and will do in a pinch if an average room is all you need. It is a good stop for tea before you hop on the train back to London or Manchester. It costs just under £100 to sleep over, although promotions are sometimes offered. For reservations, call local phone: 1423/530-797.

Stoke-on-Trent Secrets

Prices on first wares in Stoke-on-Trent are the same as in London, Manchester, and all U.K. regular retail sources.

Prices on seconds are anywhere from 20% to 80% off London prices.

The price differential between retail and factory outlet varies from maker to maker. At Spode, seconds are a flat 20% less than firsts. At Royal Grafton, they are 68% less.

Twice a year, usually in late January and August, there are sales at the factory outlets. Sales vary from place to place, but most often offer 25% off already low prices. Do note that during this same time period, there may be sales in London for which seconds have been trucked in from Stoke. The sale price in London is the everyday Stoke price; the sale price at a Stoke promotion is less than the everyday low price. But the wares that are marked down very low may be different from the ones you see in London. These special sales are not a secret, in fact, they are advertised in the upscale London newspapers like the *Times* or the *Independent*.

When you ship from the outlet to the United States (most do ship; not all will ship seconds), you will get a VAT deduction as well. If you take the goods with you, but meet the minimum requirement for a VAT refund (which varies) at the shop, you will also get the 17.5% back when you leave the country.

If you buy during a sale and qualify for the VAT, you are talking about an extra savings of 40% off discount (or 60% off retail). You can get 17.5% off retail in London, don't forget; but frankly, I like the sound of 60% off even better.

Day Tripper Tips

FROM LONDON

If you are considering visiting Stoke-on-Trent as a day trip from London, note that the price of the train ticket may exceed your savings or enjoyment of the day.

1. My best day tripper tip for those coming from London? Don't do it as a day trip! Spend at least one night.
2. This is not a casual day in the countryside. A visit to Stoke is a serious buying trip. Brides should do it, without question; those on driving trips with cars at hand should do it, without question; those who have unlimited budgets and don't mind the price of shipping should do it, without question. But if you're just going to browse, thinking you'll have a quaint day in the country, then you may want to think twice. Stoke-on-Trent is not pretty, nor are you going to have a pretty day in the country (with the exception of the visit to Wedgwood).
3. If you come from London, you will spend four hours of your day on the train (about two hours each way) and pay more than $100 for the ticket, if you don't have a BritRail pass.
4. If you have a BritRail pass anyway, and were Born to Shop, don't miss this adventure. After you've done it once, you'll begin to plan your return trip with more time, perhaps a car, and maybe a van.

Lord Wedgwood Dishes It Out

To research or date a Wedgwood plate, Lord Wedgwood suggests that you use the free charts provided by Wedgwood, any of the guidebooks that discuss dating china, or contact the Wedgwood library directly about a specific piece of Wedgwood. This can be done by mail if you can get a reasonably good photocopy of the front and back of the plate.

All Wedgwood plates have secrets in the codes on their backs; never assume that you can crack the code without looking it up. For instance, among the most valuable of Wedgwood dishes are those stamped "Etruria," not Wedgwood, as that is the location of the original Wedgwood factory. On more recently made designs, there is copyright information and a code that will tell you the date your plates were produced. Often the name of the pattern is also printed on the back. There are specific designs that were created for the export market that may bear an American copyright.

5. You have to know what you are doing in order to score big savings. Prices on best wares (that's first-quality pottery) are fixed. *The price you pay in the factory shop may be the exact same price you will get in London.* This trip is tons of fun and I can't wait to do it again, but it takes time, money, and effort to make a killing.

6. Go with a friend; it's not much fun alone. And consider renting a car if there are two (or more) of you. The drive isn't that far; you'll save on the train fare and the taxis and have much more room for lugging home your purchases. Car rentals in London can be as low as £25 for one day. Outlets are usually open later at night (till 7 or 8pm) on Thursday. If you're into a big day trip, Thursday is your day to visit.

7. Beware Euston station. If you return from Stoke exhausted and laden down with heavy break-ables, you will not be pleased to know that you may not find a cart and the taxi curb is down a steep flight of stairs. You can't get your cart down the stairs even if you have one. I cried true tears of frustration—unable to find anyone to help me and loaded down with heavy cartons of dishes; I was really miserable. It's just another reason to day trip from Manchester.

FROM MANCHESTER

Getting to Stoke from Manchester is perhaps the most perfect day trip you will ever make. For a shop-per, anyway.

1. Trains run frequently to Stoke; the running time is less than one hour. Do read the schedule care-fully, since there are fast and slow trains.
2. Because Stoke is so close, you can buy a "cheap-day return" fare, which offers one flat low-cost price for the round-trip train ticket—you just can't leave Manchester before 9:30am, but since you're so close there's no rush and you may want to save the money. Cheap-day return is less than £10! No need to use your precious BritRail pass, although if you have one and unlimited travel is the name of the game, well, go for it.
3. There is enough to do in Stoke that you may want to spend the night, so don't think that the area only merits a day trip or that the cheap-day return is all you may ever need. The day trip from Manchester gives you a good overview, but if you don't have a car, you will never get to all the outlets you want to visit in one day.
4. The Manchester train station is flat; there are trol-leys, no porters.
5. Do not exit the train station to the front where your taxi left you in the morning; if you are facing

the front with the tracks to your rear, exit to your left following signs to taxis. Drop off and pick up are in two different areas of this train station.

Shopping Hours

Hours in Stoke-on-Trent are not uniform, so work with the brochure printed by the tourist office or check the final listings at the end of this section. Most factory shops close at 4:30 or 5pm; a late night might be Thursday, and late is 6pm in Stoke. Only a few stay open until 7 or 8pm. Early means 9am, although most shops open at 9:30 or 10am. Only Mason in Hanley opens at 8:30am, making this a good place to start if you are in town at that hour.

One of the reasons you will want to spend two days in Stoke is that the shopping hours are so limited. Another reason is that you'll be having too much fun to go back to London or Manchester.

About Addresses & Shops

Some of the makers have several shops within the area, and each one is different. One can be good, the next lousy, so never figure "seen one, seen 'em all." Addresses often have no street number since the factory can take up an entire city block.

Sunday Shopping

As Britain gets more and more adjusted to Sunday retail hours, more and more factory shops are opening on Sundays. Some have always been open on Sundays during spring and summer months; others are just now opening. Call ahead, ask at your hotel, or ask at the Gladstone Museum for the latest buzz on who's doing what on Sundays.

Sometimes outlets are within the actual factories, sometimes they are in outbuildings on the factory grounds, sometimes they are in separate storefronts. A few factories have two or more shops—one for firsts and one for seconds. Having your own car in this area is empowering: It allows you to hop in and out of a number of outlets at will. Some shops will only be interesting for a minute or two; others may require a few hours. If you are driving around looking for a specific address and are a little lost, just look for a chimney. You cannot make dishes without using a chimney.

About Thursdays

Factory shops in Stoke usually close around 4pm during the week, so plan your travels accordingly. The one day for late closings is Thursday, when stores are usually open until 7pm. There's just one catch to Thursdays: If you are coming to look at Victorian reproduction tiles, the tile factory shop is closed on Thursdays.

All the more reason for you to spend at least one night in Stoke.

Shopping & Shipping

The most frustrating thing about shopping in Stoke-on-Trent is that each house seems to have a different shipping policy and prices for shipping goods can seem to vary beyond comprehension. There are three basic systems:

1. Regular international postal rates per the U.K. postal system; these prices are outrageously high. Second-class local postage is affordable.
2. A shipping scheme that is based on the number of pieces you buy, so that if you buy a soup tureen it costs the same amount to ship as a single teacup.

3. House shipping (these guys are manufacturers who ship all over the world) plans, in which you are told what the freight will be based on weight, pieces, or hocus-pocus. The best deal is at Royal Grafton.

Note: Do not ship to yourself in America but to various members of your family, making sure packages arrive with less than $50 worth of goods at staggered intervals. I recently got hit with duty that could have easily and legally been avoided, but I addressed my boxes to myself rather than to another member of the family.

Shopping Stoke-on-Trent

There are two public aspects to each pottery factory: Most factories give tours and let you see how everything is made (no children under 14 allowed due to safety regulations); all factories have outlet shops. Sometimes the outlets are in the factory; at other times they are not. Many of the factories have museums; a few factories have several shops.

Doing a tour, at least once, is a fabulous treat; seeing some of the museums provides an even

---

The Potteries Made Simple

If you've only got one day and you are traveling by train and you want to keep this simple but sublime, may I suggest that you only visit Stoke-on-Trent? You can walk into town from the train station, visit **Spode**, **Portmeirion**, and **Minton**, and have lunch at the **Blue Italian Cafe** in the Spode factory before walking or taxiing back to the station. While you'll be missing a lot of the fun (including the fabulous Gladstone Museum), you will have a very easy to handle day. And all you'll have to worry about are all those packages.

better lesson in how to separate the good stuff from the junk. The Minton Museum is small, easy to handle, and right in the heart of downtown Stoke. Spode has an absolutely incredible space called the Blue and White Room, which will stop your heart; you must write ahead for an appointment to see it. The City Museum in Hanley is a must for serious collectors; I've even been backstage with a curator and can't tell you how thrilling it is.

The goods in the outlet shops usually are marked "best wares" and "seconds." Best wares are first quality; they sell at the same prices as in London and Manchester.

Factories do close down: Some go out of business, others close on a regular rotation for holidays. Be careful when you plan your trip. Outlet shops may or may not be open when factories are closed. Common days to close are during Easter week, late June until the first week in July, the last week in August, and the week between Christmas and New Year's.

Even if a shop is open when a factory is closed, they will not be able to ship for you until the factory reopens. These factory closings can put a serious dent in your good time in Stoke; if you are planning this trip as the dream of a lifetime, please write ahead and make sure you are safe.

Finds

R. J. STEVENSON ARCHITECTURAL ANTIQUES
21 Liverpool Street, Stoke-on-Trent

Okay, so you came to Stoke-on-Trent for the china bargains, but I think you'll get into this one. Besides, it has to do with Victorian tiles—and they *are* made of china. R. J. Stevenson is a dealer that sells rebuilt and reconditioned Victorian fireplaces, bathroom fixtures, and radiators. They are real, not reproduction. You may have the toilet in working or nonworking condition; working costs more.

Peggy Davies Ceramics
28 Liverpool Street, Stoke-on-Trent

This small shop, directly across from R. J. Stevenson and only a block from Spode, is run by the son of the late Peggy Davies. Mrs. Davies remains one of the most famous names in pottery lore, having been responsible for many a Toby mug's creation. Now you can buy reproductions of her original molds directly from her son.

The work is spectacular, but it is mostly for serious collectors. A few pieces are under $1,000, but most are more, and prices can reach twice that. They are made in limited quantity; each piece is numbered. You may also commission a vanity Toby mug, which will be created in your likeness in the style of the Toby mugs Mrs. Davies made so popular. They will ship. Open Monday to Friday from 9:30am to 5pm; Saturdays from 9:30am to 1pm.

H. & R. Johnson
Highgate Tile Works, Brownhills Road, Tunstall

There's currently an upswing in interest in Victorian tiles among collectors, who are buying up whatever they can find, either for fireplaces or for decoration. The most famous of the tile makers used to be Minton, but Minton no longer makes tiles.

H. & R. Johnson bought the tile company that owned the rights to the Minton patterns, and continues to produce these same tile patterns. There is a factory shop across the street from the factory; you don't drive through the factory gates, although the guard will help you find the outlet if you need guidance. This shop is closed on Thursdays, so plan your visit carefully if you want tiles. Do note that these are repro tiles. You can usually buy old tiles (elsewhere) for less, but not in quantities. Besides, if you love tiles as much as I do, this is the kind of shop you don't want to miss.

My personal secret: I mix these tiles with inexpensive bathroom tiles bought in America. I just use a scattering of English tiles here and there for drama—works great and saves money.

STAFFORDSHIRE ENAMELS LTD.
Cinderhill Estate, Weston Coyney Road, Longton

This small factory doesn't really have an outlet store; it has an outlet display case, right there in the stock area. That's going to be fine with you when you see that these Battersea-style enamel boxes are priced at about half of what they cost in London. Many of the pieces are special orders that were never delivered. So you have to know someone named Sophie (we do) to take full advantage of the savings. Pickings can be slim or superb—it depends on the luck of the draw. This location is in a business park on the edge of Longton, and is slightly out of the mainstream.

Pottery Outlets and Shops

AYNESLEY
Sutherland Road, Longton

Aynesley has good parking and it's easy to get here; it's just around the corner from the Gladstone Pottery Museum and quite near one of the Portmeirion outlets.

Aynesley makes several patterns that are too sweet for my taste; yet I find its ceramic telephones adorable. Formal dinner plates cost about £6 ($10) each. Shipping an entire set of dishes to the United States costs a mere $100 including insurance. The shop is just one block behind the main street in Longton; around the corner from the Gladstone Museum. And only a few blocks (but drive, don't walk) from Grafton.

BLAKENEY ART POTTERY
South Wolfe Street, Stoke

This is a very small pottery, but they have some important works, and I cannot forget the pink luster pitcher that I saw here three years ago and should have bought. All items in this two-part store are discontinued or slightly damaged; they will ship with a large order. The style is rather traditional and Victorian; there is a blue and white pattern. Because of the location directly behind Minton, this is worth looking at.

COALPORT
Park Street, Fenton

There's an artsy-craftsy part of Coalport where you can watch craftspeople make pottery flowers; or there's the more serious part, where you can go shopping. Walk into the good-sized outlet, which is fancier than many, and choose from shelves of Coalport wares—Coalport cottages, lamps, white lettuce-leaf dishes called Country Ware, and zillions of gift items. The shipping policy here is based on the number of pieces.

MINTON
London Road, Stoke-on-Trent

The Minton shop is a free-standing, newish structure behind the factory; you can enter through the factory parking lot. Plushly carpeted in gray, the outlet store has some seconds and discontinued patterns, but sells mostly first quality at regular London prices. They will ship seconds. As a member of the Royal Doulton Group, Minton sells other patterns besides Minton. It also has Royal Albert crystal. Catch the China Link at the bus stop at the Minton curb if you walked into town from the train station. The museum is in the main building located directly in front of the outlet; you must walk around to the front door to enter.

MOORCROFT POTTERY
Sanbach Road, Cobridge

Moorcroft has a very specific look that you will quickly learn to identify. People seem to love it or loathe it. Either way, I must warn you that it is highly collectible and anything you can get here is a smart buy. The style is very Art Deco; the outlet is in a huge room that looks more like a greenhouse but is nonetheless charming. There's a bottle oven; there are tables filled with wares and many choices. There's a museum, too.

PORTMEIRION POTTERIES LTD.
Sylvan Works, Normacot Road, Longton

167 London Road, Stoke-on-Trent

I have good news and I have bad news. If you have the Botanic Garden pattern (I do), you will go stark raving mad in these outlets.

The bad news: Shipping is so expensive that you will only save about 25% off U.S. prices once you've landed your goods. If you can carry what you buy, you will save and save. The kind people at the front desk will work out the shipping for you before you pay; I had to put back many items.

Please note, however, that the basic dinner plate costs £4 here ($6) and $27 in the United States, so savings are huge.

There are a few Portmeirion outlets dotted around The Potteries, and stock varies. If you have the time and you collect dishes from this firm, shop them all!

The Longton shop is right behind the **Gladstone Museum.** The one in downtown Stoke is the largest of them all—practically a mini-supermarket of dishes. If you can only go to one branch of Portmeirion, it is your best bet.

Also note that you may find items in Stoke that aren't shipped to the United States, so just one or two little things—easily managed in your suitcase—may perk up your entire collection.

ROYAL GRAFTON
Nile Street, Burslem

Marlborough Road, Longton

Of the two stores, the Burslem one is better. It will get even better when a restaurant, demonstration area, and audiovisual center will open. The shop itself has already been revamped and a new visitor center is open.

However, both stores just plain feel good. There are handwritten posters with the deals of the day marked, baskets on the floor filled with treasures, shelves built into all walls, and sales help willing to check on shipping prices. They have these gorgeous little clocks, which make fabulous gifts in the $50 category. They have modern; they have old-fashioned. They have something for every taste. You will do well to fall in love with a Royal Grafton pattern.

There's only one problem with Royal Grafton; when I was there last time I asked for my VAT refund to be applied to my credit card. *It came as a check in sterling, and a payee account check at that, which means it's useless.*

🛍 SPODE
Spode Works, Church Street, Stoke-on-Trent

Spode remains one of my favorite shopping stops in Stoke, for many reasons. First of all, it is the closest factory to the train station, so you can obtain almost instant gratification. Go there immediately upon arrival. You can tell any taxi driver, "Spode, please," or you can walk—just cross the bridge from the train station and walk toward the factory chimney that says Spode on it.

Spode has at least two outlet stores in the factory—sometimes there are more, if it's a sale period. Also note that they are in the throes of planning an entire outlet minimall in their courtyard, which is part of a multiphase expansion and renovation program that already includes "The Spode Experience" (craft demonstrations) and a new reception area and souvenir shop. Of course you know my idea of a good souvenir. Service for 10.

Special Spode Savings

Spode has a special VIP discount card that gives shoppers 10% off the outlet price on goods bought at the factory. To get your card, write to Ray Elks (in care of Spode; see above listing for address), tell him you read about the discount card in this edition of *Born to Shop*, and ask very nicely if you may have such a card. Allow time for return mail.

If you have visited before, you remember the front of the block outlet shop. That shop has been transformed into Blue Italian heaven so that only this pattern is sold there. The other "old" seconds shops sells the rest of the line.

When you've shopped the two outlets at the front gate, be sure to ask if other outlets are open inside. During the big sales, empty rooms are taken over to house the overflow of the sale.

There is a pretty good selection of patterns of Spode as well as other patterns from the Royal Worcester Group. I bought Blue Italian and must confess that while I'm thrilled with my dishes, the price was only 20% less than regular retail. On the other hand, Blue Tower—a more intricate blue and white pattern—was on sale for half off the ticketed price and I went nuts. I bought a turkey-size serving platter for £15 ($25)! I kid you not! I mix up my blue and white patterns; a trend that Spode has acknowledged by selling a purposefully mixed-and-matched set of blue and white.

Blue Italian may be the most famous pattern the house has, so don't expect big bargains on this particular pattern. There are plenty of other fish in the sea. And on the shelves.

If you get to Spode for one of its famous twice-a-year sales, you'll find that everything in the outlet stores is 25% off the reduced price. Add the VAT refund and you are talking about a total savings of

60%. If you buy a lot you'll be paying for shipping, but with a 60% savings you have to figure that you are getting the shipping for free. (The 25% additional sale discount plus the VAT refund should equal the cost of the shipping.)

I've saved the best news for last: Spode has the Blue Italian Cafe, a little cafeteria decorated in fabric printed with the Blue Italian pattern. The cafe is closed from noon to 1pm when workers eat here, so arrange your day accordingly. If you don't come for a late lunch, come for tea or just a short break.

Portions are large; one day I had the fried plaice (fish) dinner, on another I had the goulash. I'm talking big hot meals to fortify you for a day of serious shopping. It also has salads, lighter fare, desserts, and afternoon tea.

With Sunday shopping now legal, Spode has climbed on board to offer retail seven days a week.

WEDGWOOD
Barlaston, Stoke-on-Trent

WEDGWOOD GROUP FACTORY SHOP
King Street, Fenton

The factory is in the "suburb" of Barlaston in Stoke-on-Trent. It appears to be part of the original farm, with a big house, lots of private driveways, many cows, a stream, and even a private train for the workers. No other place in the area is as pleasant, as elegant, as picturesque, or as worth visiting.

You must pay admission to take a tour of the workshops and grounds. But you need not enter the visitor center or pay a cent to go to the shops. The main shop sells best wares in a modern, clean, bright, one-story shop that would look good in any U.S. mall. They will pack and ship. The seconds shop, behind a pale green Quonset hut, sells seconds and is not nearly as fancy as the other shop, nor does it have the selection or stock. They will ship for you.

Wedgwood is so far off the beaten track that if you go there, you will have little time for the other outlets; another reason why you should spend the night in the area.

If time is limited, try the new **Wedgwood Group Store** that doesn't offer you the charm of the factory location but does offer all the bargains you may want or need. This new shop is centrally located in Fenton (see below). The **China Link** van service stops at this outlet, which is only five minutes from Gladstone Pottery Museum, making it a must-do for anyone in the area.

Note that Wedgwood has a new service called Wedgwood Intergift. You call Wedgwood to order any of 15 different gift items that Wedgwood then delivers directly to the hands of the intended recipient. Call local phone 1787/881-068 for information about this service.

Factory Shops

All of the following factories are closed to the public during Easter week, on May Day (May 1), during late June and early July, the month of August, and Christmas week.

AYNESLEY
Sutherland Road, Longton, Stoke-on-Trent. Open: Monday to Saturday 9am to 5pm; closed on factory holidays.

COALPORT
King Street (A50), Fenton. Open: Monday to Friday 9am to 5pm; Saturday 10am to 4pm, including bank and factory holidays except Christmas.

Please note that this has become the **Wedgwood Group Factory Shop.**

GLADSTONE POTTERY MUSEUM SHOP
Uttoxeter Road, Longton. Open: Monday to Saturday 10am to 4pm, including bank holidays; closed Sunday.

JOHN BESWICK (ROYAL DOULTON GROUP)
*Barford Street, Longton. Open: Monday to
Friday 9am to 4:30pm; closed factory holidays.*

MINTON (ROYAL DOULTON GROUP)
*London Road, Stoke-on-Trent. Open: Monday to
Friday 9am to 5pm; Saturday 9am to 4pm; closed
on factory holidays.*

MOORCROFT POTTERY (BOTTLE OVEN)
*Sandbach Road, Cobridge. Open: Monday to
Friday 10am to 5pm; Saturday 9:30am to 4:30pm.*

PORTMEIRION POTTERIES LTD.
*167 London Road, Stoke-on-Trent. Open:
Monday to Friday 9:30am to 5pm; Saturday 9:30am
to 3:30pm.*

25 George Street, Newcastle

Sylvan Works, Normacot Road, Longton.

ROYAL DOULTON
*Nile Street, Burslem. Open: Monday to Friday
9am to 4:30pm; closed on factory holidays.*

ROYAL GRAFTON CHINA
*Marlborough Road, Longton. Open: Monday to
Friday 9am to 4:30pm; Saturday 9am to 3pm,
including factory holidays.*

SPODE
*Spode Works, Church Street, Stoke-on-Trent.
Open: Monday to Friday 9am to 5pm; Saturday
and Sundays 9am to 1pm, including factory
holidays; closed on bank holidays.*

JOSIAH WEDGWOOD & SONS LTD.
*Wedgwood Visitor Centre, Barlaston. Open:
Monday to Friday 9am to 5pm, including bank
and factory holidays; Saturday and Sunday 10am
to 4pm (Easter to October); otherwise, closed on
Sundays.*

WEDGWOOD GROUP
*Factory Shop, King Street, Fenton. See Coalport
listing above for store hours.*

Chapter Thirteen

. . . .

SHOPPING SCOTLAND

Scotland really is a different country from England; if you don't believe me, just ask someone if or when Scotland will get its own parliament. Political correctness aside, you may have to roam the streets and drive the hills for a day or two to feel it—but the truth is out there, you just can't ignore it: Scotland is not England.

In Scotland, the money is a little different and the accent is a little different. More importantly, Scotland has its own traditions, a very different history, and even a slightly different look at style.

GETTING THERE

. . . .

From England

You can arrive by train or plane, or you may drive. There are no formalities involved in crossing the border.

BritRail has a Scotland-only plan called, naturally, ScotRail, which you can only buy in the U.S. This train plan is only good for travel within Scotland. You pay for the length of the pass; an eight-day pass is about $130, a 15-day pass is about $200, and a 22-day pass is about $250. This pass is also good on ferries to the various Scottish islands.

If you are coming from London or other parts of England, you can buy individual train tickets (try for saver seats on blue days, which are the least expensive) or you may use your BritRail pass. I recently purchased a four-day flexipass, which got me in and out of Scotland and saved me money; the other two train trips I took were virtually free.

Naturally, you can fly. There are commuter flights from all major English cities to both Glasgow and Edinburgh; service between Edinburgh and London is almost hourly during business hours. Birmingham and Manchester are also well connected to Glasgow and Edinburgh; from Manchester you can drive to Glasgow—it's only about two hours.

From the U.S.

You can fly directly from the U.S. to Glasgow, non-stop. The runways in Edinburgh are too short for big planes, so you have to get yourself from Glasgow to Edinburgh, an hour away. If you are going directly to Edinburgh from the Glasgow Airport, ask your hotel to arrange your transfer.

If you can manage your luggage handily, there is regular train service between the two cities.

British Airways will usually allow you to fly into Glasgow (or out of Glasgow) and into (or out of) an English gateway city, such as London, Manchester, or Birmingham, for the same price.

GETTING AROUND

. . . .

Getting around each of the major areas in Scotland is described in detail in each destination; if you are doing some major explorations, you will need and want a car. If you are chicken, and prefer big cities, Edinburgh is a walking town—you won't want or need a car to explore most of it. Glasgow is a little more spread out than Edinburgh but it does have an underground system.

If you're doing the Borders, you'll need a car. If you're headed to some of the famous islands, you'll need the ferry schedule. If you want to really see some of Scotland but not worry too much about transportation, consider a cruise. Most of the famous liners—from *Silversea* to the *QE2*—have itineraries that include Scottish ports.

Or you can book the Royal Scotsman, a luxury train that makes a four-day journey across Scotland. You get to travel in style and comfort, take day trips to castles and mills to buy cashmere, and have as many wee drams as you like, all for a flat price of just under $4,000 per person.

The Royal Scotsman flies the rails between mid-April and mid-November, and also offers a special trip around Christmas. You may also book the train from London to Edinburgh and vice versa. You sleep on the train (only lower berths), eat gourmet food, and make new friends while drinking champagne and watching the hills roll by. It's not a bad way to get around. For reservations in the U.S., call Abercrombie & Kent, 800/323-7308.

PHONING AROUND
· ·

The country code for Scotland is the same as for the rest of Great Britain, 44. To make a call from the U.S., dial 011, then 44, then the city code and phone number. The number of digits in a phone number is not regulated as in some countries; you'll find that rural Scottish phone numbers have only a few digits. Some outlying islands must be dialed through a central island operator. If you are calling from anywhere within Great Britain, add a 0 to the front of the city code. If you are calling within the same city code, dial only the local phone number.

SCOTTISH STYLE

. . . .

Before it united with England, Scotland was a separate country for many years and was closely allied with France. Thus there is very much a form of Scottish art and style that reflects local and foreign influence, a style that has nothing to do with English style.

Interestingly enough, some of it is related to Irish style because of Ireland's close proximity to Scotland. In the earliest Scottish works, a Celtic influence can be plainly seen. The needs of the land and the environment also impacted design, so that a Highland influence—engraved and carved animal heads, mountain crafts, etc.—became part of the Scottish style.

You also have to take into consideration the effects weather has on style. Weather means woollies, so Scotland is famous not only for its sweaters and cashmeres, but for all notions associated with warmth: fires and fireplaces, beds, paisley shawls, kilts, etc. You'll find that decorating styles also exude warmth. Don't expect the Scottish country house to look just like the English one—life is milder

Haggis in Style

If you don't know anything about haggis, a Scottish national dish of infamy, I'm not going to be the one to tell you about it. If, however, you already know about haggis—or feel you know far too much about it—I have a secret: You can learn to love haggis.

Ian and I spent some time with a Scotsman named Steve Abel while on the *QE2*, and he taught us an incredible trick: You pour a glass of Drambuie over the whole thing. Cut it all up, mash everything together with the tatters and neeps, and pour a shot (or two) of Drambuie over it.

in England, and Scottish style will always reflect the land as well as the people.

Indeed, the rugged edge to Scottish style is what has led it into a new vogue in the last few years—it's very "in" to have a fishing holiday in Scotland, to summer in Scotland, to get married in Scotland, to do the outdoor thing in a cottage or castle in Scotland, and to know how to carry off this salt-of-the-earth look and feel in clothes and decor.

BEST BUYS OF SCOTLAND

. . . .

Despite the fact that Scotland has been even harder hit by the recession than England, things sold in city centers rarely cost less. There are no particular bargains in Scotland. However, there are a few categories of goods whose prices are very fair and competitive; there are some things you just have to buy no matter what they cost. Like Aberlour (a single-malt whisky; see page 327).

A few of my favorite Scottish things include:

• **Scotch:** The people are Scottish; the drink is Scotch. I never even liked it until recently; now I'm devoted. Scotch is actually created from blended whiskies. A single malt is never called scotch. For more information, see "The Whisky Trail" on page 324. In terms of price, you'll find that both miniatures and full bottles cost the same in Scotland and England, and maybe slightly less (£2 to £3) at the duty free. Expect to pay £20 to £25 for a liter or so of a good single malt. Miniatures run £3 to £4 per bottle.

• **Cashmere:** Cashmere sweater factories dot the Borders and cashmeres are sold in various "outlets" all over the country. There is no question that you can save on London prices and on U.S. prices when you compare price and quality and buy the best. However, you can get lucky with a sale in

London or shop very carefully in the United States and find better prices. Quality is the word here. You can get a cashmere sweater from the J. Crew catalogue for $129. You will pay $150 for a cashmere sweater in Scotland but it will be comparable not to the $129 sweater (which was probably made in China) but to a $400 sweater.

- **Kilts:** Kilts are making a big fashion statement from Paris to Seventh Avenue these days. Do mix and match your tartans and plaids. It's chic.

SOUVENIRS OF SCOTLAND

Actually, I think my navy cashmere cardigan is a very good souvenir, but if you're thinking of the inexpensive, easy-to-pack kind, I have a few suggestions:

- A miniature of Scotch or single malt (about £3).
- A postcard with your family name, crest, motto, and/or tartan (The Clans Collection from Lang Syne, 50p).
- Gift wrap in your family tartan (£1).
- Salmon fishing flies (£2).

EDINBURGH

Edinburgh is not a large city; the shopping areas most tourists prowl are neatly divided between two parts of town and are easy to find; you are either up on the hill near the castle or down in the flats below the castle.

Edinburgh has the feel of a small town, even when you are walking on the main high street (Princes Street) and are surrounded by multiples, you still feel as though you are in a small big town. The fact that a fair number of English multiples don't have shops here just makes it more charming.

Edinburgh

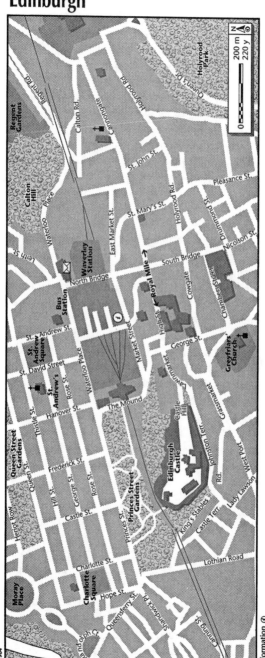

1964

Information ⓘ

Many locals go to Glasgow (say "Glas-go") to add diversification to their shopping. Glasgow has a branch store of **Istante,** the Gianni Versace line designed by his sister Donatella. No one in Edinburgh even knows who Donatella Versace is.

As an avid shopper, I can't really send you to Glasgow because Edinburgh is far and away more charming. I mean, if shopping is so bloody important, stay in London. Otherwise, enjoy Edinburgh and don't forget **Belinda Robertson**—in-town cashmere source (see page 312).

The Lay of the Land

Edinburgh was actually built as two different cities, owing to medieval problems like death, disease, and drainage. The first city (old city) was built around the castle itself, in keeping with medieval tradition. When things began to teem, a brand new city was built below the cliff of the castle, in the flats. There's a greenbelt that separates the two but no elevator.

In the new city, behind the high street (Princes Street) stores, there are rows of townhouses and then a few streets of Georgian terrace houses where rich people used to live. Some of the ones on the side streets coming off Princes Street have been turned into shops and boutiques.

Getting There

Easy connections by train from London make it possible to come to Edinburgh for a weekend, or even a day—you take the overnight train and wake up at 7am in the train station. You'd be daft to come just for a day (by train, anyway) but people do it. More frequently, the day trippers are business people who come via the British Airways shuttle. It's like traveling to Washington, D.C., from New York.

Go to Edinburgh by train, do your thing, then depart back toward London on a local train for Hawick (say "Hoyk"). Get off in Hawick and get a taxi for town. Spend, spend, spend on those cashmeres.

If you prefer a day trip to St. Andrews there are coach tours, and there's more to St. Andrews than golf, my friend—I'll be happy to tell you all about St. Andrews Woollen Mill (see page 323).

Or try the Edinburgh-Glasgow commute by train: It's only 47 minutes. I don't devote a lot of space in this book to Glasgow because I don't find it much in terms of shopping, especially for tourists. But culturally, the city is quite famous. So you might want to have a go. When you've spent all your cash, go back to the train station and proceed to London. Easy as shepherd's pie.

Getting Around

You really can walk everywhere in Edinburgh, except maybe to Leith. Do wear sensible shoes! There are a lot of cobblestones (in the castle yard), and there's one very, very big hill.

The shopping and sightseeing of Edinburgh can be tackled as one large oval from the Cally. Take the high road first and walk up the hill from the back. This gives you the Grassmarket first, while you are still strong. Come up behind the castle via the stairs (see them partially hidden in the wall?), then hit the Royal Mile. Walk toward Holyrood. If you decide to move on to public transportation, you can quit at the halfway mark, after you've finished the upper city and are near Waverley station, where you can grab a bus going along Princes Street. See my complete tour, below.

About Addresses

One word about store addresses: While they are included in each listing, you may find it very confusing since streets change names without notice. Furthermore, numbers change, so that two fabulous stores you'll want to see together anyway (**David**

Walker and **Ragamuffin**) are almost next door to each other, yet one is at 32 High Street and the other in the 200 block on Canongate. You wouldn't know they were nearby from looking at the addresses!

Sleeping in Edinburgh

There are various castles and B&Bs throughout Scotland if you want to do your tour of Scotland from the countryside. I prefer to base myself in Edinburgh and go out in a different direction each day, rather than moving from place to place.

THE CALEDONIAN
Princes Street, Edinburgh

The single most famous hotel in Edinburgh is the Caledonian, which locals call the Cally. The most important thing to do when you book your room is to request "castle view." Even if it costs extra, pay it. I cannot tell you the mystical feeling of looking out your window right into the back of Edinburgh Castle. When you see the light change—and the fog move in—and you hear the pipers play, you'll know what magic is. Aside from the fact that this hotel is drop-dead gorgeous and you will enjoy it immensely, there is a something about your castle view that will haunt you forever. The location of the hotel is also sublime, since you can walk anywhere in town from it. Rooms are in the $300 to $400 range, unless you can get a corporate rate or a package. Yes, the Caledonian is expensive, but worth every penny. A member of the Leading Hotels of the World chain. For reservations in the U.S., call 800/641-0300. Local phone: 131/225-2433.

BALMORAL HOTEL
Princes Street, Edinburgh

The Cally's archrival, the Balmoral used to be known as the North British hotel. It's now owned by Forte, which has put some money into restoration and hopes to get back into competing with the Cally again. The hotel is at the opposite end of Princes Street, across the street from the train station. Rates are less than the Cally; but then, so is the prestige. And the prices are still what is considered expensive, up to $300 per night. There is an advance sale package called Forte 30 that gives you a 30% discount if you pay for the room 30 days prior to arrival. Local phone: 131/556-2414.

The Roxburghe Hotel
Charlotte Square, Edinburgh

If you're looking for a small hotel with a good downtown location that doesn't cost as much as the grande dame hotels (and you don't mind a tour bus and coach crowd), then the Roxburghe is a winner. Double rooms are slightly over £100. A member of Best Western. For reservations, call 800/528-1234 from the United States. Local phone: 131/225-3921.

Shopping Neighborhoods

Edinburgh has five or six shopping neighborhoods, most of which connect in a U shape. There's also the port area of Leith, which I think is one of the best parts of town. The two main shopping areas are obvious, but there's more to the shopping in this small city than meets first glance.

It is possible to shop downtown Edinburgh in one day; but if you're a big spender or a slow walker and want to see the castle and a few of the sights in between, it will probably take you two days to do the various neighborhoods and feel proud of yourself. Maybe three or four.

The Castle/Lawnmarket

The Royal Mile is the main shopping drag of the upper city that stretches 1 mile from Edinburgh Castle to the palace of Holyrood. It begins at the castle door, which is called Castlehill. Then the street becomes Lawnmarket. But you'll never notice names on the streets anyway, and its just one big high street.

I actually divide the Royal Mile into two shopping areas: that portion near the castle and above George IV Bridge called Lawnmarket; the rest I call Lower Royal Mile. Many tourists poop out at Cockburn Street and head for the walkway to the new city, or just cross over at that point because it's convenient. The feel of the retail is quite different in Lower Royal Mile: I'd hate for you to miss it.

The castle neighborhood obviously houses the famous Edinburgh Castle, which, even though I rarely send you on solely cultural excursions, is a fabulous castle and is worth seeing. (Of course, they also have an excellent gift shop within the castle walls—with merchandise not found elsewhere.) On the Royal Mile outside of the castle gates, there are shops and tourist traps on either side of the street selling postcards, tea towels with pictures of Scottie dogs, sweaters, and coin purses that look like small tams. Even if they are standard tourist fare, they are kind of fun. There's one shop where the salesmen are dressed up in kilts; not only will this thrill your kids but it makes for a fun photo opportunity.

There are a couple of antique shops up here (try **Castle Antiques,** No. 330). More common are the fake sweater outlets that I loathe generically— although on an individual basis some of them are better than others. I actually enjoy poking in at **Jamie Scott's Mill Shop,** because it has a certain junky feel to it that makes me feel good. I also don't mind promotional deals like two (yes, two) sweaters for £15! There's another branch on Princes Street: I like this one better (449 Lawnmarket).

You'll want to poke in at **The Cashmere Shop,** which has several branches (No. 379 and No. 207 High Street), but the one at Lawngate (No. 379) is probably the best—although you'll have to hold out for other sources if you want serious quality. This is the kind of place you go to learn a little and maybe buy a pair of cashmere gloves. Nearby is the **Royal**

Mile Whiskies (also No. 379), where you can spend several hours. See page 308.

GRASSMARKET

Grassmarket is Edinburgh's best-kept secret. Until it's discovered, you'll find yourself in a delightful shopping area that very few people know about, even though it sits directly under the back of the castle. If this is the hottest spot in town, blame it all on sweater designer **Bill Baber** (66 Grassmarket), who has the best shop in the area (and perhaps the best shop in Edinburgh), or blame it on the recession—rents in Grassmarket are less than in other parts of town.

Grassmarket does have an open-air flea market every now and then (ask your concierge), but it has several antique and vintage clothing shops that operate every day. This is just the fun, funky part of town where people can afford to browse and shop and have a ball.

Grassmarket actually has two parts: Grassmarket, which is flat, and Victoria Street, which curves up and off to the Royal Mile from Grassmarket. Victoria Street is full of cute stores—the kind you came here to see, not the touristy ones just selling kilts and heather-tone sweaters.

LEITH

If you prefer tourist haunts where you can buy a sweater and a kilt, there are two famous ones in Leith as well. There's **James Pringle Weavers** of Inverness (70-74 Bangor Road), but before you get too excited, I must warn you that this is not the same Pringle you're thinking of. It's a large tourist trap, larger than many supermarkets, and just loaded with everything you might ever want to buy. There is a **Clan Tartan Centre** toward the rear. Prices do happen to be 10% to 20% lower than in town, but this is not a real factory outlet. If you go by taxi (about £4 one way), you can have the shop phone a taxi for your return trip or you can get there by bus from Princes Street. Open seven days a week; Sunday hours are 10am to 4pm. There is nothing, except maybe a haggis, that this store does not sell.

Kinloch Anderson, the royal kilt maker, is more famous, less touristy, and also in Leith at the corner of Commercial Street and Dock Street. See pages 313 for the store listing.

Move on to a warehouse filled with antiques at **Georgian Antiques** (10 Pattison Street) and you may need medical help after you see the selection. This looks like a mover's warehouse; furniture is stacked from floor to ceiling in a truly overwhelming manner. I'm not certain I can even explain the emotions you will go through. Some of the furniture is used, not antique. Most pieces have prices on them, some are coded. If you are looking for a certain something, get the front office to help you. They ship. If you are driving, you may want to study a map or call for directions, as the tiny streets are more like a warren and many are one way. Local phone: 131/553-7286. It is a member of the London Antiques Association (LAPADA). It opens at 8:30am on weekdays; Saturday hours are 10am to 1pm. Closed Sundays.

Then there's **Easy** and **Edinburgh Architectural Salvage Yard,** two salvage stores. The latter specializes in the usual salvage items: radiators, tubs, windows, doors, entire shower/tub combos (old ones are quite unique), toilets, faucets, etc. It is heaven. Hours are Monday through Friday from 9am to 5pm. Saturday afternoons only noon to 5pm. Closed Sundays.

LOWER ROYAL MILE/CANONGATE

This part of the Royal Mile is also loaded with stores, many of which cater to tourists. However, because these stores are a little farther away from the castle, they are not quite as touristy as the others. The number of stores selling tartan refrigerator magnets drops dramatically.

In between those that are touristy are some very fine local stores (**Hyne & Eames, David Walker**), as well as a couple of historical sights. You can take the Royal Mile all the way down to Holyrood Palace, although the shopping will peter out just a little before you get there.

PRINCES STREET

Princes Street is the main shopping drag of the new, or low, city. It sits beneath the castle. For the best shopping, connect from the high city over Waverley Bridge (which runs directly in front of the train station), then turn left and walk toward the Cally. This is an easy stroll past the department stores of Edinburgh and many branch stores of your favorite London retailers, including **Marks & Spencer, Liberty, Scotch House, Laura Ashley, Boots,** and **Next.** If you insist on paying a visit to the **Disney Store,** you'll find it also on Princes Street.

BEHIND PRINCES STREET

Real people shop Princes Street and the parallel street behind it (George Street), as well as the connecting side streets such as Hanover Street and Frederick Street. The shopping back here is not the kind I would ordinarily tell a visitor not to miss. It's nice to wander and explore; you get a much better picture of the real Edinburgh and of what it's like to be rich in Edinburgh. But if you are pressed for time, you can live without seeing this neighborhood. There is a nice branch of **Laura Ashley** for home furnishings and a few lesser multiples as well as some nice bookstores like **James Thin Booksellers.** The British Air office is on Frederick Street.

STOCKBRIDGE

In the days of villages, Stockbridge was a village
outside of Edinburgh. You'll get a much more quaint
feel for Edinburgh and find a number of stores where
prices are lower, people are friendly, and antiques
are even affordable here. Note that some of these
shops don't open until 11am or have strange hours
and open whenever they feel like it.

Number Two, one of the most famous sweater
shops in Edinburgh, is here in Stockbridge.

UNIVERSITY

Since Edinburgh is famous for its university, you
should at least know where it is, even if you don't
go there to shop. Basically, the university is below
the castle on the castle side of the high street. It's
not in the new city but sits slightly above Grassmarket on the same side, downhill from George IV
Bridge in the opposite direction of Waverley
Station. The area has jeweler's shops, shoemakers,
and photo processing shops. Not worth your time.

THE WEST END

This area really centers around the Cally as it is at
the western end of Princes Street. There is more
retail stretching out away from the castle, including
a small branch of **Boots,** some multiples like **Habitat,** etc. There is a tiny retail area just off the central
West End designation around Williams Street that
leads to Palmerston Place, where you'll find **Belinda
Robertson,** my cashmere resource.

Sweater Tips

There are about three different types of sweater
retailers in Edinburgh, with at least two of these
types found in the countryside both in the Borders
and north, toward Perth and thereabouts. Because

there are so many sweater shops, you may be confused or overwhelmed. Don't be.

FASHION SWEATERS

There are only about four high-fashion sweater retailers in Edinburgh, although more may be joining the ranks. (You'll find the good ones either in Grassmarket or on Canongate.) These sweaters are very special and nontraditional; many are one of a kind, and are hand knit and often works of art. Prices begin around £60 ($100), although don't be shocked by £200 to £350 ($300 to $500) tags. My favorites include: Ragamuffin, 276 Canongate; Hyne & Eames, 299 Canongate; David Walker, 32 High Street; Bill Baber, 66 Grassmarket.

TOURIST SWEATER SHOPS

There are a number of these. Many of them call themselves outlet stores, although they just seem to be mass merchandisers with a number of branch stores throughout the area who move truckloads of very ordinary merchandise to people who don't seem to realize how boring this stuff is.

I don't want to name names, but I'm talking shops that sell rose-colored A-line skirts and matching rose-heather Shetland sweaters that give new definition to the fashion style Ian calls "English Rose." Prices are moderate, but there aren't any great bargains, and none of these stores is an authentic factory outlet.

Most of these stores have similar names as well as branch outlets. The Royal Mile has the most offenders, but there are several on Princes Street too.

OUTLET SHOPS & JOBBERS

You'll only find these shops in the Borders; there are none in town. Except for Belinda Robertson. Please note that I got a letter from a reader who complained about Belinda Robertson, saying the stock was low when she visited. Shopper, beware: Outlets and jobbers are always a hit-or-miss kind of thing.

Remember:

- There are often good buys in cotton knits (in sweaters and polo-style shirts) as well as in Shetlands and cashmeres.
- Cashmere is sold in many plies—from single up to four-ply. A ply is a strand of yarn. The price of a cashmere sweater is directly related to how many plies are in the knit. The weight and warmth of a cashmere is also directly related to the number of plies, so a four-ply sweater may be too heavy for you if you live in California or the sunbelt. When you start comparing prices from one shop to another, make sure you are comparing apples to apples.
- Quality of cashmere differs dramatically; maybe it's the way it's knit, maybe it's the goat. Beats me. I can just tell you that there is no comparison between the top-of-the-line, fine goods sold at Belinda Robertson, and the very ordinary cashmere sold at the Cashmere Store and the like. See and touch enough sweaters, and you will soon be differentiating between "good" and "bad" cashmere.
- Men's sweaters are often less expensive than women's. Consider buying a man's sweater—who can tell? Also consider buying a man's sweater that is large enough for you to add shoulder pads if you want a fashion look.
- Sweaters that go on sale in outlets are often in color groups that have been discontinued. The very best buys we saw were on sweaters that were chrome yellow or avocado green. In all the factory outlets we visited, we never once found a simple black sweater. Barry got a sweater in a fabulous dusty water lily green, which I wanted to buy

for Ian for his birthday. The sweater came in Barry's size (very large) but not Ian's. In fact, there was little in Ian's size because he wears a common, medium-range size. Mainstream sells out in color and size.

- Twinsets may be hard to find anywhere. I've got one fabulous source for them in The Borders and there are a few other places where you may get lucky, but they are not that common.
- There are one or two shops in London that sell the same close-outs and seconds as the factory outlet shops in The Borders. The selection isn't as good as in Scotland, but if you came all the way from London just to save $10 on a sweater, you goofed. Big-name fashion sweaters (like Bill Baber), however, are 20% to 40% less expensive in Edinburgh. Olive bought Barry two cashmere sweaters in The Borders and then compared them to in-town Edinburgh prices; she saved £120!

Kilt Tips

If you are seriously shopping for a kilt to wear, I have just a few tips. There are mass-produced, tourist-quality kilts, of course. You'll have no trouble finding them, in sizes from infants to adults. They may be as inexpensive as £17 to £30 ($25 to $45) per. If you're taking this a bit more seriously, remember:

- A kilt can be off the rack or custom made. Naturally, custom made costs more—it will also have more fabric in it, which will give better drape, fit, and movement to the kilt.
- Ask how much fabric is in each kilt you look at so you can compare prices for equal pieces. Eight yards should be about right. Ask!
- A kilt need only be cleaned for two occasions in a gentleman's life: his wedding and his funeral. There is some question among locals about the second cleaning.
- If you're looking for the best price on a quality kilt, ask around for sales on "for-hire" kilts. Since

kilts have limited use in even a Scotsman's life, many gents prefer to rent. Most kilt stores have a rental department and will clean house once or twice a year with a sale of for-hire garments.

• If you are wearing the kilt to a formal occasion, you have several choices depending on your style—do it up right and get a local expert to put the whole thing together for you. Team traditional black-tie gear with the kilt; add bits and pieces of vintage mishmash and be an eccentric. Remember, if you must get it right you will need lessons. There are rites and rituals and sporrans (Scottish purses) that go with. Ask for help while shopping.

Sunday Shopping

Most stores—big multiples and touristy stores, anyway—are open from noon until 5pm.

There are very often crafts fairs on weekends, many in town or nearby, like at Hopetoun House, a stately home (part of the National Trust), which rents its grounds for these affairs.

Factory outlets are closed on Sunday.

The gift shop in the castle is (of course) open on Sunday. There is a weekly flea market on Sundays at Ingliston, near the Edinburgh Airport.

Antiques

There are a few neighborhoods for antiques, especially the less-than-serious type, which is the only kind that is still affordable. While Edinburgh is known for its selection of seriously collectible antiquarian books, you'll find more funky fun stuff either in Stockbridge or Grassmarket. Also check out West Bow, just a minute's walk from the Royal Mile.

On Victoria Street, the connecting street from Grassmarket to the Royal Mile, is **Byzantium**, an old church turned into a bazaar that has about two dozen antique dealers, a cafe, and a few artsy-craftsy-type dealers. A disgruntled reader thought Byzantium was a waste of time. As for me, when I'm out on the prowl from Grassmarket to the Royal Mile, I don't mind poking my head in—even if I don't find God. You never know.

Also, there are weekend car boot sales, a flea market near the Edinburgh airport (see above), and another flea market in Glasgow (see page 316 for more information on shopping Glasgow).

Department Stores

JENNERS
Princes Street, Edinburgh

Jenners is the local version of Macy's and Bloomingdale's rolled into one; it is right on Princes Street in the thick of the multiples and the main street shopping and could be the best stop if you only have time for one-stop shopping. Aside from the usual real-people things like cosmetics and clothes, it has a good selection of dishes, souvenirs, and needlework. Olive recommends the tartans on the second floor. Open on Thursday evenings until 7:30pm. That's called late-night shopping in Scotland. The store has salespeople who speak 10 different languages, including Polish. Just ask for help.

MARKS & SPENCER
Princes Street, Edinburgh

While you may know this English favorite from London, the Edinburgh store bears looking at for two good reasons: There's two stores. One is the basic department store with grocery; and there is a totally separate home furnishings store. This is where you can also buy bath items, as well as dishes, sheets, tabletop, wallpaper, etc. Open until 8pm on Thursdays.

Oh, yes, it has currency exchange in the main store, but the rates are bad.

Shopping Centers

At the corner of Princes Street and Waverley Bridge, roughly adjacent to the Waverley Station, is the **Waverley Market**, which is not an old-fashioned market but a new-fashioned mall. This is not to be confused with the shopping stalls that are in the train station.

Waverley Market is a new structure with three levels of stores, and because of the elevation of both the train station and the hill to the upper city, part of the mall is at ground level and part is inside the bottom slope of the hill; so there are different entrances and exits at various levels.

The Waverley Market is more a resource for locals than for tourists, but everyone will enjoy its modern stores and the offerings of its designer shops—there's everything from **Benetton** to **Jaeger** here, as well as sweater shops (**Gleneagles**), a good bookstore, and a tourist trap or two. In terms of multiples, look for **Richards, Monsoon,** and **Jumpers.** There is also a small cafeteria on the upper level for tea and cakes or sandwiches.

The **St. James Centre** is not far from Waverley Market, on the corner of Princes Street and Leith Street. It has more than 50 shops, a bank, and a hotel. This is more of a real-people shopping center.

Finds

ROYAL MILE WHISKIES
379 High Street, Edinburgh

Read more about whisky, shops, and resources on page 324, or do your own research at this small store stocked with salmon, souvenirs, and tons of whiskies in both miniature form and full bottle sizes. The help is patient and well versed; tell them your husband likes MacAllan but wants to try something similar, but new, and they will recommend, etc.

BILL BABER
66 Grassmarket, Edinburgh

Baber makes a signature sweater that immediately
tells the world you have taste—and money. The
designs are usually small geometrics or waves. The
small shop on Grassmarket is the studio—sweaters
are displayed on wooden poles, and you just keep
trying them on and gobbling them up.

There are about four or five different body types:
some cardigans, some pullovers. The colors are
muted, either dusty darks or misty pastels—there
are few clear brights. Prices are excellent for the
quality and creativity—these are real works of art.
There is usually a sale rack. If you want certain styles
changed or a different color, you can order. If this is
your one treat to yourself, look no further. Possibly
the best sweater shop in all of Edinburgh.

FORSYTH OF EDINBURGH
183 Canongate, Edinburgh

High quality and some fashion in the traditional
looks—more preppy than most; sort of the precur-
sor to Ralph Lauren. Expensive but not outrageous;
true value for cashmere and wool in all styles. One
of the best resources in town for people willing to
spend money on a top-of-the-line product.

PINE & OLD LACE
46 Victoria Street, Edinburgh

This is an excellent source for Victorian nightgowns
and white work, which are moderately priced compared to U.S. prices. Good examples of Victorian
clothing; pillowcases are about £30 ($50) a pair.

NUMBER TWO
2 St. Stephen Street, Stockbridge

One of those great tiny shops that sells nothing but fabulous sweaters, most of them either hand knit or hand loomed. For sweater freaks, this is worth the trip. The good thing about the shop is that the selection is very broad: There are solids as well as crazy colors. There are a number of sweater jacket styles as well.

HAND IN HAND
3 North West Circus Place, Stockbridge

One of the best shops in Scotland for antique fabrics, costumes, old paisleys, white work, and more. Prices are painfully high, but the quality is outstanding. It opens at 10am. On the main street, just on top of St. Stephen Street. Don't miss it. Fabulous, fabulous, fabulous.

PAVILION
6A Howe Street, Edinburgh

A small shop for artists and do-it-yourselfers who can't resist the stencil look. Stencils are sold here (beginning at £6 but escalating to a high of £20), along with paints and kits. You can buy their catalogue of designs for inspiration. At the halfway point in a walk between Princes Street and Stockbridge.

MARGARET HYNE & CAMILLA EAMES
299 Canongate, the Royal Mile, Edinburgh

One of the fanciest, richest, tweedy country look shops in Scotland, selling various designer sweaters for men and women and some tweeds and ready-to-wear. You did bring the circle pin, didn't you, Muffy? Artistic looks as well as preppy traditional styles. You came to Scotland just for this shop, you just didn't know it.

LAURA ASHLEY
Clothing: 126 Princes Street, Edinburgh
Home: 90 George Street, Edinburgh

It's hard to consider Laura Ashley as a find, but find it you will on Princes Street, with all the other big names, department stores, and multiples. The special part is the home furnishings store, a free-standing store around the corner (sort of) on George Street.

The decorator showroom it used to run has been closed down to put more goods and emphasis into this home-furnishings store. Heavy furniture and decorative things are toward the rear, while the front parts of the store have tiles, wallpaper, fabrics, accessories, etc. The store feels good. And no, I don't think it's crazy to carry wallpaper home with you, especially when you buy it on sale here.

RAGAMUFFIN
276 Canongate, the Royal Mile, Edinburgh

A sweater shop with designs from other makers as well as the house line, which comes from the Isle of Skye. I saw a lot of merchandise I'd never seen before in this warm and friendly shop, where the energy of the colors will knock your socks off. There are a few solid and traditional sweaters, but not that many. Color and artistry are the going thing; £60 ($100) can get you an awfully nice hand-knit sweater. There are hats and some accessories as well.

ROBERT CRESSER'S BRUSH SHOP
Victoria Street, Edinburgh

One of the most charming stores on Victoria Street, this shop sells all sorts of brushes—many seemingly made the way they were centuries ago. Even if you don't buy (the kids probably did not ask you to bring home a broom), this store will make you feel good for having seen it.

DAVID WALKER
32 High Street, Edinburgh

This one's a purl. (Sorry, I couldn't resist.) True talent and a way with the knit—with color, too. The most unusual fashion sweaters in Scotland are sold here; they belong in a museum or in Paris. Most are made with some mohair or some silk, so texture is part of the story. All garments are hand knit; special orders are easily arranged. Prices are fair for this kind of workmanship and high style; you get the VAT refund after spending £30. Not for the shy.

BELINDA ROBERTSON
3 Palmerston Place, Edinburgh

Robertson has a showroom on the edge of the Charlotte Square area in the West End of Edinburgh. The showroom is simply that, a room with a worktable, a desk, and some bins. It's in the front room of a townhouse; you must buzz.

Once inside, you may purchase the samples or order. Or get the address of the outlet in Hawick (see page 320). I can't promise you that the sales help is organized. The day I visited, there were no prices on half the garments I wanted and there was no one in the factory to answer questions.

There is a price guide on the wall with a color-coded dot system. There are also close-outs in bins and on racks. A cashmere T-shirt group in slightly weird but wonderful fashion colors (like lime) was marked down to £30; pale blue was £50. I bought a ribbed scarf for £25 that was the buy of the century. Gloves at £7 were also a steal.

There are samples, sample books, samples of yarns—all sorts of fun things. Prices are fair. They are not dirt cheap but they are the best you may ever find in your life for this kind of quality. For $200 you'll certainly find something special, something worth $400 in the real world.

I got a letter from a reader who found the location difficult, the stock minimal, and the whole thing an ordeal not worth the trouble. Obviously, it depends how you hit it.

THE KILT SHOP
21-25 George IV Bridge, Leith

This is not the most famous kilt shop in town, but it is a lot of fun. They sell it all, from Highland pumps to sashes and sporrans.

DISCOUNT HIGHLAND SUPPLY
7 Cowgatehead, Grassmarket

You can get the whole works here (from tam to toe) for one flat price—around £300 ($450). They also sell bagpipes. Toward the university area.

KINLOCH ANDERSON
Commercial Street and Dock Street, Leith

If you're looking for the Prince Charles Takes Balmoral look, this is it. The most famous kilt maker in the world (three royal warrants; in business since 1868), Kinloch Anderson has a retail store in the factory in Leith.

Serious kilts begin at £150, but I saw a woman's skirt/kilt on sale for $35. Of course, it was a touristy style of kilt but I liked it just fine. There're some jewelry and souvenir items. This is where I bought my tartan wrapping paper. There are also sweaters and various name-brand goods to coordinate the total look. You get your value-added tax (VAT) refund on any purchases over £35; they take all credit cards and they have a brochure in five languages.

Wearing the Plaid

A reader wrote me this tidbit: There's a store called **Schuh**, next to the Balmoral Hotel on Prince's Street near Waverly Station, that sells tartan Doc Martens. Is that fab or what?

GLASGOW

. . . .

Glasgow, long an industrial city of little charm, has been revamping its image. Millions of pounds have been spent and several of the new attractions are indeed enticing, but frankly Glasgow still has a ways to go.

There's an old saying in Glasgow: "What's there to do in Glasgow on a Sunday?" And the answer is: "Go to Edinburgh."

I think the better question is, "Why go to Glasgow?" If pressed, I'd say you go to Glasgow to spend the night and eat dinner at One Devonshire Gardens. While there's a very nice shopping center downtown, in an interesting architectural form that Prince Charles actually approves of, Glasgow has little charm to it. It has some nice museums. The shopping is not special, although it is improving and a few designers have begun to open shop. Stay tuned.

The Lay of the Land

Glasgow is an industrial city, and looks like one, so be prepared. There are some very interesting buildings, but on the whole this is not a gorgeous city. There is a downtown area with a walking street or two (Argyle Street is the main drag; Buchanan Street is the main walking street), but it's not even particularly attractive in any quaint or charming manner.

There are two big shopping centers in the downtown area. One is a rehab—Princes Square—that is gorgeous and worth seeing. This is the one Prince Charles likes. The other—St. Enoch's Centre—is more like a nice version of an American mall. Both are worth visiting while you're in town and they are only a few blocks apart.

There are two train stations in town, one for going to Edinburgh (Queen Street) and one for going to London (Central); so pay attention to ticket information. Both are downtown. There is a shuttle bus between them, should you need to make a connection.

A few blocks above Argyle Street (and within walking distance, for a good walker) are Bath Street and Sauchiehall Street, which run parallel to each other and are the other shopping streets of the city. There is a partial pedestrian area on Sauchiehall where many of the stores that are on Argyle have another branch.

Toward the outside of the city is Great Western Road, where there are a few antique shops bunched together.

Getting Around

There is a small but very clean and nice public transportation system, and it will get you to plenty of shopping experiences. It's not very convenient if you are staying at One Devonshire Gardens, but for in-city traffic it will do fine. Stations are marked with a big U; there is a convenient one next to St. Enoch's Square.

There are taxi stands in the major shopping district; otherwise, it can be difficult to flag one down on the streets. Don't be shy about calling for a radio cab. You can walk to all the downtown shopping once you are downtown.

Sleeping in Glasgow

ONE DEVONSHIRE GARDENS
One Devonshire Gardens, Glasgow

If you're going to spend some time in Glasgow and high style is what your life is all about, there is only one choice for lodging: One Devonshire Gardens, a series of three town houses strung together into the most beautiful B&B you will ever, ever see. Restored beyond its original beauty, the hotel has a famous kitchen (reservations needed), and is a favorite of those in the know. The location is outside of downtown;

take a taxi. We're talking serious money here: Rooms cost about $300 per night and dinner, which is a must-do, is over $100 for two—and can even get closer to $200. For reservations, call local phone: 141/334-9494; or fax: 141/337-1663.

Shopping Glasgow

Aside from the academic interest of seeing the two main malls in Glasgow, there are some small specialty items to shop for. These include decorative objects made in the Glasgow School mold, either originals, which are now sold as pricey antiques, or reproductions. You can hope to get lucky with antiques.

If you want to see the best of the stores, simply stroll along Buchanan Street, where the majority of the department stores, British designers, and multiples are located, although there are a few more on Argyle Street or in St. Enoch's Centre. Catch **Laura Ashley** (80 Buchanan Street), **Liberty** (No. 105), **Ciro** (No. 95), **Burberrys** (No. 64), **Jaeger** (No. 64), or **Dash** (No. 54).

Both **Gianni Versace/Istante** (162 Ingram Street) and **Giorgio Armani Emporio** (19 John Street) chose Glasgow as the location for their first U.K. ventures outside of London. In other words, they scorned Edinburgh. Supposedly, Glasgow has the second-highest retail turnover in the United Kingdom, just after London. **Muji**, which has that sensational Japanese container store right behind Liberty in London, has a branch in Glasgow (63-67 Queen Street). And speaking of the Japanese, **Ichi Ni San**—which means "one, two, three" in Japanese, in case you are wondering—is a store for nice gifts with clean lines and design elements. It's owned by the people who created One Devonshire Gardens.

There is a small antique trade, and prices can be lower than in England. The weekend flea market, the **Barras**, does not have a great reputation. Olive's friend Iona says watch your handbag. There are also some antique shops on Bath Street in the downtown area and on Great Western Road. The most fun can be had at the Victorian Village, a complex that houses several dealers on West Regent Street in the area I call "Glasgow 2," outside downtown Glasgow.

The mass-merchandised sweater mills with their so-called factory outlets have invaded Glasgow so that there are almost as many shops selling sweaters in a very commercial manner here as there are in Edinburgh or London. They're not real factory outlets. But if you need a gift or want a moderately priced, machine-made sweater, try any of them—they are either on Buchanan Street or right off it, down a little street called Nelson Mandela Place.

DEPARTMENT STORES

FRASERS
21 Buchanan Street, Glasgow

An old-fashioned, big-time department store right on the corner of Buchanan and Argyle streets, Frasers has it all in a building that will make architecture students gleeful—you can actually see the original part of the store and all the add-ons. It has everything from china to souvenirs to Ralph Lauren.

MARKS & SPENCER
12 Argyle Street, Glasgow

All of the usual, right in the middle of the real-people shopping on Argyle Street, near St. Enoch's Centre.

FLEA MARKETS

THE BARRAS
Gallowsgate, Glasgow

Held on Saturday and Sunday at Gallowsgate, the Barras is part open-air and part covered market. Hours are 9:30am to 5:30pm. Hunt down the good stuff; bargain like mad.

PADDY'S MARKET
Bridgegate, Glasgow

Absolutely all sorts of junk and stuff, new and old, much made to appeal to the large student population living on a modest budget. It's sort of picturesque, even if it's not your cup of tea. More for students and teens and tweens and those alternative retail sorts who do not wear black velvet Alice bands (headbands). Open: Monday through Saturday, 10am to 4pm. Take a taxi.

SHOPPING CENTERS

PRINCES SQUARE
48 Buchanan Street, Glasgow

It looks rather average from the outside, but it's gorgeous inside. Be sure to run up and down the stairs and around the balconies. This is the fanciest shopping center in Glasgow, and this is what all the fuss is about. Several big-time chains (Jigsaw, Butler and Wilson, Crabtree and Evelyn, Marc O'polo, Pied à Terre, Whistles) and other London designers have shops here. There is the usual central atrium space, but all the rehab work has been done according to the design principles of the Glasgow School, so there is a very modern Art Deco feel to the wrought-iron fences, etc. The details are very nice and worth your attention. There are places to eat; there are clean bathrooms and plenty of great shops. Enjoy it.

ST. ENOCH'S CENTRE
Argyle Street and St. Enoch's Square, Glasgow

Although this mall looks somewhat like a cross between a modern train station and an American mall, it has many nice branches of multiples and an assortment of big department stores. There's Boots, the Body Shop, Knobs and Knockers, BHS, Richards, and Mothercare.

SAUCHIEHALL CENTRE
Sauchiehall Street, Glasgow

This red brick bunker of a shopping center has its
back end to a pedestrian street that offers several
branches of department stores like C and A and
Littlewoods, as well as multiples like Laura Ashley
and Boots.

FORGE SHOPPING CENTRE
1221 Gallowsgate, Glasgow

This is really for locals and was devised in part
to be a destination mall—one that is open on
Sunday and provides activities for the family so
people will stay in Glasgow on the weekend instead of going off to Edinburgh. It's in the suburbs
and has 2,000 parking spaces, as well as a multi-
plex cinema and the usual mall treats. There's
also a hypermarket, if you need to do any grocery
shopping.

THE BORDERS

· ·

The part of Scotland that comes between England
and the Highlands is the lowlands; they begin with
The Borders, where all the factories are. What
do they make in those factories? I thought you'd
never ask. Sweaters, of course; cashmere sweaters.
Do those factories have outlet stores? I thought you'd
never ask.

Shopping The Borders

You may want to use some of the local guides to get
more addresses; I am purposely only listing great
stores that I know will have something worth looking at. Wear yourself out at your own pace; or stick
to the winners and enjoy yourself.

FINDS

WHITE OF HAWICK
Victoria Road, Hawick

This shop is definitely hit-or-miss. On one visit, it was disappointing. On my last visit it was, hands down, the best place I stopped at for traditional, old-fashioned sweaters. The store is not huge, but it is just big enough to have a women's department and a separate room in the rear for men's sweaters. They have large sizes for men, which are not easy to find (up to size 54). There is a catalogue. There were traditional colors such as navy, which may sound simple to find but isn't. A man's cashmere sweater, 2 ply, was £75; a woman's cardigan was £89. Absolutely the best place we visited.

CHAS. WHILLIANS
Teviotdale Mills, Hawick

This is the store that I remembered as being great, but it wasn't that hot on our last visit. There are two stores, one in the town of Hawick, which has sports-related knits and no cashmeres, and a factory shop more to the edge of town. The latter is called the Teviotdale Mills shop, and it is across the street from White of Hawick; there is a car park next to Whillians.

BELINDA ROBERTSON
Ladylaw Centre, Unit 17, Hawick

In an industrial center next door to Chas. Whillians, this factory sells the marvelous Belinda Robertson goods I have been raving about; see page 312. Do not enter the front door of the center but go around the side to your right (if you are facing the center and Whillians is to your right) and look at the doors, which are marked with numbers. The factory showroom is unit 17. The people at Whillians will guide you if this sounds complicated.

PETER SCOTT
11 Buccleuch Street, Hawick

Around the corner from the other two sources, still on the edge of town and not in downtown Hawick, Scott has a store across the street from its factory; someone will actually run over to the factory and get you something special if you so desire. I was looking for twinsets and they volunteered to go get the various parts for me.

This is top-of-the-line traditional cashmere with a few fashion items but mostly English rose styles. I bought a navy cardigan with grosgrain ribbon trim and gold rose buttons, £100. Then I got my VAT refund. Ta da!

VALERIE LOUTHAN
2 Kirk Wynd, Hawick

Not far from these other sources and not in the downtown area either, Louthan is the most fashion forthright—she actually sells cashmere T-shirts. Top, top quality and fabulous style in this tiny shop that is worth finding. Not that it's hard to find, it's just that you might be tired or broke and be tempted to write it off. Don't.

AINTREE KNITWEAR
42 High Street, Innerleithen, Peeblesshire

Olive found this shop at the end of our day. If we had gone here first thing, we may have bought out the store and gone back to Edinburgh. This source is as big as a sneeze and may not impress you at first glance. Stay a while; put down your handbag. After you've looked in the bin of markdowns and seen the fashion cashmere sweaters on the racks, get the salesgirl to explain to you the twinsets, the special orders, and the yarn book.

The yarn book has hundreds of samples; you pick and order. A twinset, both parts, costs a mere £125!

It takes about five to six weeks for your order to be made, then it is mailed to you in the United States. They are experts at mailing. Enough said?

Oh, yes, one pointer. I chose what I thought was a dusty strawberry color for my twinset. The salesgirl was all excited because that yarn had just come in. She went to retrieve it. Yuck! What was gorgeous in a one-inch sample would have been disaster in size 40. Okay, size 44. Be careful if you pick a weird shade.

Open: Monday through Friday 9am to 4:30pm; Saturdays 9am to 12:30pm or by appointment. Local phone: 01896/830-170; fax: 01896/831-265).

ST. ANDREWS

. . . .

There's more to St. Andrews than the links. There's ruins! There's theology students in cute black gowns! There's a view that will take your breath away! There's Ma Brown's Tea Room! There's the British Golf Museum (with gift shop, natch)! There's that view again. And yes, there's good shopping.

Playing the Course

I don't play golf; in fact, I care very little about golf. But I have discovered that getting onto the Old Course is very tricky and takes some consumer know-how. That's my department. If you aren't related directly to the Stuart family, or even the Windsor family, your best bet is to buy a package that guarantees your tee.

That does not mean to say you have to stay at the Old Course Hotel—the fanciest and the best known—but you will find that there are lesser hotels right there near the course that aren't perhaps your cup of tea but do come with the guarantee. Kids are not allowed on the course. You may be asked to provide local club membership, standing, and handicap.

There are small putting greens for those who must say they've done it but haven't really.

Shopping the Course

Of course, they have a pro shop at the Old Course. It's modern and not much to look at, but considering the view is outside anyway, all you want to do is run inside and gawk at the logo merchandise. There is Old Course souvenir everything. Much of the merchandise is Japanese brands. I bought colored tees for £2; souvenir golf towels cost £5; cashmere sweaters cost almost £200.

Shopping St. Andrews

St. Andrews is an adorable town with two main parts to it: the center of town and the cluster of retail stores near the Old Course. The two main drags in the heart of town are Market Street and South Street. Multiples such as Benetton, Jumpers, Simply Sweaters, etc., are on Bell Street. There are a few antique stores on North and South streets; there are a few thrift shops on South Street as well.

The streets around the course have names like The Golf Links and The Scores. Honest.

FINDS

As far as I'm concerned, there are only two stores in town anyway.

ST. ANDREWS WOOLLEN MILL
Golf Links, St. Andrews

Yes, it's a major tourist trap but it is giant fun. They give out free postcards, they have a huge mail-order business, they are prepared to do business with tourists from all over the world. The store is huge with little rooms added to little rooms and up and down stairs and tons and tons and tons of touristy items and a few nice cashmere sweaters at fair prices.

Sweaters are in bins; there's wool, there's cotton, there's cashmere; there's kilts; there's yarn on cones; there's Arrans. They have kids' stuff; there's tartan by the yard; there's sheepskin. Then there's travel blankets; Shetlands; golf sweaters; there's Pringle and big names; there's something for everyone and prices are modest. Despite the fact that this is a tourist trap, you may not have more fun anywhere else. You play the Old Course; I'll shop.

AUCHTERLONIES
2-4 Golf Place, St. Andrews

Since 1895, this has been the "in" place for the right stuff—clubs, shoes, clothes, etc. You may rent clubs, just in case you decide to suddenly drop in on the Old Course and get a tee time.

THE WHISKY TRAIL
. . . .

You can take the Disney-like ride in Edinburgh and learn all about malt whisky, or you can read my husband Mike's explanation below and then start your own Pepsi Challenge—with Scotch, of course. Malt whisky is made in pot stills in four complete stages. Do not try this at home.

1. **Malting:** Barley is screened, soaked in tanks of water (called steeps) for two or three days, and laid out on a concrete malting floor from three to seven days until "just before the shoots start to grow." Alternatively, malting is carried out in large rectangular Saladin boxes for better temperature control. Some distillers buy from centralized maltings (less expensive); others add heather at this stage (more distinctive flavor). Already distinctions between tastes are being made.
2. **Mashing:** The dried malt is ground in a mill, and the grist is mixed with hot water in a large circular vessel called a mash tun. The starch in

the malt, which is water soluble, is converted into a sugary liquid called wort and is drawn off; the remaining solid wastes are made into cattle feed.

3. **Fermentation:** After cooling, the wort is passed into huge vessels where yeast is added so that fermentation takes place; yeast attacks the sugar and converts it into crude alcohol within 48 hours; the liquid produced is now called wash.

4. **Distillation:** The wash is heated until the liquid vaporizes, rises up in the still, and passes into the cooling plant, where it becomes liquid again. The first distillation separates the alcohol from the fermented liquid. This distillate, now called "low wines," is distilled again. Neither the top nor the bottom of the mash goes into casks to be aged; only the "middle cut" is collected, bottled, and sold.

While the pot still process that creates malt whisky is intermittent, the patent still process that produces grain whisky is continuous. Grain whisky, which is also made from malted barley and unmalted cereals, is cooked under steam pressure, agitated by metal stirrers, and collected at a much higher strength than malts.

Whether malt or grain, the whisky must be aged in oak casks at least three years to be legally called Scotch whisky; in practice, few Scotches are sold before maturing for at least eight years, and some premium blends are aged for 40 or even 50 years. (Every year, as it ages, 2% of the remaining whisky evaporates; people in the industry refer to the amount lost as "the Angels' Share.") Obviously, the makers drink no Scotch before its time.

Scotch is usually characterized by the geographical regions where it is produced; each region is thought to have its own tastes and personalities. While some experts have defined as many as nine different areas, the Scotch Whisky Association recognizes just four: Lowland malts, made south of an imaginary line drawn from Dundee (east) to Greenock (west); Highland malts, made north of that line (some experts say that Speyside whiskies, made in the valley of the River Spey, are a category unto themselves); Islay malts, from the island of Islay (say "Eye-luh"); and Campbeltown malts, from the Campbeltown region.

The Whisky Challenge

Some authorities think whisky produced on the islands of Skye and Orkney deserves its own category; others think the Highlands should be subdivided into Speyside and north, east, south, and west, claiming that each region's whisky is distinguishable by its aroma and taste.

Experts immediately know the difference between the lighter Lowland malts and the peaty Islay malts (even I can tell you that difference). If you do try such taste tests, heed the experts and don't just drink the whisky. Instead, follow your nose. Like the creators of perfume, master whisky blenders are called "noses," and they can instantly identify the region and at least the decade in which a spirit was bottled, if not the exact year.

Islays may take some getting used to.

From Barry's Lips to Yours

Barry Ayre has done extensive research on the whisky trail for the *Born to Shop* team, since he lives nearby, and we let him do all the hard work and pass on his best tips to our palates. A confirmed MacAllan aficionado, Barry has recently discovered Aberlour, which he says is as good or better. (It is about the same price.) Ten years old, please.

Since we never take anyone's word at face value, both Mike and Ian have tested Barry's recommendation. They agree.

Aberlour is also available at the duty free at Heathrow.

From Michael Jackson's Lips

Michael Jackson is the author of one of about a dozen books on the subject of malt whiskies. In fact, he alone has written several books on the subject. His *Malt Whisky Companion*, which you can buy at Royal Mile Whiskies and at most bookstores, costs £11. Not only does the book have color pictures, labels, photos, and a map or two, but it includes Michael Jackson's own rating system. This system is so popular that in some liquor stores across the United Kingdom they post the list to help shoppers pick a single malt.

The two or three most highly rated cost in the £40 range, so I have never bought them. The next rankings, with scores in the high 80s, include Talisker (score 90), which I bought for Ian (£23), and Cragganmore (also a 90), which I bought for Mike (£24). Both liked these brands, but agreed that they preferred the Aberlour, which Michael Jackson rates an 83.

Whisky & U.S. Customs

American citizens may bring in one liter of whisky duty free or the equivalent, which is 20 miniatures. Miniatures may be cute, but it will cost you twice as much to get a liter's worth of liquid.

Distillery Crazy (After All These Years)

It used to be that a tourist in Scotland could hit a sweater mill or two, have lunch at a charming restaurant or inn, walk through the Highlands sniffing heather, and top off the day by dropping in unannounced at a distillery for a wee dram.

No more.

Tourists now plan visits to distilleries as if they were planning the Normandy Invasion. In the last decade, touring distilleries has become so chic that making reservations is no longer a crazy notion. It's not hard to book a tasting tour or to clamber on board something like the Glenlivet train (rather like the Orient Express).

For their part, distillery owners once scoffed at the idea of giving tours, claiming they were too busy; however, with increasing competition from wines and "white goods" (clear spirits like vodka and gin), the conservative distillers have done an about-face and have actually invested money to lure visitors.

Competition has increased to the point where distilleries are adding still more features to get more visitors. Royal Lochnagar Distillery, located on a corner of Balmoral Estate, has life-size wax models of Queen Victoria and Prince Albert, and the Cardhu distillery serves complimentary soup and sandwiches to every visitor. Most distilleries now feature video presentations in a variety of languages (English, French, German, Italian, and Spanish), full restaurants, and, of course, complimentary miniatures. Do note that while sipping and sightseeing is encouraged, there are rules as to how old children must be to enter the premises and at what age they may taste. Scotch tasting is not encouraged as a family sport.

No appointment is necessary to see many of the visitors' centers; however, with large groups (10 or more), it is always advisable to call ahead. The distilleries listed below all have visitors' centers; those marked with an asterisk request that personal appointments be made.

About that phone call: If you are calling from within the U.K., remember that 01 is part of the new phoning system. If you are calling from the U.S., drop the 0 and dial 011/44-141 for Glasgow, for example.

The numbers listed below are local phone numbers, since I assume you will be calling for an appointment once you are nearby.

Arranging a Tour

Since more distilleries are building visitors' centers, you should contact the Scotch Whisky Association in London for help in arranging an itinerary. Some tasting is done on an individual basis as a day trip or a stopover at a distillery, but tours are also available, especially in the summer season. (Although a few distilleries close for factory holidays in July and the first week of August—ask.)

Most Speyside tours (the most organized) begin, or are based in, Aberdeen. It is not uncommon for some deluxe hotels to provide a promotional deal with a few of the distilleries to create a special package for you—and they do the driving.

ABERFELDY
Aberfeldy, Perthshire. Region: Highland.
Local phone: 01887/20330.

ABERLOUR
Aberlour, Banffshire.
Region: Highland/Speyside.
Local phone: 01340/871204.

AUCHENTOSHAN
Carlisle Street, Glasgow. Region: Lowland.
Local phone: 0141/558-9011.

AUCHROISK
Mulben, Banffshire. Region: Lowland.
Local phone: 015426/333.

BALMENACH
Cromdale, Moray.
Region: Highland/Speyside.
Local phone: 01479/2569.

BLAIR ATHOL
Pitlochry, Perthshire. Region: Highland.
Local phone: 01796/2234.

BOWMORE
Islay, Argyll. Region: Islay.
Local phone: 014968/1441.

CAOL ILA
Port Askaig, Islay. Region: Islay.
Local phone: Port 014968/4207.

CARDHU
Knockando, Banffshire. Region: Highland/
Speyside. Local phone: 013406/204.

CLYNELISH
Brora, Sutherland. Region: Highland.
Local phone: 0140482/1444.

CRAGGANMORE
Ballindaloch, Banffshire. Region: Highland/
Speyside. Local phone: 018072/202.

DALWHINNIE
Dalwhinnie, Inverness-shire.
Region: Highland/Speyside.
Local phone: 015282/264.

EDRADOUR
Pitlochry, Perthshire. Region: Highland.
Local phone: 017962/095.

FETTERCAIRN
Fettercairn, Kincardineshire. Region: Highland.
Local phone: 015614/244.

GLENDRONACH
Huntly, Aberdeenshire. Region: Highland/
Speyside. Local phone: 01406/682-202.

GLENDULLAN
Dufftown, Banffshire.
Region: Highland/Speyside.
Local phone: 01340/20250.

GLENFARCLAS-GLENLIVET
*Marypark, Ballindaloch. Region: Highland/
Speyside. Local phone: 018072/257.*

GLENFIDDICH
*Dufftown, Banffshire.
Region: Highland/Speyside.
Local phone: 013402/0373.*

GLEN GARIOCH
*Oldmeldrum, Aberdeenshire. Region: Highland.
Local phone: 016512/2706.*

GLENGOYNE
*Dumgoyne, Stirlingshire. Region: Highland.
Local phone: 0141/332-6361.*

GLEN GRANT
*Rothes, Morayshire.
Region:Highland/Speyside.
Local phone: 015422/7471.*

GLENKINCHIE
*Pencaitland, East Lothian. Region: Lowland.
Local phone: 01875/340-333.*

GLENLIVET
*Minmore, Banffshire. Region: Highland/Speyside.
Local phone: 015422/7471.*

GLENORDIE
*Muir of Ord, Ross-shire. Region: Northern
Highland. Local phone: 01463/870421.*

GLENTURRET
*The Hosh, Crieff, Perthshire. Region: Highland.
Local phone: 01764/2424.*

HIGHLAND PARK DISTILLERY
*Kirkwall, Orkney. Region: Highland.
Local phone: 01856/3107.*

ISLE OF JURA
Jura. Region: Highland.
Local phone: 014968/2240.

KNOCKANDO
Knockando, Morayshire.
Region: Highland/Speyside.
Local phone: 015426/333.

LAGAVULIN & LAPHROAIG
Port Ellen, Islay. Region: Islay.
Local phone: Port Ellen 2400.

LOCHNAGAR
Crathie, Aberdeenshire. Region: Highland.
Local phone: Crathie 273.

MACALLAN
Craigellachie, Banffshire.
Region: Highland/Speyside.
Local phone: 013408/71471.

MILTON DUFF
Elgin, Morayshire. Region: Highland/Speyside.
Local phone: 01343/547433.

OBAN
Oban, Argyllshire. Region: Highland.
Local phone: 01631/62110.

ROSEBANK
Falkirk, Stirlingshire. Region: Lowland.
Local phone: 01324/23325.

SINGLETON
Mulben, Banffshire. Region: Highland/Speyside.
Local phone: 015426/333.

STRATHISLA
Keith, Banffshire. Region: Highland/Speyside.
Local phone: 015422/7471.

TALISKER
(John Walker and Sons) Carbost, Isle of Skye.
Region: Highland/Skye. Local phone:
0147842/203.

TAMDHU DISTILLERY
Knockando, Morayshire. Region: Highland/
Speyside. Local phone: 013406/221.

TAMNAVULIN
Tamnavulin, Morayshire. Region: Highland/
Speyside. Local phone: Glenlivet 442.

TOMINTOUL
Ballindalloch, Banffshire. Region: Highland/
Speyside. Local phone: Glenlivet 274.

Small Packages

Miniatures have long been savored and collected throughout the British Isles and, to a lesser extent, in the United States. If you want to sample some of the best Scotland has to offer, miniatures are a convenient and inexpensive way to go. Most cost from £2 to £4, with unusually shaped bottles priced a bit higher, as are really old whiskies.

You may bring back into the United States approximately 20 miniatures per adult as your liquor allowance.

Labels 'Я' Us

A word about label language: Makers proud of their wares lavishly throw around words like special and choice. Only the words deluxe and reserve have meaning, and are applied to premium brands.

If you are confused about prices, check the age of the liquid gold. The older, the more expensive.

Just like me.

Chapter Fourteen

· · · · · · · · · ·

SHOPPING WALES

It takes less than an hour of driving around the Welsh countryside for you to completely accept the fact that you aren't in Kansas anymore. In fact, one or two glances at the road signs in Wales, written quite plainly in Welsh, and you will handily know that Wales is not England.

By having their own language, the Welsh convince us that they are just a little more exotic than we thought. One look and you realize you're in for a treat. A second look and you're ready to buy a slate mine.

To my way of thinking, Wales actually begins in England (in Chester, to be precise) simply because all the international airports are in England. The most direct method of getting to Wales from the United States is via Manchester. So this chapter is a rather unique one: It's all about my adventures in Wales—how I got there, what consumer information I learned along the way, and yes, of course, what I bought. There are some English cities in this chapter because they are part of the Welsh experience.

Wales doesn't feel foreign to England but rather feels like the secret hidden guest room, maybe attic room or artist's studio, of a great house. The land, the hotels, the people, the slate, and the shopping are a little bit different in Wales. Even the sheep are a little bit different. The prices are better in Wales; the weekends are wonderful in Wales. There's wool, there's tapestry (that's needlepoint to Americans), there's sweaters, there's slate (even if you don't buy any just to look at it will take your breath away), there's dairy products, and there's dishes. Frankly, I don't think there's that much more to life anyway, so I'm happy enough. Oh, yes, there's books—an essential ingredient to life. But the book city is just across the border in England.

Not to worry.

MY WALES

There are borders and there are maps and you can easily verify where Wales is and isn't. A little thing like a map has never stopped me before. I have my own ideas about where Wales should be—ideas generated from two driving trips and the firm belief that parts of England are part of the Welsh experience.

So forgive me if I digress every now and then. This chapter is meant to serve as a whole tour so it does include some English edges. Chester is in England, yes, but because it is the gateway to Wales it is in this chapter. Because Hay is part of the Welsh experience it is here as well—even though you and I both know it is technically in England. Besides, if you aren't going on to London you won't have much time for stocking up on your traditional English purchases, so Chester may be the biggest English shopping spree you get.

My Wales is laid out to make sense vis-à-vis driving routes and shopping stops (limited but exceptional). It focuses on the local to maximize your pleasures, shopping and otherwise. That means that except for Chester, I don't even mention multiples or chain stores.

GETTING THERE

. . . .

It's easy as pie to get to Wales: You simply fly to Manchester.

You can fly to London or Birmingham if you want to, and it's not that much harder to get to Wales from there, but it's easier to go to Manchester where the airport is big and beautiful and the air traffic is not.

There's not much public transportation from the Manchester airport to Wales, but you can get your rental car right at the airport and hit the road (see chapter 11 for rental car agency names and phone numbers). Manchester is about 40 minutes from Chester by car; about 1½ hours from where the Cute begins in North Wales.

If you want to hit a country inn to freshen up a bit after you arrive in Manchester, I've got the perfect welcome to Wales—just down the street from the Manchester airport. Honest.

Drive yourself a few hundred yards right over to the red brick country manse hotel, **Etrop Grange,** where you can get a half-day rate, breakfast, or even stay for a few days. Call 161/499-0500 for reservations; see page 229 for more details. This is the perfect little place in the country that you are looking for in Wales; it just happens to be at the edge of Manchester airport.

GETTING AROUND

. . . .

I've actually met a woman who explored Wales by bus; not on a bus tour, mind you, but via local bus service. She just looked at a map and did what she pleased. She also had very little luggage and didn't buy much.

The way she did it was to take the train to Chester and then take small, local buses to various destinations within Wales. You'll find that there are tons of local bus routes; even little bus tour companies, so that you can book **BWS Gwynedd**, the local bus, and get from Llandudno to Conwy Castle and back very conveniently. The fare is only £1.50 one-way, so you can't beat the prices in Wales. If you are hubbing in or out of London, you can also take the bus directly to specific Welsh destinations from London via **National Express**, a British bus company. In London, call 171/730-0202 for bus information and a timetable. There are special passes and programs for overseas visitors.

If you prefer to travel by train, explore your options carefully. Since the privatization of BritRail, seemingly zillions of regional companies have taken the rails and offer various plans and tours.

Do note that Wales is famous for its restored narrow-gauge and steam trains, which travel on short runs throughout the Welsh country and are quite an experience, especially if you are with the kids. You can book a short ride or buy a pass that allows you to use all the different local trains.

Frankly, I think the whole reason you go to Wales in the first place is to drive around the country and fight with your husband over the directions. I went with Ian (who isn't even my husband) and we were barely on speaking terms at the end of our trip! Road signs in Wales (and all of England) are very different from what you're used to. You'll get lost. Nonetheless, drive: You'll love it. Roads are small and narrow; roadwork can slow you down for very long minutes. You will not make fast time over mountains or around coastal routes, so slow down and enjoy the show.

You may want to pick up a local guidebook of road rules. Otherwise, you may not realize that when you are counting lights in order to follow someone's directions, you don't count pelican crossings. And if you don't know what a pelican crossing is (this has nothing to do with birds, I assure you) then you'd better get a few lessons. Stop by the Automobile Association (AA) office in downtown Manchester, or any other branch for that matter, to pick up such a tome.

Driving is still the best method to explore Wales; just make sure you are feeling patient and generous. If we weren't driving, we would've missed the annual **Caan Sheep Auction.** If we weren't driving, we wouldn't have had the wonderful experience of driving over that teeny-tiny toll bridge (did I see a troll or just imagine it?) and paying the 5 penny fee to get onto the right road for Portmeirion. If we weren't driving, we wouldn't have been able to pull over to the side of the road and run out and get the snapshots of the man walking his cows through the streets of Brecon.

National Express does not stop for photo opportunities. Besides, driving around Wales is good for your soul.

PHONING AROUND
· ·

Despite the fact they speak a different language and you can't read the street signs, Wales is part of the U.K. and part of Great Britain. Therefore, the country code is still 44. The rest of the phone system also works exactly as in the rest of Great Britain. When dialing from the U.S., drop the first 0 in the city code prefix; within the U.K., keep the 0.

A **British Telecom** phone card will work on a Welsh phone.

SPEAKING ENGLISH
· ·

English is the official language in Wales and just about everyone speaks English. However, signs and printed materials are in Welsh and English. If you are familiar with the place-names or have a good ear, you may have no trouble with Welsh.

Since I have a tin ear, had never been to Wales before I began the research for this book, and have never met people socially who could tell me about their childhood summers at the beach in Pwllheli, well, I had a very hard time every time I opened my mouth. I cannot relate what I hear to the same letters when they are written out on a map or signpost.

Just ask Ian about the day he walked into a gas station somewhere in Wales to confirm my directions to **Betsy Coed**. You see, I told him we were going to Betsy Coed. Who could pronounce Betws-y-Coed?

I won't even begin to tell you about Porthmadog. Just ask a local to say the name of a town and write it down phonetically. I'll get you started. It's "Port-mad-dock."

ABOUT ADDRESSES

Few hotels in Wales have exact street addresses, unless they are downtown in a city center. If they are, you probably don't want to stay in them. Well, if you're on business, maybe. It's not unusual for stores to lack street numbers as well, especially if they are on the high street. Stores on side streets or off the main path are more likely to have exact numbers than those in the thick of things. It won't be a big deal once you're there. Promise.

SLEEPING IN WALES

It's rather difficult to do Wales in a day trip from England; you'll be happier to take a few days, a weekend, or even a week and stay in one or two locations. Wales does not lack for cute hotels or extravagant B&Bs.

Note that Wales survives by the tourist business: They want to attract English and Irish tourists even more than Americans. To lure their target audience, an immense number of "price breaks" and promotions are offered with a plethora of different names: weekend breaks, winter breaks, champagne breaks, etc. Any day is a good day for a deal.

Some of the fancier hotels (or castle hotels) have a two-night minimum; most have deals that include dinner. Since Wales is not the kind of place where you're going to spring for the castle hotel and then send out for a pizza, you do best to choose your hotel based on the rating of the kitchen. Most of the famous hotels in Wales became famous because they have great kitchens. Some of them only have five or six bedrooms and are primarily restaurants. If you have a special place in mind, you'd do well to book ahead or start faxing and getting friendly with the natives.

In the middle of winter you'll have no trouble, but during the summer and early fall the best places can fill up. If you have your heart set on a certain kitchen, make reservations without delay.

BODYSGALLEN HALL
Llandudno

I wish I could tell you I loved Bodysgallen Hall; surely it is one of the most beautiful hotels I have ever (and I mean ever) been to. It's a castle with a bell tower with a view with incredible gardens and orchards and it is heaven. But I found it a tad stuffy—not as warm and friendly of an atmosphere as I would have liked. Vibes are secondary to the beauty of the property and the fame of the kitchen, however.

You may stay in the hotel (or castle, whichever you prefer to call it) proper, or book one of the little cottages out back. Everything is stunning and elegant and the dining room is beautiful enough to be in a coffee-table book. The food prices are not out of line with the quality of what is served.

The hotel offers a number of price breaks, which make it an affordable splurge. A two-day breaks package is about £200 per person including breakfast and dinner. Even if you just stop by for tea, this could be a highlight of your visit. Do call for directions because it's in the middle of nowhere and I'd hate to say we were ever lost in Wales or that we ever fought over directions, but, well, we were and we did.

A good choice for seeing North Wales. For reservations, call local phone: 1492/584-466; or fax: 1492/582-519.

PLAS BODEGROES
Pwllheli

Plas Bodegroes is a tiny house with room for only a few guests to sleep over. You don't go there to sleep; you go to eat. Price for two with wine: £65.

There are price breaks that include dinner and make this an inexpensive delight. Please note that the hotel is lovely, charming, and very low key. It's not overdecorated or fancy like many of the castle properties. You dress for dinner, but the atmosphere is country, not country club. Located just outside of town. Rooms begin around £100. For reservations, call local phone: 1758/612-363; or fax: 1758/701-247.

A good choice for the Llyn Peninsula.

HOTEL PORTMEIRION
Portmeirion

One of the great travel fantasies of my life has been to visit the Hotel Portmeirion—it's the home of my dishes (Botanic Garden); it's the location where the TV cult hit *The Prisoner* was shot; it's a famous folly that has to be seen, especially when the tide is out and the magic is in.

The best surprise about Portmeirion is not that I loved it (I expected to love it), but that Ian loved it. I was afraid he would think it was American or touristy or just plain silly. The English are so reserved, you know. He loved it. Adored it. Can't wait to go back.

What's not to like? The entire village with hotel and villas and, yes, even a few stores was built to amuse the famous architect Sir Clough Williams-Ellis. The village is described as Italianate; I'd call it fairy-tale architecture with real peacocks. Please note that the entire village of Portmeirion is part of the destination; there is no "real" village. It's not like you go to the town and then there's this hotel and view. The hotel is part of the town, the town is the folly, and the whole thing is a place unto itself. If you are not a hotel guest, you pay admission. (It's worth it.)

Among the stores on the property is an outlet shop selling Portmeirion dishes at Stoke prices (when the company got too big it moved from Wales to Stoke, see page 281) and a shop devoted to souvenirs from *The Prisoner*.

Hotel prices are moderate; there are price breaks and deals—rooms can begin as low as $125 to $150. Come for tea if you don't stay here because you cannot fathom what this place is like without enjoying it for yourself. For reservations, call local phone: 1766/770-228; or fax: 1766/771-331.

A good choice for mid-Wales and Snowdonia.

LLANGOED HALL
Brecon

Fairy tales can come true, it can happen to you. The minute your helicopter lights down on the pad at this country estate built by Sir Clough Williams-Ellis (who built the Hotel Portmeirion), you will be enchanted. The hotel is owned by Sir Bernard Ashley, the widower of Laura Ashley, who bought the property years ago because it is near their factory. (No outlet store—I asked.)

Each room is decorated in Laura Ashley, but divinely so. It's not too cute. The ladies' room on the main floor is worth the stop.

You can have tea, but the kitchen is famous, so move in for a few days and just eat, play croquet, go to the nearby sheep auction, and enjoy.

Oh, yes, the name of the chef is Mark Salter and it's an "in" thing to debate which chef is better: Salter at Llangoed Hall or Chris Chown at Plas Bodegroes. The dining room at Llangoed Hall is gorgeous—from a design point of view, it beats Plas Bodegroes.

With one of its price breaks, a night in the hotel with dinner for two comes out at the unbelievable bargain price of about £100 ($150) a night. Run, don't walk. Maybe even fly. For reservations, call local phone: 1874/754-525; or fax: 1874/754-545.

A good choice for southern Wales.

CHESTER

. . . .

Chester, one of the most famous honey-pot cities in England, has been locally renowned for centuries. A walled medieval city with one of the best clock towers in Britain, it draws tourists and traffic; it is the door to Wales.

- Chester is fabulous for the first day's stop after you've flown all night from America and come into Great Britain.
- Chester is marvelous for strolling and looking in windows and poking into a few antique shops. And yes, they do have a Boots in Chester. If you don't want to spend the night, this is a good lunch stop on your way to your castle in North Wales.
- Chester is very English, but it's a good welcome to Wales. You'll catch the contrast within a few hours.
- Chester is also a good welcome to Cheshire—and there's plenty to do and see and many an antique shop to prowl, especially in nearby Boughton. See page 347.

The Lay of the Land

The walls of Chester encircle a castle and a town with medieval and Jacobian architecture of storybook proportions. The main cross streets are Eastgate, Northgate, Bridge Street, and Watergate—all of which are also the main shopping streets.

All of the English multiples, from **Laura Ashley** and **Marks & Spencer** to **Mothercare** and **Dorothy Perkins,** are in the cluster of these three streets. A small modern mall that connects from Watergate to Bridge Street is called **Newgate Row.**

There is an antique center slightly out of the center of town, in an old mill on Russell Street off the Bars. The bulk of the antique stores is in a row on Watergate, although the last time I was in Chester, many of the stores were shuttered up and the antique scene was quite depressed. This is a story of the times, not just this one city. There are antique stores to enjoy, but there aren't as many as there used to be. Watergate Row is the elevated strip of antique shops.

Although almost all of the architecture in Chester is famous (and wonderful for photographs), there is a certain style of two-tiered store built with a board-walk type of sidewalk that separates the upper and lower portions that is quite unique. It's these two-tiered stores that Chester is most famous for (called the Rows); they stretch along Bridge Street for a block or two and house many of the multiples and the city's best specialty shops. Note that most stores, especially these, have no street numbers.

Who cares? Wander and enjoy.

Sleeping in Chester

THE CHESTER GROSVENOR
Eastgate Street, Chester

The Chester Grosvenor is a member of the Small Luxury Hotels chain and I have seen its picture in the brochure for years; dreaming of the day I would someday get to Chester and this hotel—which has a reputation as the best in town. You certainly can't beat the location: right smack dab in the middle of the city center and next to the wall and the clock and everywhere you want to be.

While the hotel is dripping in elegance, it is newly refurbished and lacks soul. There are four-poster

Chester

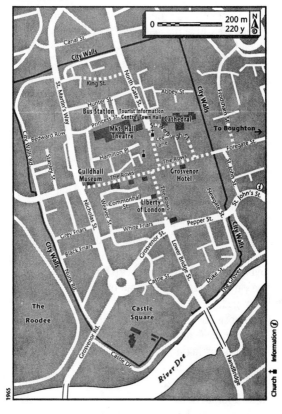

bedrooms, a health club and sauna, conference facilities, even an attached car park (which you will appreciate). But the hotel doesn't feel either completely formal or funky; it sits in the in-between neverland. Since doubles begin at £150, you might want to request a four-poster bed or push on for North Wales. For reservations, call local phone: 244/324-024; or fax: 244/313-246.

BLOSSOMS
St. John Street, Chester

Blossoms is the *other* hotel; it is around the corner from the Grosvenor, and it too is within the city walls and in a perfect location. It is not as famous and not as fancy as the Grosvenor. It's also about half the price. It's a little funkier than the Grosvenor; rooms are still of the new fake charm variety, rather than the authentic charm category. A double is £85.

For reservations, call local phone: 244/323-186; or fax: 244/346-433.

NUNSMERE HALL
Tarporley Road, Sandiway, Cheshire

This hotel is to die for; you've never seen another one like it: A country manor house has been turned into a hotel so special that Margaret Thatcher hid away here to do revisions on her autobiography.

The dining room was voted best county restaurant by the *Good Food Guide* and the room where they serve tea would make Laura Ashley and Sybil Colefax both green with envy. If you prefer tea on the terrace or a game of croquet, it can be arranged.

Nunsmere Hall is located halfway between the Manchester Airport and Chester and is a marvelous location for taking in the beauties that surround; then after a few days, you can move on deeper into Wales or North Wales. The Cheshire Polo Club is next door, m'dear.

Even if you don't book to sleep here, please come by for tea or dinner. There are weekend rates and special promotional deals and events. For reservations, call local phone: 606/889-100; fax: 606/889-055.

Shopping Chester

Chester is a good stretch-your-legs sort of shopping town. The kind of place where you say, "Good, I'm back in England and I need a trip to **Boots** and **Marks & Spencer**." A good kicking-off ground for an English shopping fix before you get into the Welsh countryside. Chester is a stroll and shop city; it's not a shop till you drop city.

Shopping Boughton:
Chester's Best-Kept Secret

While the shopping in Chester is so-so for those special items and the serious antiques are seriously expensive, there is a little-known secret that goes along with the town of Chester. Boughton. (Say "Boat-ton.")

Located about a mile from the city center, on A41 if you happen to be driving, but in the low numbers on Christleton Road if you happen to be in a taxi, is a string of antique shops on both sides of one block of Boughton.

Boughton is not as adorable as historic Chester, but you'll find its prices endearing. On first glance, the streets may seem noisy and busy, and the stores small and not very glamorous. Looks can be deceiving. Many of the stores have 10 or 12 showrooms inside that are packed with affordable fun stuff.

In fact, one dealer confided to me that the reason dealers in historic Chester have suffered is because Boughton has a big reputation with American dealers who come over on special buying trips just to stock up. Hence Boughton isn't depressed and the dealers are very friendly to Americans.

My favorite dealer is Keith at **Farmhouse Antiques** because he does marvelous windows and has a sense of humor about what he collects (top hats and chamber pots); I bought a tin bread box from him for £7 that was sensational. Carolyn had bought me one (in better condition and more unusual in shape) for £20 at a dealer outside of Manchester, but if you care about saving money, you'll head to Boughton. Also check out **Chester Furniture Cave**, a warehouse. One of the dealers there specializes in brand-new Narrow Boat painting, a type of tole work done on the barges in England. Prices begin around £8 for a small tin dish, but the work is exquisite and makes a fine souvenir of England. The pieces are signed.

FINDS

CHAINSTORE OUTLET
6 Watergate, Chester

The words *chainstore outlet* in British English mean a factory outlet store that sells Marks & Spencer goods. They are not allowed to advertise the M&S name. So the secret is out. Best of all, this new, upscale boutique has moved into the best real estate in Chester—right on Watergate—because there have been vacancies due to the recession.

The recession is officially over. The store is very tony, carries Marks & Spencer as well as a few other upscale labels such as Next and Alexon, and only has the right kind of clothes for the proper English Cheshire woman. Every item here is a winner. I got a headache trying to make a choice. A brown wool knit Marks fashion jumper (read sweater) for £25 was one of the best buys, but I could have danced all night.

NEWGATE ROW
Eastgate Street, Chester

It's not that this modern shopping arcade is the great find of the town, but it houses several real-people resources that you might find useful, especially if you are in town for a few hours or just a day and need to get a few things taken care of. There's a one-hour photo here (**City Photo**), a hairdresser, a shoe shop, and a wonderful little shop for coffee or tea or even lunch called **Paris Brioche**. The mall is L-shaped, so you enter near the Grosvenor Hotel and can exit around the corner on Bridge Street.

LIBERTY
Bridge Street, Chester

I know I promised I would only list the good local stuff and not multiples, but I have to make an exception here. There isn't a more charming sight than the local Liberty store all done up in the local architectural style. Don't miss the trade sign.

IMPERIAL CANCER RESEARCH FUND THRIFT SHOP
Bridge Street, Chester

Hey, we all have our sources. I happen to like thrift shops. I bought a pair of fabulous earrings from the 1930s here for £1; I didn't buy the Jaeger sweater for £6.50, but I was tempted.

OWEN, OWEN
Three Old Arches, Bridge Street, Chester

A tiny department store (it's a chain, no less) with a fabulous food department, take-out deli, chocolates, foods and cooking products, spices and mustards, jams, pasta, and a local farmhouse brand of food-stuffs that have great packaging and would make nice gifts to take home. They also do a variety of hampers and take-out meals. They even do hamper delivery to foreign destinations.

MADE OF HONOUR
11 City Walls, Chester

Although I had fun walking the antique shops in the town center, the most fun was happening upon this tiny antique store set right into the city wall. It's right at the clock—you can't miss it. The store isn't big and doesn't have enormous selection. It's just that it's precisely the kind of store you want to find nestled into a city wall.

ANTIQUES EXPORTERS OF CHESTER
This is more of a trade resource than a browsing adventure—the warehouse is filled. They pack and ship. Export only, just like the name says. Open by appointment only. Call 01829/741-001; address given at time of phone call.

GUILDHALL FAIR
Watergate Street

This is the once-a-week antique market—with about
20 dealers on hand. Nothing to plan your trip
around. Open Thursdays 10am to 4pm.

CONWY

Conwy is one of the first stops you must make in
Wales; it's sort of the official beginning of the Cute.
It's got a castle and a few adorable stores and a
glorious private teapot museum. It also has a few
tourist traps for souvenirs as well as little places for
tea. And clean public bathrooms.

Getting There

You can come via the slow, slightly southern back
road from Chester, which we did on one trip, and
you can come via the partially ugly, modern highway.
We went for scenic thinking it would be heaven. It
was so-so and once we discovered we could have been
on a highway and gotten somewhere in 20 minutes
and then been able to start the real part of the Welsh
adventure, we decided the highway was better.

I'd like to tell you Ruthin was worth the detour,
but, um, it wasn't. On the other hand, we went to
Ruthin for the Friday market, which I thought would
be fun. But when we got there it turned out to be
Thursday and I was a little mixed up. Ian was not
pleased. I hear from locals that the Friday market—
only held on Fridays for some reason—is worth
doing. Sorry, Ian.

Conwy begins with a view across water to the
castle; this is your true welcome to Wales.

Tea for Two

PEN-Y-BRYN
Lancaster Square, Conwy

Who could resist a 16th-century tea shop? You can get a quick light lunch or traditional tea (that's *bara brith*, to you). Located conveniently within the castle walls.

Finds

VISITOR CENTRE
Rosehill Street, Conwy

I'm not in the habit of sending you to local visitor's centers, but this one has tea (like tea-to-go or a quick cuppa, not tea for two and me for you) and lots of books (I bought one on Welsh castles for £2, which helped our tour immensely) and souvenirs and very good refrigerator magnets. And it's across the street from the public toilets. That's *toiledau*.

CHAR BAZAAR TEAPOT SHOP AND MUSEUM
Castle Street, Conwy

I was so enchanted with this stop that I made Ian go back to the car and get the cameras. Write him in care of the publisher if you want to see pictures of teapots. The museum is better than the store, but the whole production is adorable. The entrance fee to the museum is refundable against any purchase made in the shop. The shop sells mostly novelty teapots. The shop is okay; the museum is sensational.

NATIONAL TRUST SHOP
Castle Street, Aberconwy House, Conwy

Although National Trust has shops all over the United Kingdom, this one is Welsh and sells locally made crafts and decorative items. Nice place for gifts. Watch the step (down) when you enter. The store is in a 14th-century merchant home: in a word, fabulous.

BEAUMARIS

. . . .

Why in the world are we in Beaumaris? How did we even come to turn off after Bangor and get to the Isle of Anglesey in the first place? Just what is the professional shopper doing in this one-street little fishing town?

Welcome to Beaumaris, home of Elizabeth Bradley and her shop.

Okay, so I came just for the one shop. Aside from the fact that it was worth it, there's more to report. The town is adorable; there's a famous pub for lunch and there's a stroll among pastel-painted houses and along a pier reaching out into the Welsh water. There's view, there's boats, there's photo ops galore, and, most importantly, there's soul.

This is a wonderful town. Oh yes, it has a famous castle, too.

Tea for Two

YE OLDE BULLS HEAD INN
Castle Street, Beaumaris

Get out the cameras, guys. This is the shot. The inn was built in 1472; the dining room is dated 1617 and, yes, Charles Dickens ate here. Maybe George Washington did, too. You can sleep here, but if your schedule is like ours, this is where you'll stop for lunch. There's traditional pub fare (order at the bar, take a seat); lunch cost us £5 each.

Finds

ELIZABETH BRADLEY DESIGNS LTD.
33 Castle Street, Beaumaris

If you've never heard of Elizabeth Bradley, you may not be tempted to drive across most of England to get to her shop. However, if you've ever done a needlepoint kit in your life, if you've ever shopped at Bergdorf-Goodman or Harrods, then you know and have memorized the Victorian styles that Bradley is famous for.

And, of course, right about now, you want me to cut to the chase. So here it is. It's worth the drive.

Yes, prices are less than in London. I paid about £40 for a kit; the exact same kit was £49 at Harrods. The £40 price does include my value-added tax (VAT) refund. The going price with VAT was £43, I think. Obviously, one doesn't drive to Wales to save £6 or even £9. But the shop is fabulous and gorgeous and delish and, yes, you can save money. Oh, yes, the same kit costs $250 at Bergdorf's. I saved 400%, I think.

Bradley's business is located in a restored chapel in Beaumaris; this is not the shop. The shop is right on the high street (the only street in town) with an olive green storefront and gold-lettered name. The window is crammed with tapestry (needlepoint) pillows all made up and plump and sassy and trimmed with braids and pompoms and looking like the cat's meow.

In fact, there's an animal group that's very famous; the newer botanical prints were the rage when we were there. I bought the tulip to make for my husband.

The kits are all put together, you make your choice and then pick the background color you want. There are about eight choices for the background, although Bradley herself suggests black or cream. All the yarn is included as well as two needles. The canvas is 10 holes to the inch, which isn't too hard on the eyes.

About the only thing that's hard about any of this is that the kit comes in a gorgeous but rather oddly shaped square box. If you buy lots of kits (I did), they are cumbersome and when you leave the United Kingdom, you will have to show the kits at Customs to get your VAT form stamped. You may find that two or three kits are all you can carry on board and that this will limit your ability to carry much else.

And speaking of VAT, take careful pains to make sure your VAT refund goes onto your credit card. I thought I made this clear, but instead I got an

"A/C Payee" check in sterling. I couldn't deposit it in the United States; Ian couldn't cash it in Britain. It could only be paid into my account at Lloyds Bank. And I don't have an account at Lloyds Bank. The refund check still sits on my desk, an unwanted souvenir of Wales.

BETWS-Y-COED

Well, it'll always be Betsy Coed to me and I don't care what you call it. I call it adorable but with certain caveats. Boy, is this town touristy. The truth is that this is where the coach tours come, this is the main grandstand in North Wales, this is the gate to Snowdonia for retail, and Ian and I took one look at this town and one look at each other and simply said, "No."

The town has a crafts center (**Craft Centre Cymru**), a mill shop at the edge of town (**Penmachno Woollen Mill**), and gobs of tourist traps. If you've just done the fabulous mountain drive and seen the slate mine and the hills and the light and been touched to your very core, when you get to Betws-y-Coed, you are not going to want to ruin the mood.

So good-bye to Betws-y-Coed.

WELSHPOOL

The reason I was interested in Welshpool is that I have bought several sweaters in the Apple Market at Covent Garden from craftspeople who come from **Colinette Yarns**, which is based in Welshpool. Colinette Yarns are also sold at my local knitting store.

I can't say that we would have stopped in town if I wasn't waving an address in my hand, but the town is pleasant enough with a high street filled with real-people shops and several bakeries and places for tea or lunch. There's a few antique shops and while the town isn't the cutest in the world, it is very genuine.

Tea for Two

THE BUTTERY
High Street, Welshpool

Conveniently located next door to Colinette, the Buttery features Jacobean architecture, tea, and lunch.

Finds

COLINETTE YARNS
High Street, Welshpool

Colinette sells mostly yarn but also has sweaters that are already made up; if you buy from Covent Garden there's a bigger selection of sweaters. I was attracted first to the sweaters and then to the yarn itself because of the combination of texture (big, fat, thick, bulky, twisty wool), the structure of the cardigans (boxy, almost Chanel-like), and the incredible colors—all naturally dyed tones.

There are also cottons and silks, dyed in similar methods.

Prices in London for a sweater are about £60, £50 in Welshpool. A skein of 100 grams costs about £4.

HAY-ON-WYE

. . . .

So, we begin in England and we end in England; all things go around. Hay is about 20 minutes past Brecon and the Laura Ashley hotel, Llangoed Hall; it is an essential part of the Welsh tour. Hay-on-Wye is the most famous town in England for antique books.

Now then, the Wye valley is mostly in Wales, but part of it is in England and Hay is technically in England. So make Hay while the sun shines.

The Lay of the Land

Hay is actually built in a little square, so there are streets to wander and places to poke into. There's an **Antiques Centre** and there are the usual real-people shops; there's a penny candy store and everything else seems to be a bookstore. There's even an open yard where books are on shelves right out there in the fresh air and you help yourself, leaving behind payment in the wall. It's called **Honesty Bookshop**.

Because there is also a castle in town (not everyone comes to shop), there's a bit of a loop. You come into town on Castle Street, but if you continue straight on it will become Broad Street; Castle Street actually swings up to the right and turns into the high street. The main shopping is here and on Lion Street, which connects down to Broad Street. Market Square is at the other end of Lion Street. None of these streets is much longer than one block, so you can't get lost.

It's not confusing once you get there. The point is that this is not a one-street town and you will enjoy walking and shopping. And while this is one of the most famous towns in England, there is no neon sign that says This Way to the Books. Your first glance at this town may be a shrug.

Park and walk the little streets and alleys. Use the clock tower as your base and shop a square around it.

You can't miss the bookstores, the print shops, and the Used Books Bought and Sold signs. Many stores have a giveaway with a map and all the book stores and binderies listed.

Tea for Two

OLD BLACK LION
Lion Street, Hay

Right in the heart of the bookstores, this old-style pub/inn was probably put there by Central Casting. Exactly what you want, where you want it.

Finds

TRUMPS
Lion Street, Hay

It's a small convenience store, so don't get carried away with the name. They sell cold drinks and a huge array of penny candies, which will delight your children. Also a few postcards, etc.

HAY PRINTS
Castle Street, Hay

This is where you buy your own prints of Wales. (Sorry, I couldn't resist.)

HONESTY BOOKSHOP
Castle Street, Hay

You turn into the stone arch on Castle Street, across from the print shop, and there you see a grassy patch with an antique wagon and some stairs leading up to the ruins and a whole bunch of bookshelves and, yep, those books are for sale. Pray it didn't rain the day before. Paperbacks are 30p, hardcover are 50p. Put your money in the box next to the gate.

MARKET STREET SHOPS
Market Square, Hay

This is a quaint mall-strip center that must have been built to attract tourists, but don't be offended. The merchandise and stores are not spectacular, but the place is worth a visit.

ANTIQUES MARKET
Market Square, Hay

It's small but it's cute; only 18 stalls but the feel is good, and the prices are pretty fair. This part of town is attractive and the complex is open every day of the week! Weekdays and Saturdays it opens at 10am; 11am on Sundays.

Size Conversion Chart

. . . .

Women's Clothing

American	8	10	12	14	16	18
Continental	38	40	42	44	46	48
British	10	12	14	16	18	20

Women's Shoes

American	5	6	7	8	9	10
Continental	36	37	38	39	40	41
British	4	5	6	7	8	9

Children's Clothing

American	3	4	5	6	6X
Continental	98	104	110	116	122
British	18	20	22	24	26

Children's Shoes

American	8	9	10	11	12	13	1	2	3
Continental	24	25	27	28	29	30	32	33	34
British	7	8	9	10	11	12	13	1	2

Men's Suits

American	34	36	38	40	42	44	46	48
Continental	44	46	48	50	52	54	56	58
British	34	36	38	40	42	44	46	48

Men's Shirts

American	$14^1/_2$	15	$15^1/_2$	16	$16^1/_2$	17	$17^1/_2$	18
Continental	37	38	39	41	42	43	44	45
British	$14^1/_2$	15	$15^1/_2$	16	$16^1/_2$	17	$17^1/_2$	18

Men's Shoes

American	7	8	9	10	11	12	13
Continental	$39^1/_2$	41	42	43	$44^1/_2$	46	47
British	6	7	8	9	10	11	12

INDEX

A

A. Sanderson & Sons (Manchester), 249–50
Abelour whisky, 326, 329
Academy Soho (London), 129
Accommodations
books about, 12–13
Chester, 344–46
the Cotswolds, 195–97
Edinburgh, 296–97
Glasgow, 315–16
home stays, 26–27
hotel chains, 23–26, 110
London, 109–12
Manchester, 228–32
Oxford, 200–201
reservations, 23
Stoke-on-Trent, 269–70
Wales, 339–43
Windsor, 183–84
York, 258–60
Addresses, locating, 10, 44, 157, 295–96, 339
Adolfo Dominguez (London), 137
A.F. ("at fault"), 50
Afflecks Palace (Manchester), 236–37, 254
Agnés B. (London), 136

Aintree Knitwear (Innerleithen), 321–22
Airports. *See also* Heathrow Airport
Birmingham International Airport, 192, 193
duty-free shopping at, 5, 47–49
Manchester Airport, 225–26, 336
VAT refunds and, 34, 35
Air travel
baggage rules, 10, 35–37, 104–5
onboard shopping, 49
to Scotland, 288
to U.K., 14–16
within U.K., 23
Alexandra Palace Antique & Collectors Fair, 3, 102
Alexon, 67–68
Alfie's Antique Market (London), 131
Alfred Dunhill (London), 133
Alice's Shop (Oxford), 202, 204–5
Ally Capellino (London), 126, 133
American Express, 31–32
Andirons, 51

ABOUT THE AUTHOR

Suzy Gershman is an author and journalist who has worked in the fiber and fashion industry since 1969 in both New York and Los Angeles, and has held editorial positions at *California Apparel News, Mademoiselle, Gentleman's Quarterly,* and *People* magazine, where she was West Coast Style editor. She writes regularly for various magazines and her essays on retailing are text at Harvard Business School. She frequently appears on network and local television; she is a contributing editor to *Travel Weekly.*

Mrs. Gershman lives in Connecticut with her husband, author Michael Gershman, and their son, Aaron. Michael Gershman also contributes to the *Born to Shop* pages.

Want to Go Shopping with Suzy Gershman?

What does Suzy Gershman do on vacation? She goes shopping, of course. But she takes people with her. If you've ever dreamed about shopping with the world's most famous shopper, this could be your chance.

Several times a year, **Born to Shop Tours** venture forth to Suzy's favorite destinations when she takes time to really show off her best finds. The pace is busy but relaxed compared to her regular schedule; several trips are booked through cruise lines to maximize the relaxation possibilities and to cut down on the stresses of transportation and dealing with luggage . . . but you do have to carry your own shopping bags.

Excursions often include lunch at just the right charming spot (perfect for resting tired feet), trips into back rooms and private warehouses not often seen by the public, or opportunities to buy at special discounted rates reserved just for Suzy's guests.

While the schedule varies from year to year (last year, she hosted a shop-a-thon on the QE2 as she sailed from Istanbul to London), there's almost always a trip to Hong Kong, a trip to New York, and a Mediterranean cruise or two. Space is limited to ensure the intimacy of the group and experience. To find out about current plans or to inquire about arranging your own tour, call Acadiana Travel at 800/423-8661.

Frommer's Born to Shop guides are available from your favorite bookstore or directly from Macmillan Publishing USA.

To order by phone and pay by credit card, call 1-800-428-5331 (AMEX, MC and VISA cards are accepted). Otherwise, fill out the order form below.

Name _____

Address _____ Phone _____

City _____ State _____

Please send me the following Frommer's Born to Shop guides:

Quantity	Title	Price
_____	Born to Shop Hong Kong ISBN 0-02-860658-2	$14.95
_____	Born to Shop London ISBN 0-02-860659-0	$14.95
	Available in Winter 1996	
_____	Born to Shop Great Britain ISBN 0-02-860700-7	$14.95
_____	Born to Shop New York ISBN 0-02-860699-X *Prices subject to change without notice.*	$14.95

Total for Frommer's Born to Shop Guides $ _____
Please include applicable sales tax

Add $3.00 for first book's S & H, $1.00 per additional book:
$ _____

Total payment: $ _____

Check or Money Order enclosed. Offer valid in the United States only. Please make payable to Macmillan Publishing USA.

Send orders to:
Macmillan Publishing USA
201 West 103rd Street
Attn: Order Department
BS96   Indianapolis, IN 46290